Digital Activism and Design

Begüm Aylin Önder / Deniz Yengin (eds.)

Digital Activism and Design

PETER LANG
Berlin - Bruxelles - Chennai - Lausanne - New York - Oxford

Library of Congress Cataloging-in-Publication Data
A CIP catalog record for this book has been applied for at the Library of Congress.

Bibliographic Information published by the Deutsche Nationalbibliothek
The Deutsche Nationalbibliothek lists this publication in the Deutsche Nationalbibliografie; detailed bibliographic data is available online at http://dnb.d-nb.de.

ISBN 978-3-631-88094-4 (Print)
E-ISBN 978-3-631-89320-3 (E-PDF)
E-ISBN 978-3-631-89321-0 (E-PUB)
10.3726/b20371

Published by Peter Lang Group AG, Lausanne, Schweiz

info@peterlang.com - www.peterlang.com

Dedication

Globalization, especially in the last two decades, has had a significant impact on all areas of social life, starting from the economic sphere. The increasing importance of information and advancing technology have played an ever-increasing role in human life, causing humanity to feel the effects of globalization in depth. Civil voices have emerged with the development of communication technology and social movements have transcended the societies where media and democracy have changed, resulting in a major shift in the modes of action.

Today, all events and phenomena find their place on new media platforms. The proliferation of computer and internet technology has sparked the development of new media tools, which facilitate faster community mobilization and more effective action by organizations working to promote awareness. Activism is a fundamental form of action in which people act with hope for societal change. But digital activism, on the other hand, is an action type where individuals, communities, or organizations address social issues and take action on digital platforms. The possibility of reaching large audiences quickly and economically supports different types and methods of movements.

This book addresses digital activism from an interdisciplinary perspective, explaining with examples the changes in the forms of action that take place through networks. The impact of networks replacing class-based structures on action forms is examined in this book, which also provides numerous examples to help readers understand the topic. This study's interdisciplinary approach is significant.

We would like to thank all the authors who contributed to the book. Prof. Dr. Ayhan Biber and Res. Asst. Hatice Öksüz a special thanks. We are also grateful to the families who supported us every step of the way.

Prof. Dr. Deniz Yengin & Assoc. Prof. Begüm Aylin Önder

Table of contents

Preface

Social movements, which have emerged in almost every period of history against the status quo due to inequality or injustice, have started to be used to define organised and sustained collective actions towards a collective goal since the second half of the 19th century. Such social movements, which usually have a class-based structure, are organised around a certain ideology and led by a leader, have gradually been stripped of class-based organisations and left to new social movements focusing on concepts such as rights, justice and identity for political, economic and/or social change. Spanning a wide range of activities, activism is the effort of groups of people organised in line with common interests to express their thoughts and ideas about the problem through demonstration. Especially after the 1960s, the development of technology and multidimensional social and global changes such as cultural identity, equality, ecology, feminism, anti-nuclear activism have enabled the formation and diversification of new social movements. These new social movements have evolved into communities with equal rights of governance rather than having leaders at the center, despite their anti-bureaucratic organizational structure. The idea of activism has changed how people protest or oppose any circumstance or occurrence as a result of the growth of the Internet and digital technologies. Indeed, the rapid development of digital technologies has radically changed the world of communication and has had profound effects on social dynamics. One of the most prominent examples of these effects is the concept of digital activism. In its broadest sense, activism refers to a series of actions that aim to bring about social change. Research in fields such as communication, sociology, political science, art, media studies and psychology all emphasise the impact of activism on society and its potential for change. The concept of digital activism, which basically refers to the whole of interactive actions carried out through digital tools and communication technologies, has gained a new dimension by combining traditional activism practices with digital tools and platforms. In actuality, digital activism—a movement seeking social change via the use of information and communication tools—has the potential to offer quick and simple access to information in today's world where technology penetrates every part of our existence. Activist actions that originate for a cause should be realized using the codes provided by visual culture in order to increase consciousness among communities and foster a sense of shared purpose. As a matter of fact, the communication established through visual design ensures that any message conveyed on a subject is easily perceived and spread by individuals or groups. In this context, purposeful design language is very important for digital activism.

The book **"Digital Activism and Design"** was prepared under the editorship of **Assoc. Prof. Begüm Aylin Önder** and myself and is a compilation created with the contributions of valuable authors. This book is enriched with research written by experts from different fields such as communication, new media technologies, journalism and visual design. Each author addresses different aspects of digital activism and design from his/her own area of expertise and provides readers with an in-depth analysis. In this respect, the book is an important meeting point at the intersection of digital activism, communication and visual design. In this context, the book analyzes the interactions of different fields in detail and emphasises how digital activism has shaped these disciplines and played a transformative role. With its diversity of approaches and facets of digital activism, this collective study aims to provide readers with a rich perspective on the rise of social movements on digital platforms and their current impact in our rapidly changing world. It also hopes to serve as a significant resource for understanding the current role of digital activism and design and to serve as an inspiration for future research. In this context, I would like to congratulate the valuable academics who have helped us in the creation of this work titled "Digital Activism and Design", which we think will make important contributions to the literature.

Have a pleasant reading!

Prof. Dr. Deniz Yengin

Çanakkale, Turkey
June, 2024

Foreword

The concept of activism, which is partly a new concept with a history starting in 1960 and extending to the present day, means, in its most basic definition, taking action, shaping or changing. Within the scope of activism, which is basically a sociological change, it is also possible to reach various concepts such as protest, struggle, resistance and defense. As a matter of fact, activism means the struggle for the future of societies, and this change is not always innovative, but sometimes it can also emerge in line with conservative tendencies and goals. Activism as a form of action means supporting a group or community in contentious situations, in short, taking an oppositional stance. This concept, which involves qualitative social changes and reforms, can occur in all participatory social movements. Civil movement theory, as a sub-branch of activism, has a multidisciplinary structure that examines in which environments potential, cultural, economic and political situations arise, how and how they occur, and the effects of their consequences. In this context, civil movement theory has an innovative philosophy through social reforms and deals with situations that foresee or cause change.

As it is known, in today's world where communication technologies are constantly evolving, the role of the Internet in the communication process has changed to the same extent by having a fast and interactive infrastructure. As a matter of fact, after Web 2.0 technologies, the transformation of user pages into personalized ones has placed them at the center, and thus diversity has emerged in social media channels. In this way, in line with common values and interests, people can now come together not only in a physical space they determine on their own initiative, but also in cyberspace as spaceless and timeless, share their ideas through different social media tools, form public opinion and act jointly in line with common goals.

The idea of activism is understood in this context to be both a product and a cause of globalization, and changes in information and communication technology have given rise to the idea of activism taking on new dimensions. With the aid of information and communication technology, people who band together in support of shared aims and objectives within their community have transitioned to cyberspace and given rise to the movement known as digital activism. Thus, individuals can come together within the spaces created by virtual environments, perform and coordinate in a coordinated manner, especially the features of the Internet such as allowing freedoms, allowing the dissemination of information in the cross-border area without the concept of time and space, and they can transform their thoughts into widespread in a faster and shorter time together with groups like themselves. This allows for positive outcomes for digital activism. Moreover, digital activism also contributes to the development of online public support, which in turn allows for the proliferation of social and political movements. The concept of online activism, often known as net protest, hacktivism, slactivism, cyberterrorism, or cyberjamming, is ever developing and changing. A digital activist action must make use of all the codes of visual and verbal culture in order to develop a collective consciousness. A subject can be quickly understood through the use of visual codes, which are the most active way to spread ideas and opinions about it.

In this respect, this study aims to evaluate the phenomenon of digital activism and design through different texts. In this context, the study aims to be a reference source for possible studies in this field.

Prof. Dr. Deniz YENGİN & Assoc. Prof. Begüm Aylin Önder

to our families…

List of abbreviations

3D	2 Dimensional
AI	Artificial Intelligent
ARPA	Project: Advanced Research Projects Agency
BB	The Baby Boom Generation
BBC	British Broadcasting Corporation
CAWI	computer-assisted online interviewing
CD	Compact Disk
COP	Conference of Parties
DDoS	Distributed Denial of Service Attack
DPR	Donetsk People's Republic
DVD	Digital Versatile Disc
EEG	Electroencephalography
Emotiv EPOC X	high resolution, multi-channel, wireless neuroheadset. The EPOC uses a set of 14 sensors plus 2 references to tune into electric signals produced by the brain to detect the user's thoughts, feelings and expressions in real time.
EU	European Union
FI	Forza Italia
FSB	Federal Security Service
GEN	Generation
GPRS	General Packet Radio Service
GPS	Global Positioning System
GRU	Soviet Military Intelligence Organization
GSM	Global System for Mobile Communications
H	Hypotheses
HR	Heart Rate
HTCVive	American Vive Virtual Reality System
IDATE	DigiWorld Research
IFASTURK	International Financial Advisory and Audit
IT	Information Technology
Kaos GL	Kaos Gay and Lesbian Cultural Research and Solidarity Association
LGBT	Lesbian, Gay, Bisexual, Transgender
LPR	Luhansk People's Republic
M5S	Movimento 5 Stelle (Ita.) Five Star Movement (Eng.)

Mann-Whitney U test	Mann–Whitney–Wilcoxon MWW/MWU, Wilcoxon rank-sum test, or Wilcoxon–Mann–Whitney test is a nonparametric test of the null hypothesis that, for randomly selected values X and Y from two populations, the probability of X being greater than Y is equal to the probability of Y being greater than X
NTV	Nergis Television
OSCE	Organization for Security and Cooperation in Europe
PC	Personal Computer
PD	Democratic Party
RAI	Radiotelevisione
RT	Russia Today
SELF ID	Self-Identification
SMS	Short Message Service
SPSS	Statistical Package for the Social Sciences
T Test	The Independent Samples t Test compares the means of two independent groups in order to determine whether there is statistical evidence that the associated population means are significantly different. The Independent Samples t Test is a parametric test. This test is also known as: Independent t Test.
TV	Television
UHF	Ultra High Frequency
UK	The United Kingdom
UNFCCC	United Nations Framework Convention on Climate Change
USA	United States of America
V-Day	Vaffanculo Day, "F. off-Day"
VCD	Video Compact Disk
VG	Violent Gaming
VHF	Very High Frequency
VR	Virtual Reality
WI-FI	Wireless Fidelity
WWW	World Wide Web
YÖK Thesis	Council of Higher Education Thesis Center

Introduction

The history of humanity are showing that the breaking point of all economic, political and cultural processes that directly affect the life of societies began with new inventions in information and communication tools, in short, with technology-induced destruction. In ancient times, messages transmitted through drums or heliography without a messenger, cave complexes, stone surfaces or the first drawings representing the first examples of visual works in connection with technology, opened the doors to a new era by radically changing the communication infrastructure thanks to the discovery of the telegraph. As a matter of fact, immediately after the introduction of iron as a transport network, a great change occurred in the transmission of news. Following the discovery of electricity, the footsteps of this change and transformation in the field of communication began in 1837 when Samuel Morse transformed the form of communication into telegraphy with the Morse code consisting of dots and dashes. Thus, telegraph networks began to reach everywhere the railway network reached. Now, communication has gone down in history as an important step where the concept of distance has gained meaning from the beginning and communication can be done quickly wherever there is transportation. So much so that in the 19th century, the telegraph became an important tool through which individual, community and international communication could be easily carried out. This process, which marks the beginning of the "information age", has initiated a transformation in the field of communication. It has led to significant global changes by eliminating geographical restrictions on time and space. Towards the end of this century, in addition to the telegraph, with the widespread use of newspapers and photography, the global transformation of communication has reached an unpredictable speed. "Technologically, James Watt's invention of the steam engine in 1765 and its subsequent use as an energy source, economically Adam Smith's "The Wealth of Nations" in 1776 and politically the French Revolution of 1789 have been turning points (Özçağlayan, 1998: 21)." As it is known, the industrial society, which we can define as technological destruction and which was reshaped thanks to the machines working with steam as the main energy source; where the production of material products, raw materials and market ecosystem gained importance, has shown an unprecedented change after the second quarter of the 20th century and has completely reshaped the society-individual life within the globe. The use of steam power in the field of production brought about a significant increase in textile products and opened the door to new types of trade routes, this development led to the emergence of new types of urbanisation and changes in the field of agricultural activity inevitably penetrated into human life. As a matter of fact, the sovereignty of land and capital took over after this date with the proof of the maturity of technology and inventions. Henceforth, the industrial society started to change one after another with ongoing inventions that were fed by production.

The industrial society based on material production has lost its power due to rapid developments, particularly in the fields of communication and information technologies. The new society known as the "information society" is characterized by the role that information plays in society today. When considered from this point of view, the globe, which is already getting smaller day by day with the industrial revolution, has led to the emergence of knowledge-based societies in the world with these developments, and depending on the increase in the use of knowledge-based skills and advanced technology, the geographical borders of nations with each other have lost their importance, in short; globalisation has caused globalisation to touch the life of society-individuals in every aspect of life, not only in the economic field. Thanks to the developing information technologies, information has turned into a new structure that can be easily transported from one place to another, divided and even reproduced. With this development, political, social and economic structures have also been reshaped. As a matter of fact, thanks to information technologies, which are the key to control and change, the individual has started to receive and/or produce rapid responses to problems when needed. As a result, the transformation of the society in which the individual lives has become inevitable from this point onwards.

It is acknowledged that the invention of the computer during World War II marked the start of a completely new era driven by science and knowledge. Alvin Toffler emphasizes the structural change in communication technologies when outlining his theory of societal change. The first wave of Offler's theory, which he refers to as "Three Waves," is indicated by the agrarian revolution when we examine the general contours of his thesis. This primary wave refers to the agricultural societies in which hunter-gatherer groups cultivated the land, animal husbandry and the end of nomadism, in other words, settled life entered human life. Toffler emphasises that humanity, which sustains its life by growing agricultural products, has become more stable, that the population has increased significantly due to these developments and that it has ultimately complicated social structures. The second wave, which he refers to as industrial society, is the period in which production based on manual labour is replaced by mechanisation and factoryisation, and mass production plays a dominant role. In this period, the use of energy resources has increased significantly, thereby leading to a change in industrial production processes. This situation simultaneously reshaped societies and a significant economic growth was recorded worldwide. This was a time of great cities coming into being, the working class emerging, and thus, a time of constant technological and societal upheaval. The core of the structural changes in civilizations during the time Toffler refers to as the third wave is information, science, and information technology. In addition, during this time, social connections and production processes underwent a profound upheaval that ushered in the information and economic ages as well as the rise of new industries in the increasingly globalized world of commerce. As a matter of fact, as pointed out by Toffler, "the mode of production of this third wave is new communication technologies and computers (Timisi, 2003:97)." Mass production will yield to production determined by individuals, resulting in a widening of employment opportunities. While this new era, which Toffler calls the information society, was still in the process of labour around 1950, rapid access to information, education and communication technologies directly affected the concept of competition and redefined the concept of competition at the same time. Thanks to computer technologies, which were a technological gift to humanity with their invention and which are also regarded as the beginning of a new era, it has become possible to store information, to access it quickly and economically at any time, and to transmit it from person to person. As a matter of fact, "the computer is unique in its capacity to manipulate and transform information and thus automatically perform functions that previously could only be performed by the human brain without the need for human intervention (Kumar, 2013:21)." In addition to computers, significant developments in the means of communication, which have led to the emergence of the information society, have created new forms of communication that do not confine societies to time and space.

In every period of history, technology and technological tools are tools that benefit human life and contribute to the production of practical solutions to the problems faced by people. The tools or equipments produced by human beings through knowledge have created the concept of technology. In this context, it is possible to define the concept of technology as the knowledge, methodology and accumulation of knowledge necessary for something to be done. At the same time, technology is also a tool used to eliminate the desire to take nature under its patronage, which allows human beings to gain competence above their own capacity. Moreover, technology, which is recognised as having a significant impact on societies, has a driving force in the development of societies according to the view of technological determinism. This point of view holds that changes in the political, cultural, and economic spheres are caused by technology. Technological determinism holds that society's production and use of technology is always connected to both the good and bad effects of these changes. Although the steam train was the first technology to be used in communication, the technical determinist perspective only appeared in relation to modernization theories in the 1960s. Claude E. Shannon and Warren Weaver's Mathematical Communication theory and Harold Laswell's communication theory play an important role in the basis of communication technologies. In addition to these, Harold Innis's Technological Determinism theory, Marshall McLuhan's Global Village concept, Jean Baudrillard's Simulation theory and Manuel Castells' Network Society approach also hold an important place in discussions about technology. Harold Innis, known as a Canadian economist and historian who questions the underlying causes of changes in social organisation and the conditions that ensure stability in any society, has made historical studies in the field of communication and adopted a technological determinist view.

According to Innis, human beings, who have a historically passive structure, experience historical changes through technology. Innis emphasizes that with Gutenberg's invention of the printing press, the book, which replaced time-bound old media such as parchment, became a new space-bound tool. In addition, "Innis adds that the book contributed to the emergence of new secular, scientific knowledge and political elites (Di Norcia, 1990:335–337)." Marshall McLuhan, one of the foremost proponents of technological determinism, classified communication into Tribal Age, Literary Age, Print Age, and Electronic Age. He argued that these ages emerged as a result of technological advancements and fundamentally altered human life. McLuhan also introduced concepts such as the 'global village', 'the medium is the message', and 'the medium is the extension of man' within this framework. The tribal age, which he defines as the period of phonetic alphabet, created the age of literature, thus the birth of branches of science such as mathematics and philosophy became inevitable. With Guttenberg's printing press, the age of literature, in which visual word power gained sovereignty, turned into the age of printing. This age, which led to the birth of the industrial revolution, led to the beginning of the electronic age with the invention of the telegraph. McLuhan's global village thus opened its eyes to the world, and humanity, which became lonely and individualised with the book, was pushed to the background. With the invention of television, a participatory media emerged. According to him, "electronic interdependence recreates the world in the context of the global village" (McLuhan, 2014: 48). Jean Baudrillard, one of the leading names of French philosophy, developed McLuhan's "the medium is the message" discourse in simulation theory. According to Baudrillard, reality, although not actually present, can be reproduced as if it were real. According to the thinker who put forward the concept of simulation, "It is the artificial reproduction of a tool, a machine, a system, a way of functioning specific to a phenomenon through a model or a computer programme for the purpose of examination, demonstration or explanation" (Baudrillard, 2011: 9). The concept of simulation, which Baudrillard defines as hyperreality, describes an order that contains all of its features, although it is not reality itself. The thinker states that reality is now lost and people live with simulacra in the simulation universe. Simulacra means the appearance desired to be perceived. Baudrillard, who calls the period when consumption overtakes production as the simulation universe, states that the industrial and agricultural sectors have not been replaced by the communication and service sectors. While stating that McLuhan's concept of the medium is the message and that the medium and reality are mixed together, Baudrillard explains that "the mixing of medium and message is the first important and great formula of the new age" (Baudrillard, 2011: 56). The thinker also emphasises that television does not have a message through the images or indicators it transmits to societies, that television is the creator of new lifestyles imposed on societies, and that the message of television is the change of human perceptions and traditional lifestyles. Baudrillard underlines that instead of ensuring socialisation, mass media tools dissolve societies within the masses, while at the same time defining these tools as tools that cause the destruction of meaning rather than the production of meaning.

It might be argued that in information societies, when information becomes more important, work loses its connection to time and location and takes on a cultural structure that distinguishes individuals from one another. Information society is defined by Yoneji Masuda as "information civilisation," and he highlights the three primary implications of this civilisation. He claims that these outcomes are as follows: With technology, people are now able to overcome the tasks that they cannot do with their own strength. The fact that formerly performed works can be done with technology has led to the transformation of the existing social and economic structure thanks to technology.

Undoubtedly, the information technologies that spread across the globe at the speed of light towards the end of the 1960s paved the way for the emergence of a global culture as well as a global economy. In the information society, where participation and social benefit have risen to a decisive position, the previously accepted class distinction has now been replaced by a functional, multi-centred, participatory democracy that can benefit from collective participation. The polyphony that emerged thanks to these developments continued with the replacement of labour movements, which marked a period, by civil movements in which the individual aims to fulfil his/her own wishes and individualism gains importance. The 90s, when the Internet technology, which emerged with the aim of creating telecommunication and computer networks, was gifted to humanity, caused a complete change in the perception of physical space and time of humanity, reshaping individual-individual, individual-group, individual, group or society relations, and the emergence of new types of business, human, nation relations. The world, which is closely interconnected with globalised virtual networks, has rapidly undergone an effective transformation in social relations. Virtual networks have led to the emergence of virtual communities as a result of virtual spaces declaring their sovereignty. Anderson defines virtual communities as "a political community with an imagined nation that includes both sovereignty and limitation (Anderson, 2004: 20)." Manuel Castells, who combines this phenomenon with the concept of network society by revealing the common and different points of the ongoing debates on the information society, has redefined these debates in economic, political, cultural and social terms. Especially the cultural and social movements that emerged globally in the 1960s, coupled with the information technology revolution of the 1970s and particularly the processes of globalization of capitalism in the 1980s, have led to the emergence of the network society. Castells stated that information and knowledge are organised in the form of a network and that this model reveals the network society. In the last quarter of the 20th century, Castells states that a new economy in which information is at the forefront has emerged and argues that all activities related to the economy are based on technology and that globalisation has emerged as a new form of capitalism thanks to the informational economy. It is seen that the informational economy on a global scale is carried out by the government, multinational corporations or the instrumental network that establishes different ties with cultures on a global scale, and that this is based on informationalism known as information and communication. Mcluhan's global village is replaced by the concept of the global city in Castells' network society theory. The cities Castells refers to are settlements interconnected by telecommunication, rapid transport, banking and information systems, defined as a space of flows organised by networks. "What is meant by the global city is a network of spaces that express dominant functions worldwide. There are hundreds of cities in this global network in different proportions and weights. For example, Silicon Valley is not a part of financial networks, although it is a network of innovations in information technology. While London, New York and Frankfurt are the nodes of financial and business networks, they do not have much relation with technological innovation networks (Castells, 2006: 118)." Castells' term "timeless time" is used within the network society. According to him, this concept is the operation of newly formed information societies and communication technologies without the time barrier.

The rapidly developing technologies of the digital age have created a major transformation in the fields of communication and activism. As Manuel Castells puts it, the network society, in which information and knowledge are organised as networks, has emerged in a world dominated by digitalisation. With this transformation, social organisation has evolved towards a decentralised structure and new communication technologies have played a key role in the rise of social movements on a digital platform. In the network society where digitalisation is dominant, a decentralised structure of social organisation prevails and is considered among the important variables of this network society. Internet, social networks, smart mobile phones, digital applications, in short, new communication technologies have played an active role in moving social movements to a digital environment. Community protests, which can be organised in a short time through networks, have also spread to real spaces, and these communities have continued the virtual movements they have created as square movements. The digital networks mentioned by Castells play an active role in the coordination of actions. By occupying public squares or buildings with their actions that started in digital space, these communities lead to the hybridisation of cyberspace and urban space and, in Castells' words, create a space of autonomy. These actions, which are local and global, not only occupy the public space, but also transform into an interactive media structure by getting rid of history and geography in the digital space of culturally different societies. The other thinker, Van Dijk had examines the interaction-based dimensions of time and space in addressing the network society. As stated by Dijk (2006: 156), while communication technologies shape the structural characteristics of society, new media also contribute to a mutual transformation process that alters social structure. The concept of digital activism, which aims at social and political change by using the internet and social platforms that create interaction through networks, in short, digital technologies, is low- cost and has the potential to reach large masses. Digital activism, which has different types such as Slaktivism, Kliktivism, Advocacy activism, hashtag activism, info-activism, app activism, is among the methods used to ensure social transformation and raise awareness in the 21st century. Moreover, it can also have various purposes such as campaigning, which includes methods ranging from online petitions to calls for action in line with a specific goal, and community development by networking in order to act as a bridge between communities with common ideas. In addition to these positive aspects of digital activism, it can also cause misinformation, disinformation and manipulation. In this context, the spread of untrue information to large masses can deeply shake the social structure and political process. The uncontrolled spread of information through social networks can pose a serious threat by altering the true purpose of digital activism. Furthermore, in recent years, various artificial intelligence-supported software programs, such as image, video, and audio creation tools, which are readily accessible to users without any program knowledge, can significantly contribute to the dissemination of disinformation. These generated contents spread rapidly through social media within seconds and can lead to consequences ranging from social unrest to societal outrage. For this reason, ethics, trust and accuracy gain importance in activist movements, and digital media consumers should use the right sources for accurate information access. In any movement that includes action on a subject, visual elements (logos, banners, labels, videos, photos, infographics, etc.) are used to make these actions permanent in the minds of the masses, to mobilise them or to direct them to a common thought on a subject, to make a call. Considering that constantly developing new media tools allow multi-media, the design languages and visual presentations of all these tools circulated between individuals in these areas gain importance. As it is known, all kinds of communication carried out through visuals have features that can be stored, stored, reproduced, easily circulated and easily perceived by everyone. This makes the concept of visual communication universal. Visual communication, which has the feature of transferring information in a short time, can be a very effective communication tool regardless of the method used on large masses when this information between source and target takes on a creative identity.

Following the Industrial Revolution, with the diversification of mass media, human beings gained techno-vision by gaining the practice of seeing based on machines. In visual communication, the perception and interpretation of information by the target audience is very important. In this context, it is seen that this discipline has a desire to create a regular system. In this context, visual communication as a design language is fed by visual design elements such as line, texture, tone, color, form, direction and scale, and compositional principles of visual design such as contrast, dominance/focal point, balance, rhythm, shape-ground relationship, emphasis, integrity, proportion, visual hierarchy and continuity. Visual communication design has a great influence on all activist actions that arise for various purposes such as protest, support or change, such as all messages designed to make mental associations, to establish a logical relationship between facts and events, to mobilise a person, group or community.

The aim of this book, which emerged in this context, is to express the concepts of digital activism and design used in terms of activism with texts from their own perspectives, to analyze the phenomenon of "Digital Activism and Design" under many sub-headings such as information and communication technologies and systems, media policies, culture, visual arts, visual communication, mass communication media, interaction, control and transformation, and to carry out a memory study that can serve as a source for further research in this direction.

Firstly, **Assoc. Prof. Nur Emine Koç**, in this study titled *"Digital Activism on Social Media"*, explains how the activism movement developed with digital technologies has become more effective than other forms of activism and how activism mobilises collective consciousness through social media. The author also discusses the side effects of limiting or even eliminating the freedom of activist actions that take place on social media platforms, which can be controlled by the states and become a surveillance tool for both the state and companies that violate personal privacy, through the combination of censorship, surveillance and profit exploitation.

Assoc. Prof. Kenan Duman, *"Bringing together activists over cyber populism"*, The author draws attention to how cyber utopia has become an effective actor in social organisation and discusses how the interaction directly affects the individual and society, especially from the genetic features of Web 2.0 technologies. The author also examines this claim through the "Five Star Movement", which started as an activist initiative with a website in Italy and later turned into a political identity in the country and became quite powerful, and it is seen that he reveals striking data on how this movement has achieved success due to cyber culture in activist actions carried out on new media platforms.

Assoc. Prof. Begüm Aylin Önder and **Res. Asst. Bilgesu Biber,** *"Digital Activism's Impact On Gen Z: A Social Media Platform Analysis"*, the authors examine the level of awareness and understanding of digital activism among Generation Z, which is highly influenced by technology, digital inputs and outputs, has made digital a way of life, and is the primary user of social media and its tools. In the study, the authors, on the one hand, reveal the level of use of social networks by this generation, on the other hand, reveal to what extent this generation is active in activist actions carried out through social media and how much importance they attach to visual design and interaction in their level of participation in these actions. The study is considered to be important in terms of revealing how and in what direction Generation Z's knowledge, thoughts and attitudes towards digital activism are.

Asst. Prof. Büşra T. Durmuş, in this study titled *"Women plus movement as an achievement""*, analyzes the post-truth era brought about by the transformation in communication technologies in the 21st century and its impact on changes in identity acceptance, and examines the development of the women plus (+) movement both in Turkey and in the Western world by holding a mirror to the historical background and conditions of feminist women's movements. In this study, the author explains how digital activism has become effective by using new media platforms, while at the same time opening up a debate on whether the new identity acceptance brought about by the gender revolutions in Europe and America has emerged in a country like Turkey.

Res. Asst. Hatice Öksüz's study titled *"Eco-criticism in 'I Am Greta' documentary film design"* deals with the climate change crisis and climate activism within the scope of combating this crisis through Greta Thunberg's biographical documentary. In this study, the author focuses on the role of cinema from the perspective of ecocriticism in reflecting human-induced ecological destruction, climate crisis and related actions to the audience as consciousness, based on the ability of cinema to mobilize the masses as well as the function of art with visual and auditory codes, and examines the documentary film "I am Greta", which has a great global impact, through digital activism, film design and ecocritical perspective.

Erdem Koç, PhD., in this study titled *"New media and digital activism in the framework"*, examined the effect of the Arab Spring, which grew as a big wave in the social and political context centred in Tunisia in 2010 and affected many countries in the Middle East in a short time and made history as one of the first social media actions, on agenda setting as a digital activist action. In this study, the author has reached very interesting results by examining the organisation of activist movements carried out by using new media tools in the Arab Spring protests, how the protests turned into practice and how they transcended physical boundaries through discourse analysis method through case studies.

Yakup Toktay, PhD., in this study titled *"Reading hacktivism through the Russia-Ukraine War: Anonymous example"* the author examines Anonymous, one of the world's largest hacker communities, which is known as one of the important and globally recognized names of hacktivist movements and which we are used to seeing in political events by organizing attacks on the websites of state institutions for various protests, through the ongoing Russia-Ukraine war. Morever, the author examines this group, which has made a name for itself again with its cyber attacks against Russia, and discusses how digital activism has an impact on war in times of war. Analyzing the cyber-attacks against Russia by Anonymous, which caused a major transformation in the course of the war and played a leading role in gathering global support for the Ukrainian front, this study also discusses how the war became hybridized with the transfer of the war to cyberspace and how the concept of war was legitimized due to the global support for Ukraine. The study also emphasizes that these attacks have led to the emergence of negative situations such as information pollution in cyberspace.

Asst. Prof. Buket Akdemir Dilek and Asst. Prof. Muhammed Dilek, *Digital activism ın twitter post against censorship/mobing in the cinema*: '*The Bergen*' they first take the reader on a historical journey to the concepts of feminism and digital feminism and explain how women's identity became visible in Turkey with the fourth wave. In their research, the authors examined how the film "Bergen", which was directed by Mehmet Binay and Caner Alper and scripted by Sema Kaygusuz and Yıldırım Beyazıt in March 2022, based on the real life story of Bergen, one of the famous arabesque singers of a period in Turkey, resonated on Twitter, one of the digital media platforms, after it was censored by Kozan Municipality in Kozan district of Adana, Turkey. In their study, the authors analyzed the tweets posted on this platform between 04.03.2022 and 14.03.2022 using van Djik's discourse analysis method in the context of the digital activist movement and discussed how the Fourth Feminist Wave, namely Digital Feminism, makes women's struggles visible through digital platforms and social networks, how women strive to legitimise their presence in the public sphere, and activist actions that allow them to raise their voices by separating themselves from class and social differences within the framework of the findings obtained from the sample.

Asst. Prof. Orhan Faik, in this study titled *"Nomophobia triggered by digital activism and ıts place in academic studies"*, examines the concept of nomophobia, also known as the fear of cell phones, as a type of digital addiction and presents a multifaceted approach to this concept. In this context, approaching digital activism from a different perspective, the author examines how digital activist actions that have the potential to trigger nomophobia are produced through phones. The author also offers different suggestions for combating digital addiction.

Finally, **Assoc. Prof. Nur Emine Koç, Assoc. Prof. Ayşegül Akaydın Aydın, Asst. Prof. Sema Bulat Demir, Res. Asst. Elif İnceismail and Res. Asst. Meltem Başaran**, the study titled *"Virtual Reality and Digital Gaming Experiences in Turkey"* comparatively analyzed the data obtained by measuring EEG performance metrics for the experiences of digital games and virtual reality games, which have become one of the important entertainment and interaction tools today, and the users of both types of games in Turkey, and deepened the findings with interview data. In their study, the authors aim to reveal the changes in the moods of virtual game and digital game players, and on the other hand, they have carried out a study that will make a very important contribution to the academic world. Based on the data obtained by the authors, it is emphasized how digital games, which are used as a social, cultural and political tool as well as entertainment, have a potential for digital activism and create a discussion on how they can create change in this context.

I would like to thank all the authors who contributed to the book, in which different perspectives are examined under the title of "*Digital Activism and Design*," and I wish you, our esteemed readers, pleasant reading with the hope that the study will contribute to the literature.

Assoc. Prof. Begüm Aylin Önder

Istanbul, Turkey
June, 2024.

References

Anderson, B. (2004). *Hayali Cemaatler-Milliyetçiliğin Kökenleri ve Yayılması.* İstanbul: Metis Publications.

Baudrillard, J. (2011). Simülakrlar ve Simülasyon. (Translated by Oğuz Adanır). Ankara: Doğu Batı Publishing.

Di Norcia, V. (1990). Communications, Time and Power: An Innisian View. *Canadian Journal of Political Science/Revue Canadienne De Science Politique,* 23(2). 335-357.

Kumar, K. (2013). Sanayi Sonrası Toplumdan Post - Modern Topluma Çağdaş Dünyanın Yeni Kuramları, Trans. Mehmet Küçük, Ankara, Dost Press.

Mcluhan, M. (2014). *Gutenberg Galaksisi.* (Translated by Gül Çağalı Güven). İstanbul: YKY Press.

Özçağlayan, M. (1998). *Yeni İletişim Teknolojileri ve Değişim*. İstanbul: Alfa Publications.

Timisi, N. (2003). *Yeni İletişim Teknolojileri ve Demokrasi.* Ankara: Dost Publishing.

Van Dijk, J. (ed.) (2006). *The Network Society*. London: Sage Publications.

Assoc. Prof. Nur Emine Koç[1]

Digital Activism on Social Media

Abstract: Activism can be defined as the deliberate action to bring about social or political change. This action can be taken to support or oppose one of the parties in conflicting discussions. Activist movements have largely begun to occur on digital platforms in the age of digitalization. As time goes on, the phenomenon of social media becomes more and more significant in the information- and communication-centered communication processes. This is evident not only in technology-driven interpersonal or marketing communication processes, but also in the realization of communication between groups who have gathered for specific purposes and work toward a common objective. Social media tools such as wikis, social networking and content sharing sites, blogs show a user-centered structure with the advantage of Web 2.0 technology, in addition to its structure that allows simultaneous, fast and unlimited information dissemination arising from the nature of the internet, and its design and content. It offers a user-oriented, easy-to-use structure that does not require high technical knowledge in creating and operating the system. In the process, activist groups are drawn to the benefits of social media and take action to raise awareness of injustices, discrimination, and abuse in social, political, economic, or cultural issues that affect the larger social structure and to bring about behavioral changes. For activists seeking to contact a huge number of people in a short amount of time, without regard to time or location, in order to gather their ideas and form a public opinion on a particular subject, the internet, and social media in particular, is an excellent means of communication and interaction.

In this work, digital activism and its importance affecting social media users will be discussed through social communities, democracy, surveillance and control.

Keywords: Digital activism, social media, social communities, democracy, surveillance, control.

1. Introduction

Activism has been in a very important position in everyday life since ancient times. From the historical perspective, it can be seen that activism finds a place in everyday life as a form of struggle or resistance, and sometimes as an uprising or rebellion. However, no matter what nature the concept is, it always embodies

1 Istanbul Aydın University, Faculty of Communication, New Media and Communication Department, nurkoc@aydin.edu.tr ORCID: 0000-0002-3477-8019.

a field of expression. Activism, which has emerged in different ways in every era, manifests itself in a different form in today's digital world.

The European revolutions of 1848, the Paris Commune of 1871, the Bolshevik revolution of 1917, and other upheavals are now resurrecting. The impact of the World Economic Forum protests on the Arab Spring and Occupy Wall Street, as well as the widespread availability of social media, particularly in relation to digital activism, have sparked considerable debate among academics and the media (Carr, 2008: 110). In the last two decades, people around the world have started to realize the expanding use of digital technologies, computers, cell phones, and other internet-enabled devices in the struggle for social and political change (Karatzogianni, 2015: 1997). Features that make new media new; digital, interactive, hypertext, networked and virtual are included in the cluster. The most important point to note here is the position of traditional media in the cluster. Traditional media is included in the new media cluster. Within this cluster, they are only distinguished from each other by other new media features. Its new understanding continues on its way by including the traditional (Yengin & Bayrak, 2022: 41). It is inevitable that activism will find its way into the vast digital world through new media and social media in particular. It also becomes necessary for societies, ethnic groups, and other "others" to be able to most easily and directly present their own realities to the world. Demonstrations, riots, and social and political action have proliferated globally and over a wide range of reasons, particularly since 2011. A new era has begun in which society is attempting to fulfill a different dream. Over time, along with conventional media, new technology-mediated activism types have emerged as devices following cruelty or abuse, gathering and reporting information in cases of natural disasters, social justice protests and strikes, civil wars, or election processes (Karagöz, 2013: 132).

What is this concept called activism, digital activism, which is a kind of activism, digital activism environment, and digital activists? The concept of "activism" generally refers to the practices of individuals who challenge the status quo to achieve social, political, or economic change (Kahn, 2004: 88). At its foundation, activism—which encompasses social movements—begins with the 19th-century labor movements and its historical characterization.

The term "new social movements" is used to describe a variety of movements that emerged in the 1970s, including those for local autonomy, ecology, feminism, peace, and middle-class opposition to nuclear power (Ricketts, 2012: 45). "Digital activism" is a generic name given to the use of the internet by different types of activism. There are also uses of the term such as "internet activism", "e-activism", "cyber activism". When using the internet for activism, one can advocate for a cause, organize to carry it out, spread awareness among the public, lobby, boycott, take online actions like site blackouts, raise money for the cause, keep an eye on the government or businesses, and provide real-time updates to large audiences about their actions. It happens in places where there are chances to spread knowledge (social media, blogs, vlog, podcasts, videos, photo-sharing sites, etc.) (Ulram, 2017: 5). In a sense, it is an effort to change the opinions of individuals on any issue in the context of opposing or taking sides in social or political issues on the Internet. Digital activism is an experience that defines and greatly strengthens the activist identity of individuals, as the digital space allows activists to express themselves better in the issues they defend or react to (Brodock, 2010: 67). In this context, "digital activism environment" refers to both the digital technology used in a particular activism movement and the economic, social, and political context in which this technology is used and includes all social and political campaign applications that use the digital network infrastructure (Kidd, 2003: 76).

Digital activists, on the other hand, are people who design and carry out actions to inform and create a public opinion about thoughts, actions, or lawsuits on issues such as freedom of expression, human rights, or the environment. These actions are sometimes limited to digital media only, and sometimes they go down the street (Svensson, 2014: 12). As the name implies, digital activists use all digital media such as social media, newsgroups, and e-mail quite effectively (Sert, 2016: 45). In this respect, newly developed communication platforms, like social media, which have appeared concurrently with advancements in information communication technology, serve as useful instruments for virtual communities, particularly as social formation groups. The incessant advancement of technology also fortifies the adjustment of these instruments to social media platforms. Multiple-to-many tools are emerging that enable and expedite greater cooperation and action in social life, as opposed to restricting communication to one-to-one and one-to-many interactions. Such that, with these basic features, new communication technologies also show a structure that accelerates and facilitates global organization.

However, after the protests, there has also been a general transformation in people's mentality. People have come to understand the advantage of meeting for a common cause in the same environment as the pioneer of promoting issues related to social problems through social media and leading wider actions aimed at eliminating these problems (Lovink, 2003: 237). The transitivity between real and virtual streets has decisively changed and transformed the structure of both social movements and media practices. The centralized, hierarchical, strict canonical structure in the past has been replaced by a more flexible and dynamic structure with a multi-center, horizontal network of relations (Berners-Lee, 2000: 33). Social media is used by activists for their offline and online campaigns because of this. In a way, discussing activism in any form these days cannot be done without mentioning the internet realm.

As a result, online activities are referred to as internet-based, and offline acts as internet-aided. Kezban Karagöz claims that the first method involves using digital tools to help a social movement that is already in existence (2013: 142). In other words, it includes "real" actions in which the movement on the street is supported through digital mediums. The Internet-based form of social movement, on the other hand, is used to express "virtual" actions created in a purely virtual world, including new or modified forms of traditional tactics. However, Van Laer and Van Aelst also decisively emphasize that the distinction between internet-based and internet-aided actions is quite thin and permeable.

Social media has also changed the way new social movements are organized. That is, rather than being the organization that provides the communication, it is the case that the organizer is communication (Brodock, 2010: 22). While social media was used only for organizing and announcing the actions, today it has turned into an action space rather than an action sharing space. Many issues can become a field of action on social media and can go down the street (Carr, 2008: 110). In this sense, social media can function as a tool that facilitates the communication and organization of an organized social movement with real life on a local and global scale (Pickerill, 2003: 151). However, social media comes to the fore not only with these features but also with its negative features. In this context, liberal media theorists examine social media in the context of opportunities and advantages it creates in the socio-political field, such as "participation", "interaction", "liberation", "making a public space", "democratization", "critical theorists", "medical commercialization of communication", "virtualization of the public sphere", "standardization of interaction", "creation of a society of control and surveillance" (Uldam, 2017: 6). As a result, a lot of problems now that digital activism has impacted our lives so much call for us to reconsider how activism affects social life. It is possible to identify three crucial factors to create boundaries in this context, despite the fact that there are numerous difficulties and regions to be taken into consideration. These include advancing social awareness, which enhances social connection, encouraging participatory democracy, which promotes economic-political interaction, and opposing democratic surveillance and control, which eliminates anonymity.

Social participatory democracy

Two main issues are discussed in the literature regarding the importance and potential of the internet, especially social media, for active citizenship and social participation. The first issue is what level of online activism can reach the real world and be counted as political participation. Some researchers believe that Facebook and Twitter are becoming an important means of breathing and making alternative voices heard in undeveloped and oppressed countries and make public protests visible with masked human rights violations (van de Donk, 2004: 45). Protest movements were to create their counter-networks, despite the hegemonic efforts of the power communication networks, they are engaged in a struggle that can render the power networks ineffective or dysfunctional. The strength of these movements is based on their success in creating a network (Brodock, 2010: 69).

As seen, although the word digital activism has recently been used as a synonym for protesting or opposing, this concept also includes numerous political orientations (Chadwick, 2013: 92). The most important reason for this is that it soon became a channel for political activity, even if it was initially used by many for networking and entertainment purposes. It is possible to give the example of the 2004 Orange Revolution in Ukraine, the 2007 protests in Burma, the 2008 strike movements in Egypt, the 2009 Iranian election protests, and the 2010 Arab Spring. Especially in the Arab Spring, Tunisian street vendor Mohammed Bouazizi was subjected to police violence and burned himself in the square where the city hall was located, which caused intense reactions. Bouazizi's "self-immolation" image, captured with mobile phone cameras, quickly spread through the Internet's social networking sites and satellite television. It was the first time that an appeal had been raised from the Tunisian people, who had been subjected to all kinds of rights violations by authoritarian administrations for many years, and who were living illegal lives in silence. With this movement, passive networks became active (Joyce, 2010: 56). In this context, social networks performed two related functions in the Arab Spring; it was used to organize protests and made the protesters' demands internationally visible. Both of these actions were carried out silently and around the back, without being caught by the authorities, just as in the practices of inactive social movements At this point, social media tools such as Facebook.Twitter, YouTube, and Flickr acted as back streets for the activists by keeping the activists out of sight and protecting them from the wrath of the administration, on the other hand, by enabling the rapid mobilization of the people. In this context, the activism seen in the Arab Spring emerges as an old phenomenon in terms of its methods and a new phenomenon in terms of its actors and tools (Brodock, 2010: 123).

In the face of such digital activism, the ruling regime tries everything from increasing the censorship of traditional news media such as newspapers and television to blocking or delaying access to popular social networking sites such as Twitter and YouTube. However, since controlling the flow of information is more complicated on social media than on traditional media, platforms such as Facebook, Twitter, and YouTube are becoming a global information front in such actions (Carr, 2008: 112). Carr analyzed the discourses underlying new media institutions' use of the term "platform", which means an open space where everyone can have their voice heard, and found that all the income of sites like YouTube is derived from advertisements and that users do not earn any income for the videos they produce and circulate late. Therefore, as new connections are opened in this way and more freedom of expression areas are created, it is foreseen that protests will continue in the near future (Carr, 2008: 116).

In summary, given that social media has advanced to an unprecedented level in terms of social interaction, speaking, and involvement, it is reasonable to argue that networking and restructuring inside these platforms have emerged as the most significant instruments for social and political participation. However, as social media and activism become more entwined, the boundaries between online and "real" political spaces are beginning to crumble (Pearson, 2015: 925). Although it is not the solution for every problem, Facebook and other social media tools provide activists with an imperfect but effective weapon to counter pressure (Joyce, 2010). Looking at the existing examples and research, it is seen that social media facilitates activism considerably, offers faster and easier communication at less cost, allows for new connections and collective identity creation, and creates a sense of community.

Creating awareness of social communities

The infrastructure of digital activism is based on the digital network, which is a group of interconnected devices that use digital code to transmit information. The beauty of networks is that the connection is scattered. Networks not only connect us to the center but also connect us to each other (Joyce, 2010: 2). The turning point has been the growth in the use of mobile phones to access the web. It is now obvious that many people have mobile phones, even in economically developing countries. Most phones have internet capabilities, so the digital divide is at a lower level than in the past (Laer, 2010: 232). The characteristics of mobile phones for activism, and the portability, and prevalence of mobile phones make them attractive to individual activists and advocacy groups. On top of that, mobile phones are ideal for activism because communication can be maintained even when mainstream media is cut off. Many, who previously relied on mass media to share information, are now able to participate more actively in the public sphere by using mobile devices and other social media tools (Laer, 2010: 233). On the other hand, the Sensation programs for mobile devices expand the ability of the common man to actively follow corporate issues, police enforcement, and government. As time passes, it gets harder to conceal incidents like corporate criminality, police brutality, and corruption since everybody with a smartphone can act as an observer. In terms of internet activism, websites aim to increase public awareness of a problem by using information to create an awareness effect. Websites are very important for the visibility of the problem by being on the agenda of the public (Sert, 2016: 134). In this direction, people engage in activist movements aimed at taking sides to publicize their ideas, raise awareness, protect their rights, and avoid what they perceive as threats. Signature campaigns, social media accounts and groups, campaigns to be the most talked-about topic on social media (especially on Twitter), media campaigns, and similar activities are among the main activities of the type of activism aimed at being a party. This type of activism has recently been more commonly referred to as "hashtag activism". Headlines that are opened on social media and many messages related to some topics are made to attract attention to the subject (Gurak, 2014: 8).

Nowadays, activists are actively using social media tools to ensure the rapid spread of news to a wide audience, both locally and nationally. Events that seem too small or insignificant can create a butterfly effect on social media and create big repercussions. Therefore, social media tools provide an alternative and powerful platform for the transmission of messages related to global and local problems, especially against mainstream media. In this context, the act of "Do not touch my internet" against the Information and Communication Technologies authority s secure internet regulation is important in terms of understanding the power of social media. Social media tools such as Facebook and Twitter, which are used especially effectively in this action, have made it easier to organize and direct the movement (Turhan, 2017: 27). As can be seen, digital activist movements bring new forms of organization. It creates a decision mechanism by bringing together people who agree on the same line to solve the problems that exist in society (Koç, 2022: 645). On the topic, a broad sphere of influence is developing that requires global attention. People who get together voluntarily to defend, uphold, and express their rights and interests establish activist formations with the intention of altering the status quo from the global networks that the internet has generated. It is possible to give the events of Şule Çet and MasterChef competitor Murat Özdemir as examples of the fact that the subject to be drawn attention to creates a wide range of influence. Some topics that are covered up or not emphasized much can be made visible on social media through digital activists. It is even possible to initiate legal processes, arrest someone, and interfere with the incident upon reactions given on social media. For example, although the suspicious death of Şule Çetin in the Plaza was covered up by saying it was a suicide, it returned to trial for alleged murder after being an agenda topic on social media. Similarly, after Murat Özdemir videotaped and published how he tortured a parrot, he became the subject of an agenda on social media and was detained. In this sense, images or written explanations that are still wanted to attract attention and go viral lead to a different dimension of events.

Surveillance and control

According to Turhan, technologies carry a fairly significant degree of risk, as in many things in life. Therefore, regardless of how reliable and private a site's content will be, it is important to ensure that there is a method by which information can be leaked. Because it should be remembered that social media platforms such as Facebook or Twitter were established to make a profit rather than to organize people (Turhan, 2017: 29). Evgeny Morozov describes this aspect of the internet in his book "The Net Delusion" as "the dark side of internet freedom" and emphasizes the anti-democratic control of technology. Morozov draws particular attention to the fact that digital technology provides new methods of control, surveillance, and persecution for oppressive governments (Morozov, 2011: 201).

It is emphasized by certain scholars that new information and communication technologies are not limited to the usage of activists. Because governments can restrict access to the resources and infrastructure required to use these technologies, they can stop the use of these technologies that they see as a danger. Additionally, if governments have access to private personal information in new media networks, the information obtained from it may be used to identify and/or track various activists and protesters. The fact that government agents were able to identify and apprehend prominent digital activists is compelling proof that there has been some level of digital monitoring. This has a chilling impact that normally works to lower actors' inclination to employ technology. Hacktivists are specifically targeted by national intelligence services and, if apprehended, subject to severe criminal penalties (Denning, 2000: 17).

Moreover, the results of the sharing of different views on social media clearly reveal that social media is being watched and tried to be taken under control. Through their investments in surveillance and censoring technology, governments and corporations have the ability to illegally interfere with people's personal and social lives. It follows that governments with internet control are not surprised when actions conducted online are banned. Likewise, platforms such as Facebook and Twitter can meet the demand of governments and apply censorship. This social media is a mass communication tool that can be easily controlled rather than a revolutionary tool (Denning, 2000: 19). Considering this dimension, it would not be wrong to say that with the technological dimension, more opportunities are provided for more comprehensive surveillance. For example, regimes in Iran, Bahrain, and Syria use Facebook to uncover opposition networks and capture activists. China, Russia, and Saudi Arabia are investing heavily in surveillance infrastructure; use national trainees as tools for cultural management. In fact, the US Department of Defense states that cyber terrorism has replaced terrorism as a primary security concern (Kahn, 2004: 90). Accordingly, it is known that between 2003 and 2009, 30 countries arrested 161 bloggers a total of 202 times. Most of the arrests have a clear political motive. It is known that bloggers were persecuted for political reasons in 162 of these 202 cases and only 37 were prosecuted. In this sense, activists are often accused or slandered on the grounds that they either take actions to overthrow the state or the current regime or are spies. Such an accusation brings both a long prison sentence and a heavy moral burden to the accused person (Kahn, 2004: 92).

Aside from these, a lot of governments impose restrictions on activists' ability to go abroad, both virtually and physically. Whereas Saudi Arabia forbids many of its activists from traveling abroad, China forbids activist critics from going anywhere, not even to accept prizes. Upon their return from overseas activism, some activists find themselves detained for hours at airports for no apparent reason. Their personal goods, particularly laptop computers and memory devices, are frequently seized, and they may even be repeatedly summoned to the police station.

Governments have the power to censor digital content, keep an eye on what their citizens do online, and have an impact on people's offline life. In this regard, the commercial nature of digital communication technologies, their auditability by governments, and their transformation into monitoring instruments for governments and corporations disregarding individual privacy can curtail or even completely eradicate the freedom that these technologies will bestow upon people and social movements (Gunkel, 2005: 596). The real question, therefore, is how the tools that make up digital forms of action can continue to be used in the face of the intertwined nature of censorship, surveillance, and commercialization. It is necessary to find the answer to the question of how governments can go beyond the censorship, surveillance mechanisms of the industry, and the combination of profit and exploitation. Without a fight for digital rights regarding internet policy, the chances of digital technologies to support social movements to some extent will be diminished.

Conclusion

Many developments have occurred as a result of the growth and adoption of digital technologies. Particularly with social media, which has ingrained itself into daily life, people are better organized and able to contact with one another more swiftly, inexpensively, and effortlessly. Using social media, a larger audience can be reached in less time, and the word gets out there faster. These settings, which welcome people of all ages, actually open the door for virtual surroundings to eventually take the place of actual locations.

The activism movement, which is developing with digital technologies, also appears as a digital version of self-expression and brings the struggle to social media platforms. Qualifications such as digital activism or social media activism, which are used to describe different forms of activism using digital technology, mean that individuals inform each other through social media, organize around this information, and take action over social media. Thanks to digital activism, the understanding of collective consciousness and support is being established, an agora space is being created. It is evident from this angle that digitalization has changed the nature of activism. However, this reconfiguration has both advantageous and disadvantageous aspects. Because digital technologies both support and amplify social movements and, at the same time, name people and make them visible. Digital activism can be used to reinforce anti-democratic authority or cause disorder, but it can also be used to upend political systems and make people laugh.

References

Berners-Lee, Tim. (2000). *Weaving the Web: The Original Design and Ultimate Destiny of the World Wide Web by Its Inventor*. New York: Harper Collins Publishers.

Brodock, Katharine. (2010). *Digital Activism Decoded The New Mechanics of Change* (Ed. Mary Joyce). International Debate Education Association.

Carr, Nicholas. (2008). *The Big Switch: Rewiring the World, from Edison to Google* (pp. 110–117). W. W. Norton: New York.

Chadwick, A. (2013). *The Hybrid Media System: Politics and Power*. Oxford, UK: Oxford University Press.

Denning, E. Dorothy. (2000). Activism, Hacktivism, and Cyberterrorism: The Internet as a Tool for Influencing Foreign Policy. *Nautilus Institute. A revised version appeared in The Computer Security Journal*, XVI(3), 15–35.

Gunkel, J. David. (2005). Editorial: Introduction to Hacking and Hacktivism. *New Media & Society*, 7(5), 595–597, Sage Publications.

Gurak, J. L. (2014). Trust and Internet Activism: From Email to Social Networks. In M. McCaughey (Ed.), *Cyberactivism on Te Participatory* (pp. 7–19). New York: Routledge.

Joyce, M. C. (2010). *Digital Activism Decoded: The New Mechanics of Change*. New York, USA: International Debate Education Association.

Kahn, Richard ve Kellener, Douglas. (2004). New Media and Internet Activism: From The 'Battle of Seattle' to Blogging. *New Media and Society*, 6(1), 87–95.

Karagöz, Kezban. (2013). Yeni Medya Çağında Dönüşen Toplumsal Hareketler ve Dijital Aktivizm Hareketleri. *İletişim ve Diplomasi*, I(1), 131–157.

Karatzogianni, Athina. (2015). *Firebrand Waves of Digital Activism* (1st ed., pp. 1994–2014). UK: Palgrave Macmillan.

Kidd, Dorothy. (2003). Indymedia.org: A New Communications Commons. In artha McCaughey & Michael D. Ayers (Eds.), *Cyberactivism: Online Activism in Theory and Practice*. New York: Routledge.

Koç, E. (2022). Eğitim ve Öğretim Faaliyetlerinde Sosyal Medya Platformlarının Kullanılması: Hashtag İncelemesi. *The Turkish Online Journal of Design Art and Communication*, 12(3), 643–654.

Laer, J. Van, & Aelst, P. Van. (2010). Cyber-protest and Civil Society: The Internet and Action Repertoires in Social Movements. In Y. Jewkes, & M. Yar (Eds.), *Handbook of Internet Crime içinde* (pp. 230–254). London: Willan Publishing.

Lovink, Geert. (2003). *Dark Fiber: Tracking Critical Internet Culture* (p. 237). Cambridge, Mass.: MIT Press.

Morozov, Evgeny. (2011). *The Net Delusion: The Dark Side of Internet Freedom* (1st ed.). NewYork, NY: PublicAffairs.

Pearson, C., & Trevisan, F. (2015). Disability Activism in the New Media Ecology: Campaigning Strategies in the Digital Era. *Disability & Society*, 30(6), 924–940.

Pickerill, Jenny. (2003). *Cyberprotest: Environmental Activism Online*. Manchester: Manchester University Press.

Ricketts, Aidan. (2012). *The Activists' Handbook*. London: Zed Books.

Sert, Nuray Y. (2016). Aktivizmin Kavramsal Gelişimsel ve Araçsal Açıdan İncelenmesi. In Nuray Yılmaz Sert (Ed.), *Aktivizm Toplumsal Değişimin Yeni Yüzü*. İstanbul, Değişim Publishing.

Svensson, Jakob. (2014). Activism and Radical Politics in The Digital Age: Towards a Typology. *Convergence: The International Journal of Research into New 126 Media Technologies*, XXII(2), 1–16.

Turhan, D. G. (2017). Dijital Aktivizm. *Süleyman Demirel University Social Sciences Enstitute Journal*, 26, 26–44.

Uldam, Julie. (2017). *Digital Activism: After the Hype* (pp. 1–8). New Media & Society. Special Issue.

van de Donk, W., Loader, B. D., Nixon, P. G., & Ruch, D. (2004). *Cyberprotest: New Media, Citizens and Social Movements*. London, UK: Routledge.

Yengin, D., & Bayrak, T. (2022). *Yeni Medya Kuramları 101*. İstanbul: Der Publishing.

Assoc. Prof. Kenan Duman[1]

Bringing together activists over cyber populism

Abstract: In the past century, activism movements have undergone transformations alongside global social, political, and technological developments. With the advent of the Internet, activist actions were discussed in the context of technology use in the early studies, and it was assumed that the masses were strengthened, and democracy was given a healthy structure by digital technologies. This process, known as "digitalization," has been embraced as a "cyber utopia." Especially the emergence of interaction with Web 2.0, access to information and the involvement of users in a social purpose support this idea. Today, new media platforms have become the primary address for organizing in the realm of new social movements. Activist actions that take place in the platforms have had different initiatives in many countries. This study examines the digital activist efforts of the Italian "Five Star Movement," which began as an activist endeavor with a website and achieved the status of a major political party in Italy. The study argues that the political success of the Italian "Five Star Movement" is largely dependent on cyber culture. Furthermore, it emphasizes that the movement was formed as a grassroots movement based on participatory democracy through internet networks.

Keywords: Cyber-utopianism, digital activism, Italian politics, 5-Star Movement, digital democracy.

1. Introduction

Activism is known as an activity that aims to bring about social or political change and is often used together with the concept of protest or dissent. The starting point of activism is social movements. Over the last 100 years, there has been a transformation in social, political and technological developments and activism movements around the world. At the same time, awareness of social and environmental injustices occurring in various parts of the world in the digital age is becoming increasingly widespread. Although the internet and social media are criticized for many issues, especially fake news, they also help citizens from all corners of the world to access information and get involved in a social or environmental cause. Karatzogianni (2015) states that the internet has always allowed people to create new communities and share resources. According to

1 Istanbul Arel University, Faculty of Communication, Visual Communication Design Department, kenanduman@arel.edu.tr ORCID: 0000-0001-5338-9150.

Karatzogianni, more and more groups are now turning to different ideological and practical tools and creating collaborative platforms to achieve social change.

A new form of collective action has begun to develop, especially with social networks and digital tools. The period after 2004 is at the center of these developments. While these actions are generally described as digital activism, this type of activism allows individuals to connect with each other for a core cause, while also having the power to connect many people nationally or internationally. Joyce (2010: 2) describes digital activism as an economic, political and social content that draws attention with its instrumental structure advanced by digital technology infrastructure. In the context of this definition, digital activism can be considered as a situation in which efforts are made to raise awareness through digital technologies, especially the internet, and to be a voice in public opinion. Action against a public event, which is the basis of the concept of activism in the traditional sense, can be done more easily with digital activism.

Digital activism defines a form of activism used for mass political or social actions after the internet and digital media (URL-1). As of the early 1990s, online activists have been using the Internet as a tool to instantly reach large audiences beyond local or regional borders and distribute information. In 2004, with the introduction of Web 2.0 technology, broader examples of digital activism began to be seen. With the developments in broadband technology, it has been seen that the internet has quickly turned into a field that reflects and strengthens protests. As of this period, different digital activism tactics such as e-mail, social network campaigns and hacktivism have begun to be used. As a result of these studies, the internet and social networks have increased individual and social awareness of a particular problem by allowing the amplification of political messages. Internet platforms, which initially serve the primary purpose of personal and social relationships, soon prove to be a useful tool for producing and disseminating meaningful content as part of a larger struggle that leads to social change (Treré & Kaun, 2021).

Digital activism has also transformed forms of political communication and political protests over the last two decades. Especially after 2005, as smart phones became widespread, there was a change in the way political events, protests and movements were organized. Such activities have become a part of everyday life, with the new possibilities of digital activism helping to mobilize millions of new supporters for a wide variety of causes. Karatzogianni (2015) points out that in this new era, where new forms of digital activism have emerged, the current world of politics, social movements and campaigns has changed, and internet and mobile technologies have come to the fore to offer an alternative way of arranging social and economic structure.

> (...) We've become used to the idea of digital activism and social media being used to publicise and grow political movements, such as the Arab Spring uprisings in the Middle East and the anti-austerity movement Occupy. Activists, such as those in recent French labour protests, can now live stream videos of their actions using apps such as Periscope while online users contribute to the debate. In Barcelona, the party of new mayor Ada Colau drew up its electoral programme with the help of over 5,000 people, in public assemblies and online, including the formation of network of cyberactivists, SomComuns. (...) So-called hacktivist organisations such as Anonymous regularly attack the computer networks of the rich and powerful, and even terrorist organisations such as Islamic State. The recent Panama Papers follow similar revelations by Wikileaks and Edward Snowden as examples of "leaktivism". Here, the internet is used to obtain, leak and spread confidential documents with political ramifications. The Panama leaks have led to protests forcing Iceland's prime minister to step aside and calls for similar action in the UK (Karatzogianni, 2015).

There have been different attempts in many countries with activist actions, which have become an important extension of new social movements in the new digital age and where networks are used for organizing purposes. In this study, the digital activist work of the Italian Five Star Movement, which started as an activist work with a website and became the first party in Italy, and its internet infrastructure and direct democracy experiments were examined in the context of cyber populism.

1.1. Social movements, web 2.0 and digital activism

As technology permeates the world in the 21st century, activism experiences an expansion from the grassroots to the internet. With digital activism, people use various digital media such as the internet, mobile phones, proxy servers, blogs, online petitions or social networks to convey their messages (Gerbaudo, 2017: 481). Platforms such as MoveOn.org, founded in 1998, Seattle protests in 1999, GoPetition, founded in 2000, and Change.org and Avaaz.org, founded in 2007, are known as early examples of digital activism. In particular, the Seattle protests against the World Trade Organization have begun to gain traction through new platforms, such as protesters using e-mail to organize during counter-protests. Digital activism has become a global focal point with the Arab Spring protests that began in late 2010. People in the Middle East and North Africa passing through a series of revolutions utilized social networks to convey information about the protests, by means of videos recorded on smartphones. Wikileaks, which coincided with the same period, enabled digital activism to be discussed in the mainstream media and the public.

Activists use internet and new media technologies in different ways for their main actions and stances. Morozov (2007) collected these actions under 8 main headings. It is seen that activists turn to new media to access information and increase the quality of action. Activists often use new media tools to draw public attention to the problem that is the subject of action. While the main public issues were in the hands of a group of elite groups during the mass communication period of the 20th century, with the internet, people from many different groups have managed to bring issues outside the mainstream to the public agenda. This period also draws attention as the beginning of the decline of public determining media, as well as the decline of most traditional institutions. Activists use new media tools to reach volunteers in aid efforts, facilitate crowd gathering, and improve outreach. In addition, new media tools have become very important to create new members for topics, agendas or organizations. One of the important issues of activism is to generate income from actions. Compared to the traditional period, activists use new media tools to raise funds for post-digital media actions and to create new action methods. Apart from these forms of use, new media tools are used to communicate with other non-governmental organizations, to communicate with political party representatives, to accelerate actions and to provide assistance in logistics.

Castells (2016), in his studies on network society, attached great importance to the communication style of the user within the network. According to Castells, a new form of interactive communication has emerged with the advancement of internet and network technologies in the post-1990 period. Especially in the post-Web 2.0 era, users have created their own mass communication systems through text messaging (SMS), blogs, wikis, podcasts, etc. Castells (2016: 65) defines this new form of communication as "mass self-communication". According to Castells, "mass self-communication" refers to an interaction in which the person has the opportunity to reach an audience, but in which message production depends on the person himself, in which the person directs message reception, and in which the acceptance and assembly of content from electronic communication networks depends on the person's own choices. The logic of mass self-communication mentioned by Castells combines face-to-face communication with digital tools and mass media. Castells states that this logic of communication deeply influenced global and local activist movements between 2000 and 2010. While many different and creative forms of digital-based activism have emerged in the new media age, new social movements defined as "digital activism" have begun to appear with new communication technologies.

Karatzogianni (2015) describes digital activism in four main stages in a historical context. According to him, digital activism started in 1994, transformed with the events of September 11, reached its peak with the Arab Spring uprisings in 2011, and entered its fourth phase with the Wikileaks revelations in 2013. The first phase of Digital Activism covers the period between 1994 and 2001 and is seen as the roots of digital activism. The first example of activism in this period was the Zapatistas, who changed tactics from guerrilla warfare to online activism in 1994. Then, during the 1999 Seattle World Trade Organization protests, demonstrators used their mobile phones to stream directly to the Internet and broadcast live video. Protesters have used the Web extensively for street protests as well as mobilization and online direct action (Özkula, 2021). During these anti-globalization protests, activists came together and Indymedya (Independent Media Center) was established. Indymedia is a citizen journalism project that supports activism and challenges mainstream media news and commentary perspectives. Citizen journalism projects that emerged from Web 2.0 were formed when users who did not receive special training in media production recorded and reported events. The "gatekeeper" role of traditional news editors; blogs have been overtaken by You Tube or other freely publishing citizen journalists (Laughey, 2010: 165–166).

The second phase of digital activism was between 2001 and 2007. After the September 11 Events in the United States in 2001, a major change began in global politics. Activism is also affected by this situation. In this period, which is known as the rise of digital activism, while Web 2.0 technologies were integrated into the system, cyber conflicts were observed in the context of activism. MoveOn, which started as an e-mail community in 1998, is among the first pioneers of digital activism. Their digital and traditional work against the American invasion of Iraq in 2003, and their work in Barack Obama's 2008 campaign in the US elections. Again, in the protests in the Philippines for President Joseph Estrada to step down in 2001, in the demonstrations after the presidential elections in Iran in 2009, in the protests in Moldova in 2009, and in the Arab Spring events in 2011 and 2012, primarily SMS and e-mail messages were used. and the use of social networking sites are the most important examples of the use of new media in social movements (Özkula, 2021).

Karatzogianni (2015) points to the period between 2007 and 2010 as the third phase of digital activism. According to him, this is the period when digital activism spread. In this process, the actions taken by countries through hackers, especially as they realize the power of the internet, draw attention. The new era is a period in which tensions begin on the network, beyond just the struggle over land. In the network-centric world, which has become accessible to everyone, new concepts such as cyber protest, cyber terrorism, cyber crime and cyber conflict are introduced in the context of activism. Van Dijk (2016: 147) states that during this period, Russia, China, the USA, Iran and Israel were accused of cyber attacks, but nationalist and opposition action groups were behind these actions. The period after 2010 is seen as the fourth phase of digital activism. The most important activist event of this period is WikiLeaks. Wikileaks is a disclosure platform founded by Julian Assange in 2006. Fuchs (2016: 291) states that Wikileaks aims to reveal the inappropriate behavior and crimes of governments and global companies subsidized by online donations. The large-scale power-oriented surveillance debates put forward by Wikileaks and other leak networks have been important in the spread of digital activism. Karatzogianni (2015) pointed out that this new period after 2010 has drawn digital activism, which is a field of alternative media, into general politics.

1.2. Going against the system in digital cyber populism

Cyber populism is a form of political movement in which discourses opposing the system and order are spoken through digital media tools. "Cyber populism", which is close to concepts such as techno-populism, populism 2.0 and web-populism, is a new phenomenon and has seen its development from the end of the 20th century to the present. In the post-1990 period, as the Internet became more widely used in daily life and became widespread, the ability to share it with users through Web 2.0 was effective in the development of cyber populist actions. With the rapidly expanding social media platforms of Web 2.0 and its aftermath, access to the general audience restricted by mass communication has become much easier. The age of mobile communication has also offered its citizens new opportunities for political participation in democratic processes and, ultimately, the creation of a new public sphere focused on discursive and participatory practices.

Gerbaudo (2017: 477) points out that in the two main waves of digital activism called Web 1.0 and Web 2.0, there are two different waves of protests, the anti-globalization movement and the square movements that started in 2011, each with its own dominant ideology. The Arab Spring is the peak of this process. However, the point that should be noted here is that, especially in the post-2008 period, the dominant activist ideology began to evolve towards cyber populism. As a result of this turn, Gerbaudo (2017: 477) states that the first and second wave of digital activism experienced a transition from cyber-autonomism to cyber-populism, the two defining techno-political orientations. Cyber-populism, sustained by the populist turn of the movements after 2011, views the internet as a "popular space" that should be adopted by ordinary citizens, withdrawn from consumption activities and encouraged towards the purpose of popular activation against neoliberal elites. "(...)This shift that substantially modifies the way in which activists conceives of and utilise digital media goes a long way towards explaining the differences in digital activism practices, and their contrasting views of the internet as a tool and site of struggle.(...) (Gerbaudo, 2017: 477)"

Cyber-populism is a populist ideology formed in the age of digital media that can be reached directly to the user. Populist actions here are implemented by politicians or political movements on platforms that are used free of charge by users. The Five Star Movement in Italy, La République En Marche in France, Alternative for Germany (AfD) in Germany, Podemos in Spain, and "One Nation" in Australia, which emerged after the World Wide Web 2.0, can be exemplified as cyber populist political movements (Bickerton & Accetti, 2021).

2. Post-republican Italian political order and the Five Star Movement

With the Italian Union in 1861, Italy became a single country again after Rome. Although Italy was the winning side in the First World War, it suffered many casualties and faced great economic and social chaos as a result of the destruction of the war. As a result of this situation, the country experienced political instability. In 1922, the National Fascist Party led by Mussolini came to power in this environment of chaos, and the Mussolini era began in the country, which would last until the end of the Second World War. Italy, which entered the Second World War with Mussolini, had an unsuccessful war, and as a result of the defeats that followed, Mussolini fell from power in 1943. After losing World War II, Italy experienced a major economic and social collapse. In 1948, the Italian people approved a new constitution and transitioned to a republic (Duman, 2013).

The period from 1946 to 1993 in Italy was called the "First Republic", and the period after 1993 was called the "Second Republic". While the period of the First Republic (1946–1993) is considered to have a relatively more stable structure, the period after 1990 is seen as more transitional and problematic. An important history of the country, which has had more than 60 government changes since 1948, is coalition governments. In fact, the country, which traditionally had a parliamentary structure between two or three parties from the 1950s to the 1990s, completely changed after the "Clean Hands" operation, which was a corruption investigation in the early 1990s. Many political parties disappeared in this investigation, which resulted in the end of the period described as the "First Republic". After this period, technocrat prime ministers and cabinets began to appear, as well as constantly changing governments. After the "Clean Hands" (Mani pulite) operation, new actors and formations emerged, such as Silvio Berlusconi, who served as prime minister in different periods for a long time, and the Northern League. In the new period called the "Second Republic", two major mass parties, mainly represented by the Democratic Party (PD) and Forza Italia (FI), became the main political actors. In the elections after 2010, political formations such as the Five Star Movement and the League Party ranked in the top three places and a new era began in Italian politics (URL-2).

2.1. Five Star Movement

As a political party, The Five Star Movement was established in Italy in October 2009 by political activists Gianroberto Casaleggio and Beppe Grillo, who is also a comedian. Beppe Grillo, the inspiration of the movement, is also a blogger. The Five Star Movement has also progressed as an internet-based movement. As the first spark in the history of the movement, Beppe Grillo's invitation to the masses to Meet Up social network meetings for communication and coordination at the local level on his blog in July 2005 is of great importance (URL-3). During the emergence of the movement, the event that made Beppe Grillo draw attention throughout the country on June 14, 2007, was his organization of the V-Day (Vaffanculo Day, "F. off-Day") regarding the election law. It shows that it is different from the dynamics of a political formation (Bailo, 2015: 552). The emergence of the movement in terms of politicization took place in 2009 with the text called the Florence Declaration. The name of the movement refers to the five main areas of interest: water, sustainable transportation, sustainable development, free internet access and the environment (Manucci & Amsler, 2018: 115). The party has made a name for itself in Italian and European politics as an advocate of green politics, progressivism and direct democracy. The characteristic features of the party include populism, anti-corruption, anti-environment and anti-EU ideas. Unlike other parties, the party has introduced practices such as participatory and direct democracy, e-democracy, and free access to the internet.

After its emergence in 2009, it was seen that the Five Star Movement gradually started to get important results in the regional and local elections in Italy between 2010 and 2012. In fact, in the Italian local elections held in 2012, the Five Star Movement reached between 10% and 20% of the votes, especially in the cities of Northern Italy such as Genoa, Verona, Parma, Monza and Piacenza (URL-4). The real breakthrough of the Five Star Movement was the 2013 general elections. The movement received 25.5% of the votes in the general elections it entered for the first time in 2013 and became the second largest party in Italy after the

Democratic Party (Natale & Ballatore, 2014: 106). The most important promises of the Five Star Movement in the general elections are the necessity of placing politics on a moral basis, the importance of direct democracy and opposition to the austerity measures of the Monti government implemented in the country (Franzosi et al., 2015: 111). In the 2014 European parliament elections, the Five Star Movement again took second place, receiving 21.15% of the votes. "Participate, choose, change!" in the 2018 general elections. The Movement, which entered with the motto, received the most votes with nearly 33% of the votes. The Centre-Right Coalition received the most votes in the elections, but since no political group or party could achieve an absolute majority, the election resulted in the suspension of the parliament (URL-5). While the period between 2019 and 2022 was filled with government crises for the country, the European parliament elections were held in 2019 and the Movement's vote rate decreased to 21%. The political Movement, which stayed away from coalitions, supported the Conte Government, the 65th Italian Government, during this period. However, there was a lot of turmoil during this period and the political leader of the Movement, Luigi Di Maio, resigned from this position. Coalition Government, Political Crises, Global Developments The movement revealed negativities and the vote rate in the elections held in 2022 was 15%.

2.2. Grillo's Beppegrillo it blog and digital direct democracy essays

Beppe Grillo, the co-founder of the Five Star Movement, is known as a television celebrity before his political side. While the actor, born in 1948, was known as a national television face during the emergence and development of Italian television, his comedy and sketch styles are known to be more political. While Grillo has made satirical comedies on television, he has also worked as an activist and campaigner in theatres. Grillo's satire touched on the corruption of Italian politicians and big corporations. He was dismissed from RAI, the Italian public service broadcaster, after sketches targeting the Italian Socialist Party (Natale & Ballatore, 2014: 107). After this development, Grillo did not appear much on television. After this situation, Grillo earns his living by performing stand-up shows in Italy. In January 2005, he founded his own website, beppegrillo.it, and started blogging.

Grillo, who concentrated on blogging and politics and political communication studies in the post-2005 period, turned into a political leader after 2009 (Natale & Ballatore, 2014: 107). Grillo has been one of the most prominent examples of the populist rise that emerged in Europe in the 2010s. Grillo's bloc and the political formation that followed changed the political climate in Italy after the second republic and led to the birth of this new national movement. In this parallel process, which coincides with the changes in the internet communication behavior of the masses after the Millennium, the works of Grillo and his friends are about combining physical space and the digital world. The contents of Grillo's blog are about morally cleansing the Italian parliament and the importance of freedom of access to information and communication (Natale & Ballatore, 2014: 16).

Beppegrillo.it is updated daily with the latest comments and opinions on topics of both national and international interest. Beppe Grillo regularly conducts interviews, references and quotes with experts in different fields who offer their opinions and comments through his blog multimedia platform, and publishes video interviews and texts together. While Grillo can communicate directly and effectively with voters and sympathizers through his website, he accepts the internet as a tool for direct democracy. Unlike politicians who reach the masses through mass media and election venues in the traditional structure, they use the internet as a medium through which they can communicate directly with the leader. The blog that Grillo was able to establish directly with the Movement's supporters also served his anti-elite attitude and populist discourse in a positive way. While Beppegrillo.it was used as a gathering tool by activists in the first period, it became the main information tool and, in a sense, the "spokesperson" of the party in the post-2009 period. In the last two hundred years, the transmission tool of political parties, which first started with newspapers and magazines and then evolved with radio and television, has started to change with blogs, micro blogs and web pages, and Beppe Grillo's blog can be mentioned as one of the leading examples of this (Musso & Maccaferri, 2018).

One of the significant factors that distinguish Grillo's blog from other pioneering examples is that it goes beyond the mere use of the internet in political communication. Because Grillo's blog united online and offline on a common ground at the national level (McDonnell, 2013). Blogging and the internet have been an important catalyst in political organizing. Beppe Grillo's success in creating meetups with Meetup.com and bringing users together for discussions about issues in their area both online and physically are important examples of political communication. An important situation here is that users started to spend more time on the internet, especially in the Web 2.0 period after 2004, and the golden age of micro blogs coincided with the same time. After 2009, this process accelerated even more with the 3G and mobile revolution. Grillo has encountered a group of users who are enthusiastic about this new public space. Of course, explaining this situation only with technological developments would mean missing the dynamics of Italian politics. In this regard, both technology and political context must be evaluated together. After Grillo's blog went live, users started to spend time with the blog in a wide geography. Afterwards, interactive comments began to be written at Grillo's local meetings and in discussions on his internet forum. After these discussions held over the internet, they continued with a meeting held in a real physical location. Under the influence of online activities, users decided to go to physical discussions and subsequently participated in the local offline activities of the movement. As in all public space discussions after Web 2.0, there has been a similar debate on this issue, and it has been seen that the internet does not completely constitute the public space but has a function that facilitates and complements physical activities (McDonnell, 2013).

Direct democracy is known as a democratic form of government in which citizens can directly exercise legislative power without any political mediation or representation. This form of democracy, which was seen to be practiced in Ancient Greece and Ancient Rome, was seen in the Middle Ages and the Modern Age with very different forms and original local solutions. Forms of direct democracy are defined as all procedures that imply the cancellation of any mediation in the exercise of "power of the people" (Florida & Vignati, 2013). The theme of "direct democracy" regained strength in the Enlightenment. Jean-Jacques Rousseau defines direct democracy as the only form of government in which the sovereign people express their general will. Rousseau, who wanted the new society to be established on the basis of "common interests", saw it necessary for selfish individuals to transform into "citizens" who desire to serve society through direct democracy (Rousseau, 1993: 29–35). It has become a step that can support the direct expression of citizens' will without a mediator. This situation has produced a result close to Rousseau's ideal. Gallo (2021) mentions the Five Star Movement initiated by Grillo as one of the most important experiments in the context of direct democracy in the modern Era. Grillo states that with the widespread use of internet technology, direct democracy has become possible and allows citizens to participate in political decisions without the mediation of politicians and political parties (Florida & Vignati, 2014).

> The term direct democracy describes a new relationship between citizens and their representatives, […] Current democracy operates on the principle of delegation, not direct participation: With the vote, the voters' relationship with the candidates and the choices they will exercise ends […] The Internet is redefining the relationship between citizens and politics by allowing access to real-time information on any phenomenon and control over processes activated by central or local government. Direct democracy reveals the centrality of the citizen (Casaleggio, 2004: 23–25).

This formation, which acted outside party and association ties and without the mediation of guiding or representative organisms, consisted of a group of educated urbanites. The Five Star Movement placed anti-environment and anti-particracy at the center, encouraging the direct participation of citizens united in the management of public affairs through internet-driven direct democracy. While the grassroots mass is gaining the ability to produce new messages autonomously, it is seen that the groups are rapidly mobilizing and organizing. Social networks, blogs and the internet are not only central to Grillo and the Five Star Movement's understanding of democracy, but also the party's communication process and organizational model are based on this "structural" element. While the Five Star Movement was going for a political organization with the aim of a major change in Italian political life in 2009, it tried a new form of internet-based direct democracy (Ceccarini & Bordignon, 2016: 135). Almost all of the 15-year activity of the Five Star Movement, which became one of the most important political actors in Italy in a very short time, was carried out online. It was observed that the formation is far from traditional media tools such as newspapers and television, and that the candidates did not give interviews on television or in the press for a long time. Starting with the blog of the founder Grillo, the movement aimed to represent the views of the public through an online voting and discussion portal for direct democracy on the internet. The movement has used online voting since 2012 to determine its candidates in Italian and European elections. Candidates are determined as a result of these elections, which are held through a web-based application accessible to members registered on the party's website (URL-6). With the online platform, users who support the Movement can discuss the legislative proposals on the agenda and give their approval for approval or rejection. Decisions taken on the online platform are then presented to the Parliament (Deseriis, 2017: 48). For example, the election law of M5S and the election of the presidential candidate were determined through online voting. In addition, the decision to abolish a law against immigrants was taken by the decision of the members, contrary to the views of Grillo and Casaleggio, the leaders of the Movement (URL-7). While political chaos continued in Italy in 2019, Five Star and the center-left Democratic Party (PD) agree on a draft program to govern Italy. However, the Five Star Movement needs the support of approximately 100,000 members to become a member of the coalition. 79.3% of the 79,634 members using the online voting platform called Rousseau voted in support of the coalition (URL-8).

It has also been revealed in different studies that the Five Star Movement uses the internet as a potential alternative web-based civil platform to transmit alternative content and challenge mainstream media communication on its own ground (Mosca & Vaccari, 2013). According to Mosca and Vaccari's (2013) analysis, comparing the voters and candidates of Italian political parties with the voters and candidates of the Five Star Movement, it was concluded that the Five Star Movement considered the internet to be the most reliable media in terms of political information. Secondary sources as important as the Beppegrillo.it blog in message distribution and organization of the Five Star Movement are Twitter and Facebook. The process parallel to the movement's emergence date shows its golden age in mobile and social networks. Twitter and Facebook have greatly helped spread Grillo's blog posts and Movement messages. Social networking platforms served as an important megaphone for the messages Grillo and the Movement pioneers sent. Through these two social media platforms, Grillo has enabled him to communicate "directly" with his voter base, as well as the public and the media (Bordignon & Ceccarini, 2015: 463).

Considering the historical development of the Five Star Movement's direct democracy efforts since 2005, which emerged at a time when representative democracies were being questioned, there is a significant difference between the 2005–2012 period and the post-2013 period. It is stated by many critics, especially the Old Movement administrators, that the Movement encountered distortions, unlike its initial idea, in the process of gaining political power. In particular, Casaleggio Associati, the company that manages the Five Star Movement's internet network, has often been accused of not being transparent and centralizing. Again, the Movement's voting platform "Rousseau" caused controversy due to both security and number of users (Mosca, 2015).

2.3. Cyber populist rhetoric of the Five Star Movement

Populism is known as a political philosophy or form of discourse that assumes that the interests of the people are suppressed and hindered by an elite layer in society and that state organs should be removed from the influence of this elite layer and used for the benefit of the people and their development as a society. In short, populism is also defined as "political ideas and activities that aim to gain support from ordinary people by giving them what they want" (Cambridge). Throughout history, Populism has displayed itself in many different forms from the end of the 19th century to today. Curently, it appears that the growth of the internet and the emergence of populism have a considerable repercusions impact. Populism always occurs as an indicator of the lack of democracy, that is, "representation" (Revelli, 2017).

Since the emergence of the Internet, the concept of digitalization has also been accepted as "cyber utopia". In the first studies on Web 1.0 and 2.0, it was pointed out that the internet and mobile technologies were an important force in the empowerment of the masses and the development of democracy. According to this idea, it is believed that digital technologies will help create a decentralized, democratic and liberal society. Cyber-utopianism serves as a basis for cyber-populism. Electronic democracy proposals proposed and implemented by cyber-populist parties have been seen as an idea that motivates cyber-utopians. Pazzini (2019) points out that in the post-Web 2.0 period, the internet space is used by populists as one of the lowest common denominators to build a common identity. Here, the user, who is the addressee of populism as a manifestation of the situation of modern social network societies, is being adapted again. In this manner, the capability to connect becomes the lowest common denominator and the common person is somewhat reshaped to adopt him/herself to the other online users of the Internet. Therefore, all unsatisfied demands converge at one point and their common elements are found through the internet. Thus, it plays a key role in the discursive construction of people. The online interaction and idea sharing efforts of the Five Star Movement, which Grillo and Casaleggio initiated with the idea of direct democracy, can be interpreted as a mass democracy effort in activism. Especially in this period when Web 2.0 interactively draws the user into the process, the fact that messages can be liked, re-posted and shared on their own micro blog page has provided significant convenience for activist movements acting collectively. Pazzini (2019) draws attention to the concept of fluid democracy in this process, which is based on the idea of collective knowledge, where sharing ideas and changes can lead to better results. In a liquid democracy, voting power is exercised by delegates rather than representatives. By these means, cyber populists maintain that they can banish the need for representation rather than enact direct democracy.

When we look at the political history of Italy, we can often see examples of populism, the Five Star Movement and the Northern League as a continuation of the centre-right populist political school that Berlusconi started in the 1990s after Clean Hands. In this very period, the increasing impact of the global economic crisis in Italy, developments within the European Union, immigration policies and the accompanying developments created a populist wave. In the studies of Natale and Ballatore (2014), it was determined that the Five Star Movement intensively used cyber-utopian rhetoric in its promises of better environmental and political space regulation via the internet in examples of direct democracy. One of the main starting points of the Internet in the context of democracy is transparency. Criticizing Italy's recent political developments, Grillo and Casaleggio (2011) define the internet as a transparent, unified, coherent entity with its own logic, laws, activism and destructive agenda. One of the main efforts of Casaleggio and Grillo is the remoralization of Italian politics, which they see as problematic. In this context, both leaders criticized Italian politics and politicians with populist discourses. According to Casaleggio and Grillo, the internet inherently reduces corruption and encourages transparency. Unlike political parties, online communities are characterized by solidarity and transparency (Casaleggio & Grillo, 2011: 46).

The Five Star Movement is an important example of the charismatic leadership connections of mass parties such as Grillo combined with the media (Deseriis, 2017). Grillo is a political entrepreneur who is very successful in mobilizing the masses as a result of his acting talent (Bordignon & Ceccarini, 2013). Grillo was able to effectively convey populist discourse with his personal rhetoric ability. Grillo, who conveys sections and examples from his own lives in a satirical language in his discourses, also underlined his rejection of the elitist style of politics by using daily language and was able to establish the image of "one of us" in the eyes of the voters (Sokullu). Luidi di Maio, who replaced Grillo in 2017, continued an extremely aggressive populist line. The movement exhibited all the characteristics of a classical populist party, such as demagogy, cultural vulgarity, anti-systemism, criticism of political figures' disconnection from the public, and charismatic leadership.

The spread of fake news on the internet, the gap in education, the negative effects of the economic crisis and the emergence of international terrorism are frequently listed among the factors that lead to the rise of populism. The Five Star Movement has also been accused by major western media outlets of being linked to the spread of fake news on the Internet. The Five Star Movement, especially Beppe Grillo, expressed an opposing opinion about the compulsory vaccination of governments during the Covid 19 epidemic. Grillo and his Movement have been accused by media outlets of contributing to the spread of conspiracy theories about vaccines. As a counter move, the Five Star Movement and its leaders criticized the press for publishing "fake news" about them and filed a lawsuit against many journalists (URL-9).

3. Conclusion

The Five Star Movement, founded in Italy in 2009 by activist actor Beppe Grillo and web entrepreneur Gianroberto Casaleggio, quickly attracted attention in Italian politics after 2010. The Party, which managed to become the second largest party in the 2013 general elections, became the party with the most votes in a short time. The internet played a major role in the emergence and rise of the Five Star Movement. Blogs, social networks and websites were used to organize the movement and create a voter base. This is of great importance for early internet and network studies. While the Five Star Movement's direct democracy-based efforts draw attention as a different experiment in Italian and European politics, a unique and consistent discourse has been created by interacting with the voters. The Five Star Movement experimented with the internet-based form of direct democracy while organizing for a major change in Italian political life. Starting with the blog of the founder Grillo, the movement aimed to represent the views of the public through an online voting and discussion portal for direct democracy on the internet. The Five Star Movement has made populist promises such as better environment and regulation of Italian politics in order to gain the support of the public and voters via the internet. Grillo, the leader of the movement, was able to effectively convey the populist discourse with his personal rhetorical talent. Additionally, the Movement was accused of producing fake news in Italy in the post-2016 period.

References

Bailo, F. (2015). Mapping Online Political Talks Through Network Analysis: A Case Study of The Website of Italy's Five Star Movement. *Policy Studies*, 36(6), 550–572.

Bickerton, C. J., & Accetti, C. I. (2021). *Technopopulism: The New Logic of Democratic Politics*. USA: Oxford University Press.

Bordignon, F., & Ceccarini, L. (2013). Five Stars and a Cricket: Beppe Grillo Shakes Italian Politics. *South European Society and Politics*, 18(4), 427–449.

Bordignon, F., & Ceccarini, L. (2015). The Five-Star Movement: a hybrid actor in the net of state institutions. *Journal of Modern Italian Studies*, 20(4), 454–473.

Casaleggio, G. (2004). *Web Ergo Sum*. Sperling & Kupfer.

Castells, M. (2016). *İletişimin Gücü*. İstanbul: İstanbul Bilgi University Press.

Ceccarini, L., & Bordignon, F. (2016). The Five Stars Continue to Shine: The Consolidation of Grillo's "Movement Party" in Italy. *Contemporary Italian Politics*, 8(2), 131–159.

Deseriis, M. (2017). Technopopulism: The Emergence of A Discursive Formation. TripleC: Communication, Capitalism & Critique. *Open Access Journal for A Global Sustainable Information Society*, 15(2), 441–458.

Duman, K. (2013). *Türkiye ve İtalya'da Özel Televizyon Yayinciliğinin Başlangıcı ve Deregülasyon Sürecinin Karşılaştırılması* (Yayımlanmamış Doktora Tezi). İstanbul: İstanbul Üniversitesi Sosyal Bilimler Enstitüsü.

Franzosi, P., Marone, F., & Salvati, E. (2015). Populism and Euroscepticism in The Italian Five Star Movement. *The International Spectator*, 50(2), 109–124.

Florida, A., & Vignati, R. (2014). Deliberativa, Diretta O Partecipativa: Quale Democrazia Per Il Movimento 5 Stelle? *Quaderni di Sociologia*, 65, 51–73. https://doi.org/10.4000/qds.369

Fuchs, C. (2016). *Sosyal Medya: Eleştirel Bir Giriş*. İstanbul: Notabene Press.

Gallo. (2021). Rousseau e il M5s? La democrazia diretta non può avere "custodi". *Serve un nuovo modello per evitare grumi di potere*. Erişim Tarihi: 02.07.2023.

https://www.ilfattoquotidiano.it/2021/05/22/rousseau-e-il-m5s-la-democrazia-diretta-non-puo-avere-custodi-serve-un-nuovo-modello-per-evitare-grumi-di-potere/6204351/

Gerbaudo, P. (2017). From Cyber-autonomism to Cyber-populism: An Ideological Analysis of the Evolution of Digital Activism. TripleC: Communication, Capitalism & Critique. *Open Access Journal for a Global Sustainable Information Society*, 15(2), 477–489.

Grillo, B., & Casaleggio, G. (2011). *Siamo in Guerra: Per Una Nuova Politica*. Chiarelettere.

Joyce, M. (2010). *Digital Activism Decoded: The New Mechanics of Change*. New York: Idebate Press.

Karatzogianni, A. (2015). *Firebrand Waves of Digital Activism 1994–2014: The Rise and Spread of Hacktivism and Cyberconflict*. Springer.

Laughey, D. (2010). *Medya Çalışmaları: Teoriler ve Yaklaşımlar* (Çeviri: Toprak, A.). Kalkedon.

Manucci, L., & Amsler, M. (2018). Where the Wind Blows: Five Star Movement's Populism, Direct Democracy and Ideological Flexibility. *Italian Political Science Review/Rivista Italiana Di Scienza Politica*, 48(1), 109–132.

McDonnell. (2013). The Real Innovation in Beppe Grillo's Campaigning Is Not His Use of Social Media, But His Success in Using The Internet to Bring Together Activists at The Grassroots Level. https://blogs.lse.ac.uk/europpblog/2013/04/23/innovation-beppe-grillo-internet-campaigning-m5s-social-media-meetup/. Acsessed Date: 07 September 2023.

Morozov, E. (2007). *New Media Essentials*. Prague: Transitions Online.

Mosca, L., & Vaccari, C. (2013). Il Movimento e la rete. *Contemporanea*, 221, 169–196.

Musso, M., & Maccaferri, M. (2018). At the Origins of the Political Discourse of the 5-Star Movement (M5S): Internet, Direct Democracy and the "future of the past". *Internet Histories*, 2(1–2), 98–120.

Natale, S., & Ballatore, A. (2014). The Web Will Kill Them All: New Media, Digital Utopia, and Political Struggle in the Italian 5-Star Movement. *Media, Culture & Society*, 36(1), 105–121.

Özkula, S. M. (2021). The Problem of History in Digital Activism: Ideological Narratives in Digital Activism Literature. *First Monday*, 26(8).

Pazzini, E. (2019). Grillo and the Vacuum: Understanding the Project of the Five Stars Movement. *Canadian Journal of European and Russian Studies*, 13(1), 21–37.

Revelli, M. (2017). *Populismo 2.0*. Giulio Einaudi Editore.

Rousseau, J. J. (1993). *Toplum Sözleşmesi* (Çeviri: Vedat Günyol). İstanbul: Adam Press.

Treré, E., & Kaun, A. (2021). Digital Media Activism: A Situated, Historical, and Ecological Approach Beyond the Technological Sublime. In Gabriele Balbi, Nelson Ribeiro, Valérie Schafer, & Christian Schwarzenegger (Eds.), *Digital Roots: Historicizing Media and Communication Concepts of the Digital Age* (pp. 193–208). Berlin.

Van Dijk, J. (2016). *Ağ Toplumu*. Epsilon Press.

URL-1: https://www.britannica.com/topic/digital-activism Accessed Date: 12 June 2023.

URL-2: https://www.mfa.gov.tr/italya-siyasi-gorunumu.tr.mfa. Accessed Date: 07 September 2023.

URL-3: http://www.beppegrillo.it/2005/07/incontriamoci_m_1.html. Accessed Date: 22 August 2023.

URL-4: https://www.corriere.it/Speciali/Politica/2012/elezioni12/SEAS/amministrative/comunali/20120506000000_2_COMUNE_29_60.shtml. Accessed Date: 12 June 2023.

URL-5: https://www.dw.com/en/italy-election-to-result-in-hung-parliament/a-42823814. Accessed Date: 22 August 2023.

URL-6: https://www.movimento5stelle.eu. Accessed Date: 12 June 2023.

URL-7: https://www.corriere.it/politica/14_gennaio_13/grillo-lancia-consultazioni-reato-clandestinita-dissidenti-politica-non-sia-videogame-b474ad60-7c49-11e3-bc95-3898e25f75f1.shtml

URL-8: https://www.bbc.com/news/world-europe-49563798. Accessed Date: 07 July 2023.

URL-9: https://www.cjr.org/analysis/italy-five-star-movement.php. Accessed Date: 12. June 2023.

Assoc. Prof. Begüm Aylin Önder[1], Res. Asst. Bilgesu Biber[2]

Digital Activism's Impact On Gen Z: A Social Media Platform Analysis

Abstract: Throughout history, the unstoppable progress of information and communication technologies has not only influenced human and social life in economic, sociological and cultural terms. It has also led to differences in the needs of generations born in different eras and whose goals change according to time and conditions. Generation Z, whose date of birth is described in the literature as 1995 according to some sources and 2000 and later according to others, can use these technologies actively and multipurpose in today's world where digital technologies have become an essential part of life. In particular, due to the increasing number of users of the interaction-based Web 2.0 and the promise of being pluralistic and democratic, social media platforms are used very effectively by Generation Z when it comes to questioning and demanding rights, especially when it comes to social events. In this context, this study aims to determine the level of awareness and understanding of digital activism. Generation Z, which is heavily influenced by technology, digital inputs and outputs, was born into the digital world as the primary users of social media and its tools and adopted the digital platforms and digital technology as a way of life. In addition to this main aim of the study, the objectives of the study include exploring the level of use of social platforms by Generation Z and their attitudes towards social networks in relation to issues that can be considered part of digital activism, their level of participation, whether they consider themselves digital activists and whether they think that visual design and interaction are important when participating in such posts. The results of the study are intended to shed light on the knowledge, thoughts and attitudes of the generation in question towards digital activism and contribute to the literature.

Keywords: generation z, digital activism, social media, visual communication, social awareness.

1. Introductıon

The fact that each generation throughout history has more knowledge and skills than the previous one can be seen as a result of the development of information

1 Istanbul Arel University, Faculty of Communication, Visual Communication Design Department, begumaylinonder@arel.edu.tr ORCID: 0000-0002-0314-2843.

2 Istanbul Arel University, Faculty of Fine Arts, Cartoon and Animation Department, bilgesubiber@arel.edu.tr ORCID: 0000-0002-88795973.

and communication technologies. This development leads to differences in cultures, values, the relationship of individuals with their social environment and, depending on all this, to differences between generations. The emergence of computer and Internet technologies and the fact that they have become accessible to individuals in a short period of time have changed the way people exchange information and have initiated a change that is large enough to affect the way business is conducted, relations between countries, and the private and social lives of people.

Conceptualizing the generation (https://sozluk.gov.tr) as a group of individuals aged around twenty-five to thirty makes these changes and transformations clear. These human communities, which appear as generations and have a common age group, world-view and values, have gained importance especially since the 1990s (Önder, 2021: 143). In this context, Generation Z is one of the generations that is the focus of interest in many areas today and is referred to by researchers with different year intervals and names (digital natives, i-kids, net generation, digital-born, zoomer, iPhone generation, millennium generation, etc.). Generally associated with technology, Generation Z is considered to be the children of an era equipped with all kinds of technological devices and is clearly different from all other generations with these characteristics. Characterized by the digital culture we live in, Generation Z is defined as individuals with high thinking skills who learn by exploring, doing and experiencing the language of digital tools. People of this generation have a tendency to meet and interact in online environments with people they have not previously met in a physical environment (Erkırlı, 2022: 152–153). With the social networks where interaction-based communication takes place, Generation Z effectively utilizes social media platforms with their innate learning abilities, unlike previous generations.

The growing influence and number of social media users has undoubtedly led to activist actions becoming more active and spreading through social networks. Activist initiatives on social media platforms have become a formidable force in mobilizing large masses. Today, representatives of Generation Z can easily use the Internet and social media platforms to express their views on their daily lives and even on social or global issues. In this regard, it can be observed that the generation has a participatory attitude, especially in social mobilizations where they come together for a specific purpose. Users of digital networks have the ability to communicate their support or opposition to environmental, social, political, and economic issues, inform each other, facilitate organization, and make their voices heard through activist actions on digital platforms. Generation Z has been described as a social justice-minded, tech-savvy, well-educated, and creative generation in many studies. As one of the most multicultural generations, Generation Z individuals have grown up with an awareness of many issues such as human rights, animal rights, gender equality, and the climate crisis. For this reason, as stated by Sparks and Honey (2015: 46), unlike previous generations, members of Generation Z have a sense of social responsibility, are sensitive to global issues, and are determined to change the world. In this regard, they exhibit digital activism-oriented behavior, both in accessing information and in the actions in which they participate. Social mobilization, which brings people together for a specific goal on issues that directly affect society, enables collective attitudes and behaviors through digital platforms. The concept of digital activism, which has gained prominence in this context, is a set of activist discourses and actions that bring people together and mobilize them through technological means of communication. In this context, it would not be wrong to say that Generation Z, which follows and uses technology and experiences digitalization most intensively, plays a leading role in such actions.

Based on these points, the main objective of this study is to determine the level of awareness and understanding of digital activism among Generation Z, which is highly influenced by technology and digital inputs and outputs, has made digital a way of life, and is the primary user of social media and tools. Furthermore, this study aims to find out the extent to which Generation Z uses social networks, how they communicate on social networks about digital activism issues, the extent to which they participate in posts, whether they consider themselves digital activists, and whether they consider visual design and interaction important when participating in activism-related posts. In this context, the study aims to uncover Generation Z's habits in using new media tools and their attitudes toward digital activism.

1.1. The effect of social mobilizations and technological developments in historical perspective

There have been social mobilizations in almost every period of history. These mobilizations are about resisting current processes, in short, drawing attention to the existence of another reality, different from the existing one. In particular, the importance that the social science literature attaches to the concept of "social mobilizations" is a kind of interpretation based on establishing a relationship with a more modern period. Social movements are perceived as a consequence of profound changes emerging as individuals strive to cope with the increasing rationalization brought about by modern life. Within this framework, these movements that arise alongside transformations within society are seen as a response against rationalization. It can be said that social mobilizations in search of equality, freedom, human rights and social justice have emerged against many common economic, social and environmental problems since humans have lived together. Moreover, such mobilizations sometimes lead to revolutionary change and sometimes appear as resistance to change. Social mobilizations are usually characterized by a series of activities, such as protests, strikes, rallies, or civil disobedience, aimed at raising awareness of social problems, creating pressure, and/or making efforts to change or maintain the current prevailing situation. These actions are demands for change by the masses who come together for a common goal to those in power. Over time, these mobilizations can become effective in the mentality of societies, paving the way for change or resisting possible or expected change by dominating the preservation of existing rights or status. Of course, the reasons for these actions can occur in different ways and in different areas at different times.

From a historical point of view, technological development and changes in the means of communication are indicators of how and by what means these forms of action will take place. At this point, the means of production become important. It is well known that the structuring of societies is based on the organization of production activities. In this context, the aims of production, how and by whom it is carried out, and for whom or what this production serves, make it inevitable that societies create a unique order. Means of production, forces of production and relations of production, which are the basic elements of production, are the building blocks of this order of production. Human labor, as the most basic element of the means of production, and nature, as the most primitive object of labor, have undergone various developments from ancient times to the present. Therefore, it can be concluded that the relations between individuals in a society are generally characterized by the means of production. When a new means of production appears, this situation determines the new production process and also enables the emergence of new types of production relations. From the agrarian society to the invention of printing, many technological means of communication and a variety of means of production have been invented to facilitate social life. The transformed forms of production that accompanied the invention of these new means of production have led to the emergence of relations of production that can harmonize with each other on a cooperative basis or, on the contrary, come into conflict with each other, thus significantly shaping the social structure. Every new means of production leads to the emergence of differences due to the change in the forces of production and thus to the change in the relations of production. As Hançerlioğlu (1986: 453) states, the structure of society changes with the mode of production, so that socio-economic formations differ.

As it is known, the 19th century signifies a global transformation. With the emergence of new forms of management and production in societies and new technological requirements, humanity has witnessed two major movements of change and turbulent processes in this era: The French Revolution and the Industrial Revolution. In the capitalist system, which is criticized for its aim of creating mechanical human beings, especially in Marxist thought, the owners of power are those who own the means of production. In this system of thought, the ownership of the means of production affects the social structure, but this mechanization simultaneously leads to the exploitation of the working class. The Marxist system of thought, which focuses on the necessity of achieving an order in which everyone has equal rights, defines those who own the means of production as a determining factor in the formation of the general structure of society. Moreover, each substructure, which is accepted to form the basis of a society, has its own superstructure. Just as people produce to live and produce tools to facilitate production, political, philosophical, religious, legal, moral, etc. ideas and institutions are produced within the social relations in the superstructure (Erkan 1993: 28). The superstructure, which includes political organization, art, science, morality, religion and all kinds of thought systems, consists of phenomena and formations that are determined depending on the economic substructure. The rise of this idea, which stands against capitalism, has led to the emergence of social organizations unprecedented in history. Concepts such as social injustice and equality, which were criticized based on the machine-oriented development of modernism, led to the emergence of a series of social actions. This concept was first used in Western European countries with labor movements (Işık, 2015: 17). These collective actions, which are seen as active in changing the social structure and can also be defined as political mobilization, have undergone a significant transformation in the information society. Developments in communication technologies have transcended geographical boundaries and time barriers, causing local identities in society to organize and gather under one roof to form an integrated structure. It is widely accepted that the information society is more flexible than the industrial society, which feeds on causality, and that relative arguments have more favorable explanations (Toffler, n.d.: 105–107). It can be said that there are structural transformations in the functional and polycentric information society and at the same time these developments increase social or political mobilizations. Individuals in the information society are more entrepreneurial, creative and productive. In this respect, individuals seek to prove themselves. Individuals, who have become increasingly isolated due to the industrial society, have a more active identity, which is an indicator of these efforts in the information society. At this point, information technologies, which develop unpredictably from day to day, guide the individual in these efforts. In this way, individuals can voluntarily come together with like-minded people who share common values in society and, through these communities, become the subject of the social order on a voluntary basis.

Negative situations caused by industry, such as competition, war, unemployment, and fascism, have affected individuals on a social and even global scale, causing anxiety about the future. The mass consumer society, the last stage of the industrial society, is being replaced by the mass information society (Erkan, 1993: 69). This can be explained in terms of the production line. The mass production based on "produce, store, sell" in the industrial society is fed by the "sell, produce, deliver" approach in the information society. In this way, the concept of "value" comes to the fore. The main activities that create wealth are neither the allocation of capital to production nor labor, both of which are poles of economic theories of the nineteenth and twentieth centuries (…). Now surplus value is created by efficiency and innovation, both of which are the application of knowledge to work (Drucker, 1993: 18).

Along with the mechanization brought about by the Industrial Revolution, Industry 2.0 continued to have an impact throughout the 20th century. During this period, the cultural bombardment brought about by the information age and capitalism directly affected people's lifestyles on a global scale. With this interaction, changes in people's habits in their subjective and social lives became inevitable (Önder, 2021: 33–34). Societies that are changing socio-economically due to information have become an indispensable element of competition today. Technology and information used in personal production provide societies with sociological and economic development.

Capitalism is based on the transmission of information over long distances through networks (Stevenson, 2003: 11). This makes sector-specific information unique. In digitalized societies, information can be disseminated and stored in the desired way in a short time, owing to the possibilities offered by proximity and timelessness. This situation not only leads to changes in business and management structures from an economic point of view but also has an indirect and profound impact on the lives of individuals, who are the building blocks of society. So much so that the change in management styles, the increase in production and efficiency, and the emergence of the need to develop new types of technological tools have led to other social, political, and cultural developments in the social structure. Moreover, this situation has created societies that are interdependent in the globalized world. Thus, political, cultural, economic, and social integration among countries has emerged based on these activities in the information society. Various terms such as "third industrial revolution," "atomic age," and "space age" have been used to describe the process that follows the Industry 2.0 process. As Aksoy noted, the era of automation began with the combined use of electronic information and technologies and the use of programmable machines in production for the first time in the Industry 3.0 period. This era lasted until the 2000s (Aksoy, 2017). The Internet, one of the most important inventions after computer technology, enabled the beginning of a revolutionary data exchange in the information field. In the 2000s, the use of the internet, which started with Industry 3.0, began to encompass the developments in the communication field. The period of Industry 4.0, also known as the Fourth Industrial Revolution after 2011, is referred to by various names, such as "Information Age" or "Digital Age". Internet usage has continued to grow during this period. However, it has undergone a digital transformation. Globalization and technology-based borders have become more intertwined during this period, and both the public and private spheres have changed due to the use of artificial intelligence and robotic systems. Yıldız expressed the main goal of Industry 4.0 as: "Industry 4.0 aims to take over production with robots that communicate with each other, detect the environment with sensors and realize needs through data analysis, and produce higher quality, cheaper, faster and less wasteful production" (Yıldız, 2018). The transition period from Industry 4.0 to Industry 5.0 is referred to as the process of "transition from digital production to digital society" (Yıldız, 2018). In this transition period, cooperation between humans and robots is planned, as artificial intelligence is now fully integrated into human life and society. The aim of this cooperation is to improve the human resource capacity (Yücebalkan, 2020: 242). In the literature, Industry 5.0 is also referred to as a "super smart society" because it can produce and effectively use information-based solutions to many of the global problems that humanity and societies have to deal with.

With the information society, changes have become visible and social movements have diversified in terms of form and interaction. Now, groups have begun to reconstruct both the forms of action and the areas in which the action is carried out in each issue they consider to be problematic. The information technologies that individuals can easily access and use in the digitalized society and their qualitative structure have also changed their intellectual structure. Moreover, this change in the intellectual structure of the individual can cause a change in his behavior and even in the traditions of the social structure. Individuals in different parts of the world have been able to access information in the cheapest and fastest way due to the fact that computer technologies have become available to ordinary individuals, cheaper in a short period of time and spread on a global scale, the emergence of interconnected computer networks with the Internet revolution, and the personalization of information and the possibility of interaction. In this context, any local event or phenomenon that takes place in one society can be transmitted across borders in a matter of seconds. This allows new types of associations and movements to emerge, and even the same movements to emerge in other societies facing similar problems, ultimately replacing social quality with global movements. The Internet, which was initially a tool for gathering information, has in a short period of time expanded its scope and begun to be used as a tool for storing and disseminating information. The Internet has also been instrumentalized as a space for social movements, contributing to the diversification of mass media. Social movements might not necessarily be endowed with ample resources. However, the Internet can help them gain a strategic advantage by using the Internet to compete with other nationally organized, resource-rich movements. Activities around an issue in cyberspace can trigger physical activities and have an impact on large masses. In this way, all kinds of activities with activist characteristics show that the Internet is a fast resource for the exchange and circulation of information. Individuals can carry out virtual actions on social networking platforms or virtual games owing to the Internet, which enables individual actions. These actions can lead to the emergence of movements with others concerned about similar issues. Moreover, in addition to social media platforms, social movement actors create specific websites to organize and disseminate events or phenomena that they support or oppose among individuals and even communities. Other methods used to communicate and share information with like-minded people or to raise awareness about the event/phenomenon include websites such as Indymedia, founded in 1999 during the Seattle protests, or Zynet, founded in 1995 with the slogan "the spirit of resistance lives on" and still active today. Moreover, because of the interconnectedness of platforms and websites, any action initiated on one platform can be transferred to other platforms and websites, and thus the issue can become a determinant of the agenda in areas with different user profiles. By means of digitalization and the diversity of mass media, activist actions of all kinds can find the power to create large audiences.

With the loss of the mass influence of traditional media, individuals have preferred to exist in networks of personal choice, mutual interaction, and social stratification, according to Castells (2003: 496). Thus, in the current system, it has become possible for a person to be both a receiver and a sender on the same communication ground, to switch easily from one to the other, and to reduce the mental distance between different sources. Social media was first used intensively in the context of social movements in the Middle East and North Africa in 2011. As people used social media tools such as Facebook and Twitter to communicate and organize, these movements gave rise to terms such as the "social media revolution". From another perspective, the communities formed by online activists are easily dispersed. Unlike traditional audiences, they often set short-term and highly achievable goals.

While mass media and the Internet have diversified and facilitated participation in social or global issues, it is also necessary to consider individuals' access to and use of these technologies. In this respect, similarities and differences between generations may lead to differences in the level of participation in activism or the forms of activism. Before addressing these differences, it would be appropriate to examine the characteristics of the generations.

1.2. The concept of generation and characteristics of generations

This development, which ranges from computer games to mobile phones, from smart devices to wearable technological tools, from augmented, virtual and mixed reality technologies to the easy and widespread use of artificial intelligence, has led to an unprecedented and serious disruption and transformation of the communicative and cultural memory, ways of thinking, perception and acquisition of individuals and thus of societies. As a result of all these developments, the gap between generations has widened.

First of all, according to the definition of the concept of generation in the literature, the common view of all studies is that each generation is renewed every twenty years. As already mentioned, economic, political, sociological and technological changes in the world are based on the ability of societies to shape the future on the basis of past events and, in this context, to adapt or improve existing opportunities to the requirements of the time. Therefore, as a result of every change in society, generations are formed with a common age range and a common world view. The phenomenon of generations has gained importance especially after the 1990s and has become a subject of interest in every field in the 21st century (Önder, 2021: 143). There is no common consensus on the classification of generations. In addition, there may be differences in the age ranges defined for generations. However, the general opinion is that a few years do not make a big difference in the definition of generations. The idea of naming generations, which was proposed by the Census Bureau due to the growing population in the U.S., was a great success at the time because of the products and services the marketing industry sold to them as they reached adulthood. After this period, all generations were named.

The Lost Generation is known as the first generation of the 20th century. The years 1883–1900 are accepted as the age range of this generation. The Lost Generation has a high sense of belonging. Karahasan (2018: 24) expresses his thoughts about the Lost Generation as follows: "The children of the Lost Generation have gone down in history as patriotic, hardworking, thrifty, traditional, obedient to authority, and highly respectful of work." The Greatest Generation (1900–1924) is the generation that lived through global events that affected the masses, such as World War II and the Great Depression. There is little need for institutions in this generation, which has a civic-minded personality. In the literature, the Silent Generation refers to individuals believed to have been born between 1928 and 1945. Although the children of this generation are known as traditionalists, they are also known as the Silent Generation because they grew up during the World Wars. The Baby Boom (BB) Generation, born between 1946 and 1964, is also known as the Boom Generation, the Me Generation, the Baby Bombing Generation, or the Sandwich Generation. This generation is also known as the Digital Nomads. Individuals in this generation use technology out of necessity as a result of their digital habits. This generation consists of individuals who adhere to the traditional structure. Generation X, also known as the transition period, is considered to consist of individuals born between 1965 and 1980. Members of Generation X were introduced to computers and then Internet technologies with digital disruptions. As a result, they are averse to digitalization. In addition, individuals of this generation are known to be idealistic and hardworking. Generation Y individuals, also known by various names such as Millennials, Nexters, and Next Generation, were born between 1981 and 1996. Comfortable with digital technologies, this generation uses technology as effectively as they do print resources, as does Generation X. Children born in the 1980s grew up with desktop computers, game consoles, and MP3 players. Their adolescence coincided with the early years of the internet (Karahasan, 2018: 26). Generation Z, the focus of this study, is a generation that has made digital life their way of life. Researchers define Generation Z as a generation that is directly involved in social issues, technologically equipped, educated, and creative (Trevino, 2018). Some studies use 1995–1996 as the birth year of Generation Z, while others use 2000 as the base year. In this study, individuals born between 1997 and 2012 are considered Generation Z. Members of Generation Z are part of a global and multicultural generation that has grown up with an awareness of gender equality, climate change, and many socioeconomic factors. "Members of Generation Z, also known as the Internet Generation, are defined as the generation with the highest synchronization of motor skills such as hands, eyes, and ears in human history (Keleş, 2011: 131,

132)." As Sparks and Honey (2015: 46) state in their report, unlike previous generations, Generation Z individuals have a high sense of social responsibility, are sensitive to global issues, and want to change the world. Generation Z knows no limits in their access to information and solves their problems mostly by communicating online. In other words, this generation, which lives in an area without physical borders, can criticize any institution, person or organization. This is made easier and more visible by the way Generation Z tends to use virtual environments. Therefore, it is possible to say that this generation has a positive attitude, especially on social media platforms. This aspect of their use of social media shows that members of Generation Z are also digital activists.

2. Methodology of the research

2.1. Objective

This study aims to determine the level of awareness and understanding of digital activism among Generation Z, who are highly influenced by technology, digital inputs and outputs, have made digital a way of life, and are the primary users of social media and tools. In addition to this main objective, other objectives of the study include exploring the level of use of social networks by Generation Z, their communication styles on social networks regarding issues that can be considered within the scope of digital activism, their level of participation in posts, whether they consider themselves digital activists, and whether they think that visual design and interaction are important when participating in posts with activism content. Based on the results, this study aims to explore the knowledge, thoughts, and attitudes of Generation Z about digital activism.

In this context, the research questions are as follows

- What are the habits of Generation Z in using new media tools?
- What is the attitude of Generation Z towards digital activism?

Accordingly, the fourteen hypotheses of the survey are as follows;

H1: Generation Z is concerned about social issues.

H2: Generation Z has a high level of participation in digital actions on social media.

H3: As Generation Z's internet usage increases, so does their participation in digital activism actions.

H4: Members of Generation Z who participate in digital actions on social media do so primarily to help solve social problems of concern to society.

H5: Generation Z prefers new media tools over traditional mass media tools to address social issues that affect society.
H6: Generation Z reproduces content using simple applications to participate in digital actions.
H7: Generation Z shares existing content created by others with their environment to participate in digital actions.
H8: Generation Z believes that simple applications are effective and sufficient in terms of design when producing content for digital actions.
H9: Generation Z believes that brands should produce content for social issues.
H10: Generation Z values design as much as content in digital posts about social issues.
H11: Generation Z supports the posts of activists, politicians, political leaders, or thought leaders on social issues that affect society by sharing them on their own accounts.
H12: Generation Z prefers digital activism to physical activism.
H13: Generation Z believes that humorous content produced for digital activism is effective.
H14: Generation Z believes that digital interaction is important in social media activism.

2.2. Population, sampling, and limitations

- Turkey is divided into 81 provinces and seven regions. Some cities in some regions are more populous than others due to economic, educational, trade, etc. characteristics. In this context, the voluntary participants of the study consisted of people living in twelve different cities in Turkey. The first city where the participants of the study reside is Istanbul, which is located in the Marmara Region, which has the highest immigration in terms of economic size and therefore has a very dense population. The second is Ankara, which is located in the Central Anatolia Region and is the capital city. The third is Izmir, which is located in the Aegean Region and is considered to be the third largest city in Turkey. The fourth city is Edirne, which is located in the Thracian part of the Marmara Region. The fourth is Bursa, which is known as the fourth most populous city in the country in terms of population density and is located in South Marmara in the Marmara Region. The fifth is Antalya, which is known as the capital of tourism, especially in the summer months, and ranks fifth among Turkey's most populous cities. Kayseri, located in the Central Anatolia Region and known as a center of trade and industry, is one of the fourteenth most populous cities in Turkey. Samsun, also in the metropolitan category, is located in the central Black Sea Region. Trabzon, located in the Eastern Black Sea Region, is the twenty-seventh most populous city in Turkey. Erzurum is located in the Eastern Anatolia Region and is considered to be the third largest city. Malatya has metropolitan status in the country and is located in the Eastern Anatolia Region. Finally, Gaziantep, located at the intersection of the Mediterranean Sea and Southeastern Anatolia in Turkey, is rich in industry, education and trade, and is also the ninth most populous city in the country, occupying an important position between Anatolia and the Middle East.

- The population of the research is Turkey. However, since it is impossible to reach the entire population in terms of cost and time, the sample of the research was limited to 384 individuals consisting of male and female individuals belonging to Generation Z living in twelve provinces of Turkey (Istanbul, Edirne, Izmir, Bursa, Ankara, Antalya, Kayseri, Samsun, Trabzon, Erzurum, Malatya, Malatya and Gaziantep), born between 1997–2002 and having different educational backgrounds.
- The online survey technique was used because of its ability to reach a larger number of participants in a short period of time and at the same time.
- The variables addressed in the research are limited to the reliability and validity periods of the measurement tools used in the application.
- All data obtained in the study are collected within the rules of ESOMAR and the Researchers Association of Turkey and are used only for analysis and reporting purposes.
- The participants live in twelve provinces of Turkey: Istanbul, Edirne, Izmir, Bursa, Ankara, Antalya, Kayseri, Samsun, Trabzon, Erzurum, Malatya, and Gaziantep. Therefore, replication of the research in different geographical areas may contribute to more generalizable findings. Moreover, the small sample size is another limitation considering that the population is quite large.
- The limitation that social science research cannot be completely empirical also applies to this study.

2.3. Data and ınformation collection method

In the study, the survey technique, which is one of the systematic data collection tools, was applied and a survey form was prepared for quantitative research purposes to reveal the impact of digital activism on Generation Z. The study was limited to a total of 384 randomly selected voluntary females and males from Generation Z. The questionnaire form was prepared in a standardized and structured manner for the attitudes and tendencies of the participants toward digital activism. Based on the main topic of digital activism, the questionnaire form was prepared as a multiple-choice and 5-point Likert type of closed-ended questionnaire. The questionnaire consists of 59 questions in total. To determine the demographic characteristics of the participants, 6 multiple-choice closed-ended demographic questions were included. Then, 8 multiple-choice questions were asked to evaluate the participants' Internet and social media usage habits and/or purposes, 32 multiple-choice questions to learn the participants' knowledge about digital activism and evaluate whether they are digital activists or not, and 13 5-point Likert-type questions to reveal the participants' attitudes toward digital activism. After a pilot interview with 10 people before the study was conducted, no problems were observed, and with the final expert approval, the field research preparation for the study was started. The survey was conducted online with 384 people between 18.08.2022 and 29.08.2022, provided the sample characteristics were appropriate. The interviews were conducted using CAWI (computer-assisted online interviewing) methodology. In the first part of the questionnaire, which includes socio-demographic content, the participants were filtered according to the identified characteristics. According to the filtering results, the questions in the second and third sections were asked.

2.4. Preparation of the questions in the questionnaire form

The survey, designed to determine Generation Z's habits in using new media tools, as well as their attitudes and knowledge about digital activism, consisted of demographic questions and closed-ended 5-point Likert multiple-choice questions. Control questions were also included in the questionnaire form, and the results are discussed in detail in the corresponding section. In order to clarify and make understandable the questions posed by the researchers to the participants and the characteristics to be determined, the following Table 1 method was used.

Table 1. Characteristics to be tested with the questionnaire items

Scope		Items	Characteristic
Section 1: Filtering Section			
General Characteristics of Generation Z	1	Gender	Demographic Information
	2	Marital status:	
	3	Age	
	4	Province of residence:	
	5	Occupation:	
Section 2: Assessing Internet and social media usage habits and purposes			
Generation Z's assessment of their Internet and social media usage habits and purposes	1	Do you use the Internet?	Generational characteristic; knowledge of experience and goals
	2	How much time do you spend on average per day on the Internet?	
	3	How often do you connect to the Internet? (*Hypothesis H3*)	
	4	Do you use social media applications?	
	5	How much time do you spend on average per day on social media? (Choose only one)	
	6	Which of the following is your favorite social media application?	
	7	How often do you check your social media accounts? (Choose only one)	
	8	Which of the following is your purpose for using social media platforms?	
	9	Which of the following mass media do you use most to get information about social issues? (*Hypothesis H5*).	
Section 3: Generation Z Participants' Knowledge of Digital Activism and Their Assessment of Whether They Are Digital Activists			
Participation, Involvement, and Attitudes of Generation Z Toward Digital Activism	1	Which of the following connotations does the word activism have for you? (multiple answers possible)	Cognitive Involvement (control questions)
	2	Have you ever heard the term digital activism?	
	3	Do you think digital activism raises public awareness?	
	4	Would you define yourself as a digital activist?	
	5	Which of the following social media applications do you use most for digital activism? (Check only one)	
	6	Where do you get information about digital activism activities? (multiple answers possible)	
	7	How do you prefer to get information about current events on social media? (multiple answers possible)	
	8	Do you follow people or organizations (opinion leaders, NGOs, associations, politicians, etc.) on social media to support an ideology or a social movement in virtual environments? (*Hypothesis; H11.*)	

(*continued on next page*)

Table 1. Continued

Scope	Items		Characteristic
	9	Do you support digital activists on online platforms related to social or global issues? (If your answer is no, go to question C.11.) (*Hypothesis; H11.*)	
Items for Generation Z's Participation, Involvement and Attitudes Toward Digital Activism	10	How do you support digital activists taking action on topics that address social or global problems (*Hypothesis H11.*)?	Cognitive Involvement (control questions)
	11	Do you physically participate in real-life events (demonstrations, rallies, protest marches, sit-ins, etc.) to support a digital action on social media?	
	12	What is the most preferred way for you to support any kind of digital action on social media platforms? (*Hypothesis; H4.*)	
	13	Do you think that activist actions on social media are successful?	
	14	Do you think that visual design is important in content such as posters, photos, articles, and videos used in activist actions on social media? (*Hypothesis; H10.*)	Level of Involvement in Design (control questions)
	15	Do you think that the visual design of content such as posters, photos, articles, and videos used in activist actions carried out on social media are sufficient? (*Hypothesis; H8.*)	
	16	Do you think that the content produced using techniques such as humorous tagging, drawing/ illustration, caps, gifs, and video are effective in activist actions carried out on social media? (*Hypothesis; H8, H10, H13.*)	
	17	Do you think that digital interaction is important in activist actions carried out on social media? (*Hypothesis; H14.*)	Cognitive Involvement (control questions)
	18	What is your purpose for participating in social media activist actions? (*Hypothesis; H4.*)	Assessment of Attitudes
	19	Which of the following do you prefer to support activist actions on social media? (Hypothesis; H7.)	
	20	Please indicate which activist organizations you know. (Multiple answers possible)	
	21	Which of the following global and social issues concerns you the most? (*Hypothesis; H6.*)	
	22	Which of the following activist actions organized around global or social issues are you familiar with?	
	23	Do you prefer brands that support activist actions on social media?	
	24	Would you be interested in interactive content from brands that support activist actions on social media platforms? (*Hypothesis; H9.*)	

Table 1. Continued

Scope	Items		Characteristic
Items Related to the Importance and Attitudes of Generation Z towards Visual Design in Activist Actions	25	Are you interested in using humor in content produced for activist movements on social media platforms?	Generation Z's attitudes toward using new media tools
	26	Do you share posts using relevant hashtags to support activist actions on social media platforms?	
	27	Do you create and share relevant content (caps, videos, photos, collages, literary content, etc.) to support activist movements on social media platforms? (If your answer is no, go to question C.29.)	
	28	Do you use design tools (mobile collage applications, Canva, Photoshop, video editing tools, Adobe Illustrator, line drawing software, sticker applications, etc.) to create and share content about global and social issues?	Generation Z's approach to using new media and design tools
	29	Do you think that designs created by others on global and social issues should be attractive?	
	30	Do you think that designs created by others on global and social issues should be easy to share?	
	31	Do you think that designs created by others on global and social issues should be compatible with all types of technological devices?	
Generation Z's Participation, Involvement and Attitudes towards Digital Activism	32	Do you think that instant messaging applications (WhatsApp, Bip and Telegram) are important for communicating news about global and social issues?	
Section 4: Assessing Participants' Engagement with Attitudes Related to Digital Activism			
Scope	**Items**		**Characteristic**
Items related to Generation Z's level of participation in digital activism	1	Digital activism is used in place of street activism or physical mobilization.	Levels of Participation in Digital Activism
	1	Digital activism raises awareness and helps change situations.	
	1	Digital technology plays an important role in my activism.	
	1	Digital activism is successful in mobilizing people to take to the streets when an authoritarian government is the target of a campaign.	
	1	I use digital tools every day to raise awareness about my activism.	
	1	I trust the accuracy of the information I get on social media.	
	1	If I see an environmental petition campaign on the street, I sign it.	

(*continued on next page*)

Table 1. Continued

Scope	Items		Characteristic
	1	If I see an online petition campaign related to global or social issues, I sign it.	
	1	I interact with my followers or visitors (by sharing their posts, commenting on their posts, replying to their emails, etc.).	
	1	I engage with social issues outside of social media.	
	1	The Internet provides a unique and revolutionary opportunity for democracy and free speech.	
	1	The agenda of issues is the same on social media as it is on the street.	

2.5. Characteristics of the participants

The research was conducted with a total of 384 individuals living in twelve different cities in Turkey, with an equal gender distribution and born between 1997 and 2002. The survey questionnaire aimed to determine how and for what purpose Generation Z individuals use new media tools, as well as their knowledge and attitudes towards digital activism, regardless of their level of education.

2.6. Sociodemographic characteristics of participants

The socio-demographic characteristics of the participants, who belong to the Generation Z group, are evenly distributed by gender, and voluntarily participated in the study regardless of their educational status, were measured using a total of six (6) variables and multiple-choice questions through the filtering questions of age, gender, marital status, educational level, and occupation.

2.7. Data analysis

Considering that the number of users is increasing day by day in today's world where the Internet surrounds human life, this study adopted the CAWI methodology, which is one of the survey application methods often preferred in academic research. The study was conducted online, and validity and reliability analyzes were conducted by considering the hypotheses before analyzing the data. The descriptive statistics technique was used to analyze the data obtained through quantitative questionnaire study. One sample t-test was applied for one group in the 5-point Likert type scale questions in the questionnaire form. The data obtained were analyzed through SPSS (Statistical Package for the Social Sciences) program and frequency and percentage distribution graphs were processed in Microsoft Excel. Then, the data were analyzed and converted into graphs by the researchers and reviewed by experts. After this stage, the researchers interpreted and analyzed the data through tables.

3. Findings and evaluation

3.1. Demographic characteristics

The Table 2 below shows the gender and marital status of the participants according to the research data.

Table 2. Distribution of participants by gender (left), distribution of participants by marital status (right)

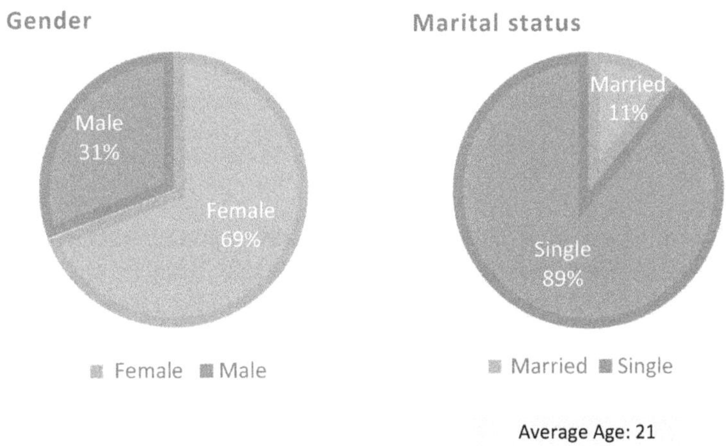

69 % of the sample is female. The average age of this group is 21 and they are all from Generation Z. Therefore, the majority are single (89 %).

3.2. Level of education, occupation and location

The education levels and occupations of the participants are shown in the tables 3 below. 34 % of Generation Z participants are high school graduates. 24 % have an associate degree and 35 % have a bachelor's degree. The remaining minority have either a primary school diploma or a postgraduate degree.

Table 3. Distribution of participants by education level

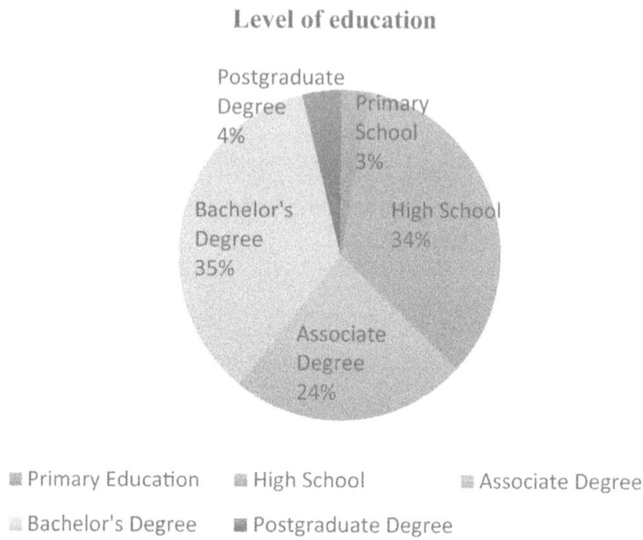

In order to ensure a nationally representative sample, participants from each province were included according to the population of the provinces within the NUTS 1 scope, taking into account the *Classification of Territorial Units for Statistics (CUTS)* or *Nomenclature of Territorial Units for Statistics (NUTS)*[3] criteria. The Table 4 and Table 5 below shows, 41.53 % of the 118 male participants and 36 % of the female participants were students, with an average student population of 38 %. 19 % of the participants work and study at the same time.

3 "The NUTS classification is based on three criteria. The first is based on the previous regional classification of the country. For example, a classification made according to the geographical characteristics of the region is also used to create NUTS regions. The second is to classify areas with the same potential by grouping them together (e.g. regions with intensive agricultural activities). The third criterion is population. NUTS Level 1, Level 2 and Level 3 regions have population thresholds of 150,000, 800,000 and 3 million inhabitants respectively. Taking into account the criteria of population, geography, regional development plans, basic statistical indicators, socio-economic development ranking of provinces, 12 Level 1, 26 Level 2 and 81 Level 3 NUTS regions have been defined in Turkey (Taş, 2006)".

Table 4. Distribution of participants by occupation (left), distribution of participants by NUTS1 provinces according to the Nomenclature of Territorial Units for Statistics (NUTS) (right)

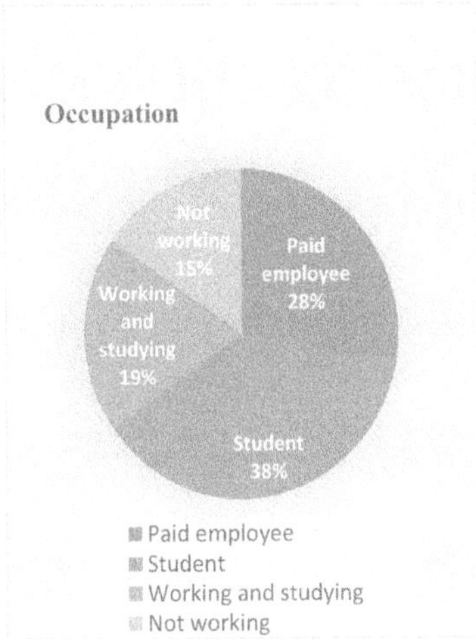

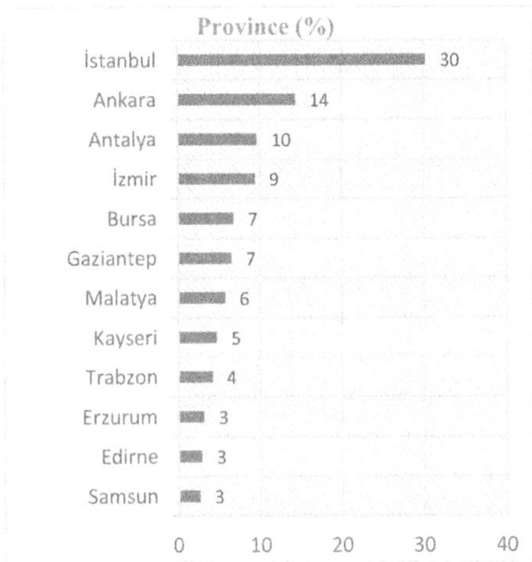

Table 5. Distribution of participants by gender, education level and occupation

		Gender		Level of Education					Occupation			
Total		**Female**	**Male**	**Primary Education**	**High School**	**Associate Degree**	**Bachelor's Degree**	**Postgraduate Degree**	**Paid employee**	**Student**	**Working and studying**	**Not working**
Base	**384**	**266**	**118**	**11**	**131**	**91**	**136**	**15**	**106**	**145**	**74**	**59**
Paid employee	27.6	29.7	22.88	45.45	16.79	24.18	34.56	66.67	100	0	0	0
Student	37.76	36.09	41.53	9.09	49.62	30.77	36.03	13.33	0	100	0	0
Working and studying	19.27	17.67	22.88	0	14.5	29.67	18.38	20	0	0	100	0
Not working	15.36	16.54	12.71	45.45	19.08	15.38	11.03	0	0	0	0	100
Total	**100**	**100**	**100**	**100**	**100**	**100**	**100**	**100**	**100**	**100**	**100**	**100**

3.3. Internet usage habits

The table 6 below shows in detail the distribution of participants according to their Internet usage habits based on their responses to the questions "Do you use the Internet?", "How much time do you spend on average per day on the Internet?", and "How often do you connect to the Internet?"

Table 6. Frequency of Internet Access (left), Distribution of the Participants by Time Spent on the Internet per Day (right)

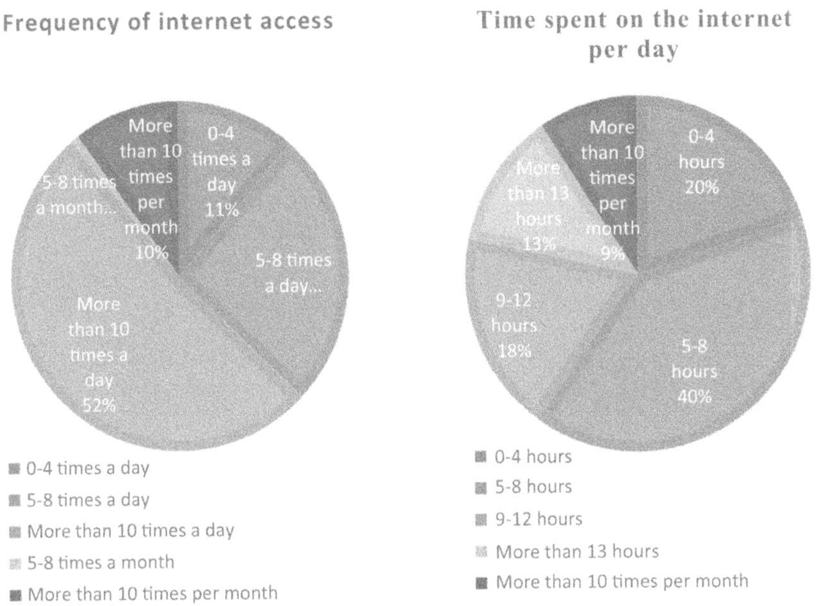

The Table 7 below shows, the average time spent online by Generation Z in the sample is seven (7) hours per day, and they go online an average of eight (8) times per day.

Table 7. Distribution of participants' ınternet use habits by gender and education level

"Do you use the Internet?"	Total	Gender: Female	Gender: Male	Level of Education: Primary Education	Level of Education: High School	Level of Education: Associate Degree	Level of Education: Bachelor's Degree	Level of Education: Postgraduate Degree
Base	384	266	118	11	131	91	136	15
Yes	100	100	100	100	100	100	100	100
No	0	0	0	0	0	0	0	0
Total	100	100	100	100	100	100	100	100

The 384 respondents use the Internet regardless of gender or level of education.

3.4. Social media usage habits

The table 8 below shows participants' responses to the questions "Do you use social media applications?", " How much time do you spend on average per day on social media?", and "Which of the following is your favorite social media application?"

Table 8. Distribution of participants by time spent daily on social media

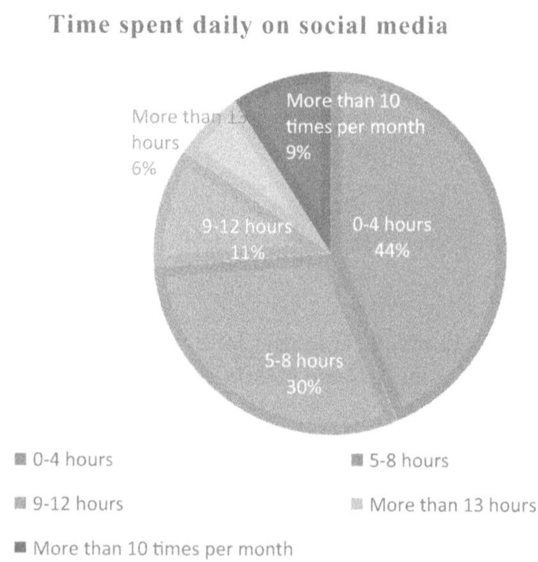

According to the data (e.g Table 9) obtained from the study, the average time that Generation Z spends on social media is 5–6 hours per day.

Table 9. Distribution of participants by social media platforms they use

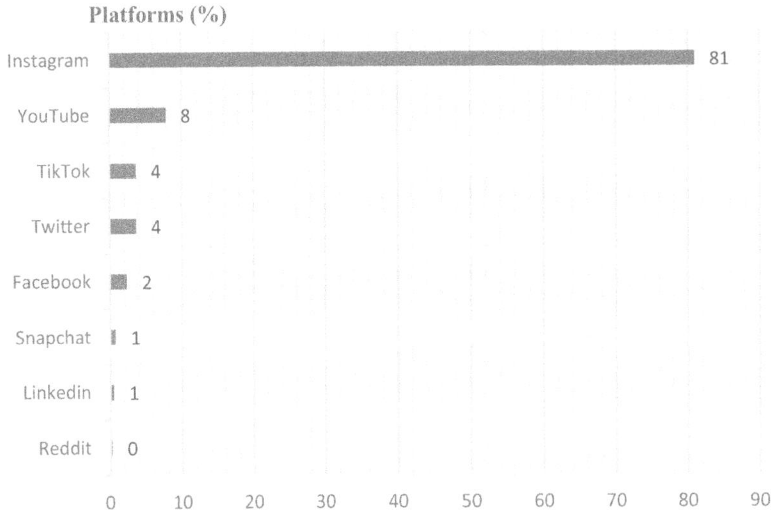

The Table 10 below shows, instagram is used by 81 % of participants, YouTube by 8 %, TikTok and Twitter by 4 %. Only 2 % of participants use the Facebook platform, while Snapchat and Linkedin are used by 1 % of participants.

Table 10. Distribution of participants by frequency of checking the social media platforms they use

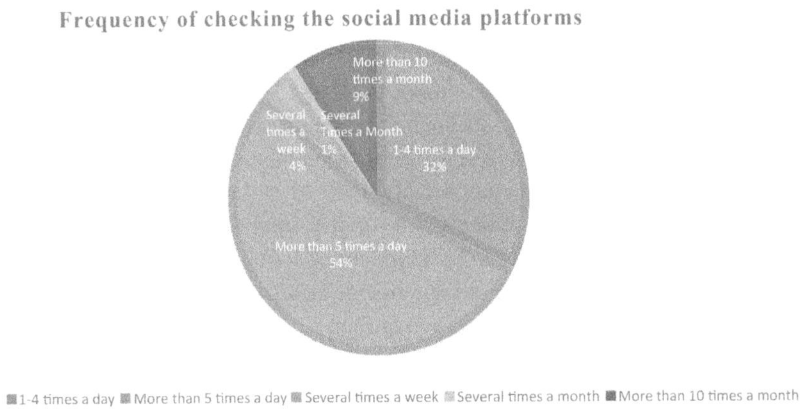

Based on participants' responses to the question "How often do you check your social media accounts?", it was determined that participants check their social media accounts an average of seven (7) times per day. While 36 % of respondents check their social media accounts between 1 and 4 times per day, only 1 % of respondents check their social media accounts several times per month.

3.5. Purpose of social media use

The table below shows participants' responses to the question "Which of the following is your purpose for using social media platforms?"

Table 11. Distribution of participants by purpose of social media use

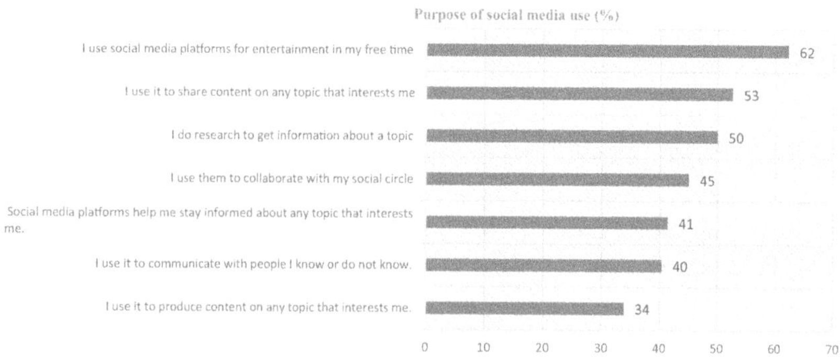

The Table 11 below shows, Generation Z's primary purpose for using social media is to have fun in their free time (62 %). While 53 % of participants said they use social media to "share content on a topic that interests them," 50 % of participants said they use social media platforms to "do research to get information about a topic". While 45 % of respondents answered "I use these platforms to collaborate with my social circle", 41 % said "I use social media platforms to stay informed about any topic that interests me". While 40 % of respondents said they use social media platforms to "communicate with people I know or do not know", 34 % of respondents said they use these platforms to "produce content on any topic that interests me".

3.6. Participants' mass media preferences

The table below shows the distribution of participants' responses to the question "Which of the following mass media do you use most to get information about social issues?"

Table 12. Distribution of participants by mass media preferences

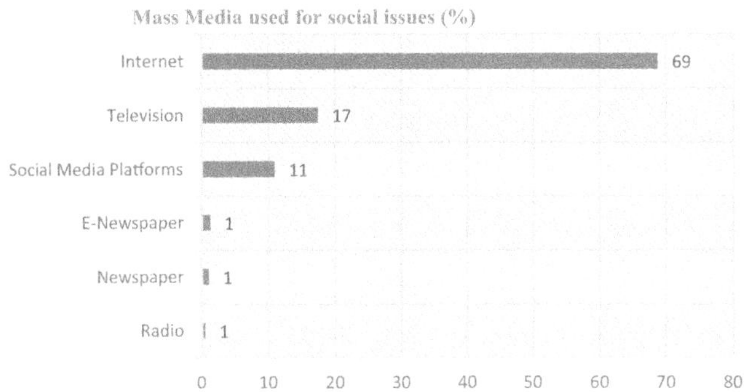

The Table 12 below shows, the Internet ranks first with 69 % of the mass communication tools used by Generation Z for social issues. Television comes in second with 17 %, while social media platforms come in third with 11 %. The use of e-newspapers, newspapers and radio is 1 %. In this context, the hypothesis proposed by the researcher and coded as H5 "Generation Zers prefer new media tools over traditional mass media tools to address social issues that affect society." was confirmed.

3.7. Generation Z participants' knowledge of digital activism and their assessment of whether they are digital activists

In response to the question, "Which of the following connotations does the word activism have for you?", 62 % of respondents answered "taking action to solve a social problem". The Table 13 below shows, While 31 % of the participants answered the question as "forming public opinion to solve a social problem", 28 % answered as "showing sensitivity to solve a social problem", 20 % answered as "demonstrating to solve a social problem" and 16 % answered as "boycotting to solve a social problem".

Table 13. Participants' knowledge of the of "activism"

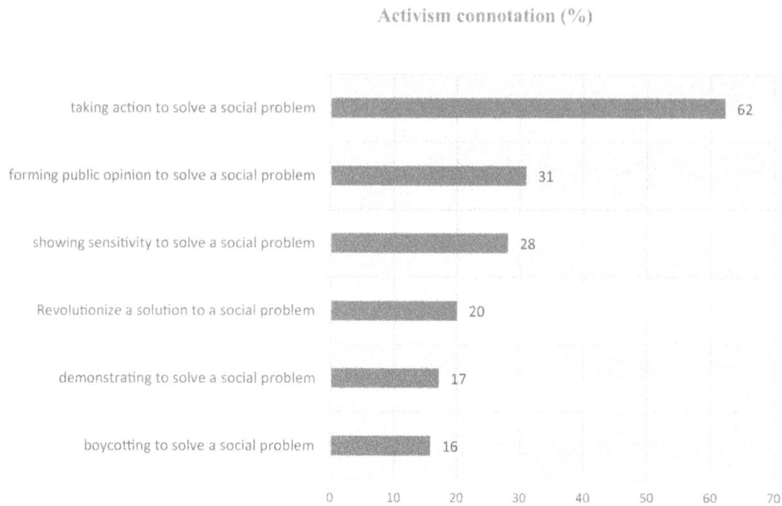

The Table 14 below shows, According to the survey, which included 266 female and 118 male participants, the connotation of digital activism does not change as the level of education of Generation Z individuals increases. In other words, 69.12 % of 136 bachelor's degree holders, 57.25 % of 131 high school graduates, 60.44 % of 91 associate's degree holders, 60 % of 15 bachelor's degree holders, and 54.63 % of 11 primary school graduates gave the same answer as "taking action to solve a social problem".

Table 14. Participants' knowledge on the connotation of "activism"

Which of the following does the word activism bring to mind?		**Gender**		**Education**					**Occupation**			
Total		Female	Male	Primary Education	High School	Associate Degree	Bachelor's Degree	Postgraduate Degree	Paid employee	Student	Working and studying	Not working
Base	384	266	118	11	131	91	136	15	106	145	74	59
Taking action to solve a social problem	62.24	64.29	57.63	54.55	57.25	60.44	69.12	60	70.75	62.07	56.76	54.24
Forming public opinion for a solution to a social problem	30.99	33.08	26.27	36.36	21.37	37.36	33.82	46.67	38.68	19.31	45.95	27.12
Revolutionize a solution to a social problem	20.05	21.43	16.95	36.36	19.08	20.88	16.91	40	32.08	13.79	22.97	10.17
Boycott to solve a social problem	15.89	16.92	13.56	9.09	16.03	20.88	11.03	33.33	22.64	8.28	22.97	13.56
Demonstrating for a solution to a social problem	17.19	18.42	14.41	18.18	12.98	18.68	19.85	20	25.47	7.59	22.97	18.64
Showing sensitivity for a solution to a social problem	28.13	30.45	22.88	9.09	25.95	29.67	30.88	26.67	33.02	22.07	37.84	22.03
Total	**174.48**	**184.59**	**151.69**	**163.64**	**152.67**	**187.91**	**181.62**	**226.67**	**222.64**	**133.1**	**209.46**	**145.76**

The Table 14 below shows, the percentage of those who have heard of the concept of digital activism is 36 %. Awareness of the concept among young people is 59 %. The percentage of digital activists is 33 %.

Table 15. Percentage of people who have heard of "digital activism"

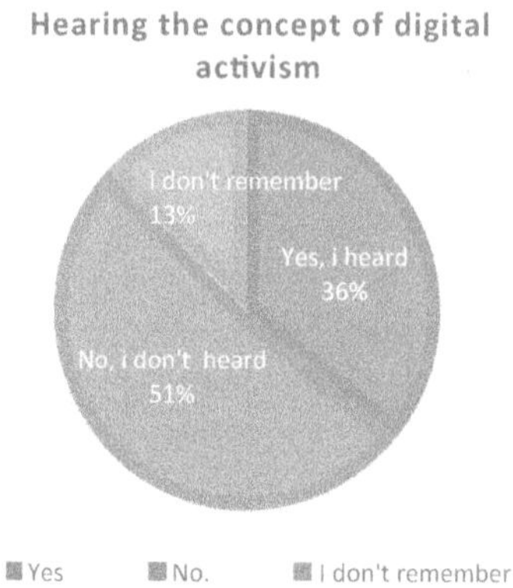

In response to the question "Do you think digital activism raises public awareness?", the Table 15 below shows, 59 % of the participants think that it raises awareness, while the rate of those who answered "I don't know" is 33 %. It was found that 8 % of the participants were of the opinion that the concept does not raise public awareness.

Table 16. participants' views on whether the concept of "digital activism" raises public awareness

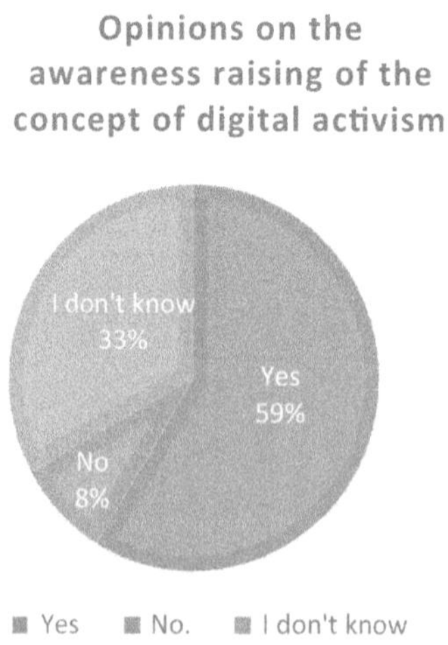

In their responses to the question "Would you define yourself as a digital activist?", The Table17 below shows, 44 % of Generation Z participants are undecided, while 33 % of them define themselves as activists. 23 % of Generation Z respondents do not define themselves as activists.

Table 17. Participants' views on "being a digital activist"

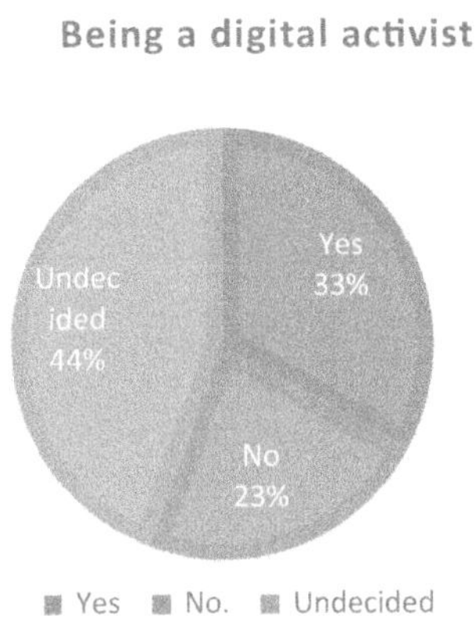

The Table 18 below shows, 35.71 % of the 266 female participants and 27.12 % of the 118 male participants define themselves as digital activists. When analyzing the activist status of the participants according to their educational level, 46.32 % of the 136 Bachelor graduates are undecided. 72.73 % of the 11 high school graduates identified themselves as activists. 46.67 % of the 15 postgraduate participants answered "yes". The same percentage were undecided.

Table 18. Distribution of participants' views on being a digital activist by gender, education, and occupational status

Would you define yourself as a digital activist?		Gender		Education					Occupation			
	Total	**Female**	**Male**	**Primary Education**	**High School**	**Associate Degree**	**Bachelor's Degree**	**Postgraduate Degree**	**Paid employee**	**Student**	**Working and studying**	**Not working**
Base	**384**	**266**	**118**	**11**	**131**	**91**	**136**	**15**	**106**	**145**	**74**	**59**
Yes	33.07	35.71	27.12	72.73	22.9	37.36	35.29	46.67	52.83	20.69	36.49	23.73
No	22.66	21.43	25.42	18.18	30.53	20.88	18.38	6.67	13.21	28.28	22.97	25.42
Undecided	44.27	42.86	47.46	9.09	46.56	41.76	46.32	46.67	33.96	51.03	40.54	50.85
Total	**100**	**100**	**100**	**100**	**100**	**100**	**100**	**100**	**100**	**100**	**100**	**100**

The Table 18 below shows, While 52.83 % of the 106 paid employee participants define themselves as digital activists, 50.85 % of the non-working participants are undecided.

Table 19. social media platforms most frequently used by participants for "digital activism"

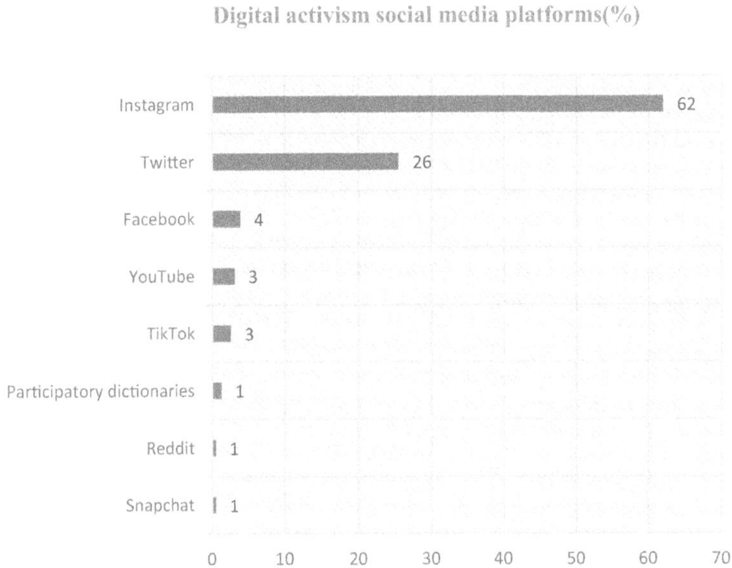

The Table 19 below shows, in response to the question "Which of the following social media applications do you use most for digital activism?", Instagram is the primary social media platform for digital activism among the Generation Z at 62 %. Twitter is the platform of choice for 26 % of respondents, while YouTube is the platform of choice for only 4 % of respondents.

Table 20. *Participants' sources of information on digital activism events*

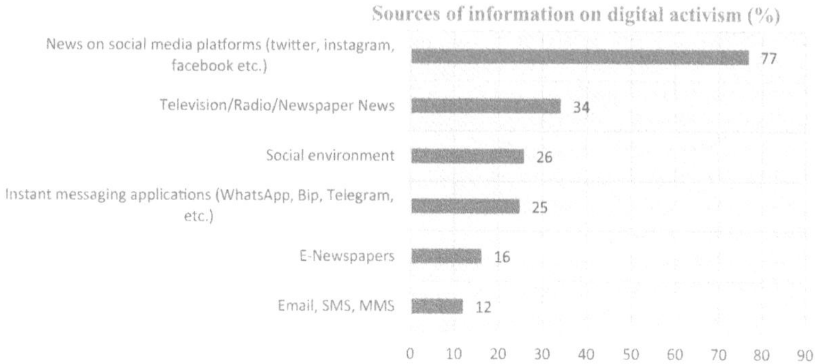

The Table 20 below shows, 77 % follow news on these platforms to learn about digital activism. Among Generation Z respondents, 34 % use traditional media such as television, newspapers, and radio, 26 % use their social circles, and 25 % use instant messaging applications to get information. According to the responses to the question, "How do you prefer to get information about current events on social media?", 67 % of Generation Z members follow virtual social movements on social media.

Table 21. Participants' habits of using social media in digital activism

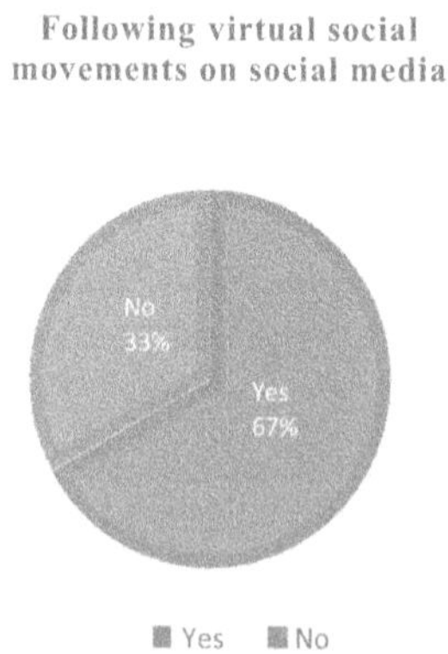

The Table 21 below shows, Of the 384 participants, 66.93 % answered "yes" and 33.07 % answered "no" to the question "Do you follow people or

organizations (opinion leaders, NGOs, associations, politicians, etc.) on social media to support an ideology or a social movement in virtual environments?" The proportion of males who said yes was 56.78 % and the proportion of females who said yes was 71.43 %. While 28.57 % of the female participants answered no, 43.22 % of the male participants answered no. In terms of educational level, 136 of the participants were bachelor's degree graduates, 131 were high school graduates, 91 were associate's degree graduates, 15 were post-graduates, and 11 were primary school graduates. The vast majority of high school graduates, 90.91 %, support the posts of activists, politicians, political leaders, or opinion leaders on social issues by sharing them on their own accounts. (e.g Table 22)

Table 22. Participants' habit of following people or organizations that support digital activism in virtual environments

Do you follow people or organizations (opinion leaders, NGOs, associations, politicians, etc.) on social media to support an ideology or a social movement in virtual environments?		**Gender**		**Education**				
	Total	**Female**	**Male**	**Primary Education**	**High School**	**Associate Degree**	**Bachelor's Degree**	**Postgraduate Degree**
Base	**384**	**266**	**118**	**11**	**131**	**91**	**136**	**15**
Yes	66.93	71.43	56.78	90.91	58.02	69.23	72.79	60
No	33.07	28.57	43.22	9.09	41.98	30.77	27.21	40
Total	**100**	**100**	**100**	**100**	**100**	**100**	**100**	**100**

The Table 23 and Table 24 below shows, According to the answers to the questions "Do you support digital activists on online platforms related to social or global issues?", "How do you support digital activists taking action on topics that address social or global issues?" and "Do you physically participate in real-life events (demonstrations, rallies, protest marches, sit-ins, etc.) to support a digital action on social media?", Digital activists are supported by 78 % of participants. However, even if they do not support activists, 31 % of respondents take part in physical actions to support social movements.

Table 23. Participants' support for social movements (right) and participation in physical actions (left)

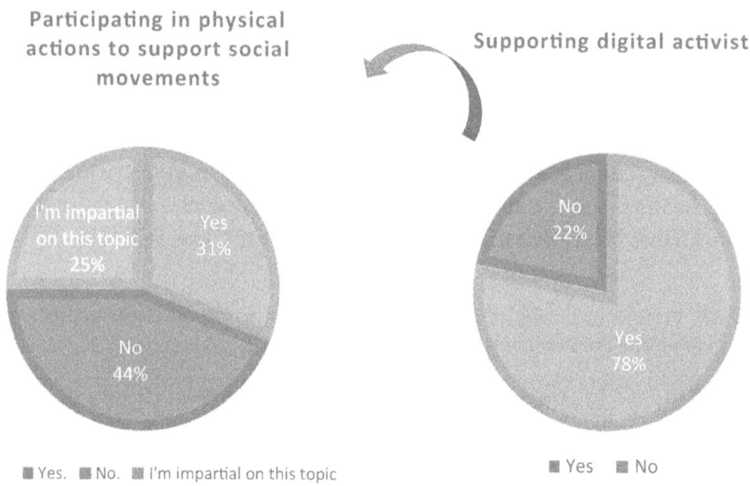

Table 24. Participants' support for activists taking action in social/global movements by gender, education and occupation

"How do you support digital activists taking action on issues that address social or global problems?"		**Gender**		**Level of Education**					**Occupation**			
	Total	**Female**	**Male**	**Primary Education**	**High School**	**Associate Degree**	**Bachelor's Degree**	**Postgraduate Degree**	**Paid employee**	**Student**	**Working and studying**	**Not working**
Base	**384**	**266**	**118**	**11**	**131**	**91**	**136**	**15**	**106**	**145**	**74**	**59**
By liking the content that is shared by the activists on their personal accounts.	58.07	62.78	47.46	72.73	45.8	60.44	68.38	46.67	68.87	51.72	60.81	50.85
By reposting content shared by activists on their personal accounts	39.84	44.36	29.66	9.09	35.11	39.56	49.26	20	50.94	33.79	45.95	27.12
By commenting on the content shared by activists on their personal accounts	32.81	34.59	28.81	18.18	26.72	32.97	38.97	40	47.17	17.24	50	23.73
By reorganizing the content shared by activists on their personal accounts through graphic production collages, photos, caps, gifs, video production, etc.	22.14	25.94	13.56	36.36	10.69	23.08	30.88	26.67	33.02	10.34	33.78	16.95
By providing feedback on the content shared by activists on their personal accounts via private message or e-mail.	15.63	18.8	8.47	9.09	6.87	19.78	19.85	33.33	27.36	6.21	21.62	10.17
Total	**168.49**	**186.47**	**127.97**	**145.45**	**125.19**	**175.82**	**207.35**	**166.67**	**227.36**	**119.31**	**212.16**	**128.81**

The Table 25 below shows, In response to the question “What is your favorite way to support a digital action on social media platforms?”, 58 % of the 384 participants answered “By liking the content that is shared by the activists on their personal accounts”. 39.84 % answered “by liking or re-sharing graphic productions shared by others on social media”. The same percentage of participants, 39.84 %, responded as “by liking or re-sharing graphic productions of content shared by others on social media”.

Table 25. Participants' support for digital action on social media platforms by gender, education, and occupational status

"What is the most preferred way for you to support any kind of digital action on social media platforms?"		**Gender**		**Level of Education**					**Occupation**			
	Total	**Female**	**Male**	**Primary Education**	**High School**	**Associate Degree**	**Bachelor's Degree**	**Postgraduate Degree**	**Paid employee**	**Student**	**Working and studying**	**Not working**
Base	**384**	**266**	**118**	**11**	**131**	**91**	**136**	**15**	**106**	**145**	**74**	**59**
By liking or re-sharing content shared by others on social media	57.55	63.91	43.22	72.73	55.73	56.04	62.5	26.67	52.83	61.38	67.57	44.07
By liking or re-sharing graphic productions of content shared by others through social media	57.55	63.91	43.22	72.73	55.73	56.04	62.5	26.67	52.83	61.38	67.57	44.07
By reorganizing with collages, photos, caps, gifs, video productions, etc.	13.8	12.41	16.95	0	9.16	18.68	16.18	13.33	19.81	6.9	13.51	20.34
Commenting on the content shared by others	9.38	6.39	16.1	18.18	16.03	5.49	5.88	0	8.49	13.79	4.05	6.78
Providing feedback on content shared by others via private message (DM) or email	3.91	4.14	3.39	0	4.58	0	2.94	33.33	6.6	1.38	5.41	3.39
By participating in petitions organized by others	5.99	5.26	7.63	9.09	6.11	7.69	4.41	6.67	4.72	7.59	5.41	5.08
By remaining silent	9.38	7.89	12.71	0	8.4	12.09	8.09	20	7.55	8.97	4.05	20.34
Total	**157.55**	**163.91**	**143.22**	**172.73**	**155.73**	**156.04**	**162.5**	**126.67**	**152.83**	**161.38**	**167.57**	**144.07**

The Table 25 below shows, 13.8 % of the participants use methods such as collage, photography, caps, gifs, video production, etc. in their digital activism-centered action participation and circulate them by re-sharing. In terms of education level, 18.18 % of primary school graduates responded "by writing comments under the content shared by others" in such actions.

Table 26. Whether participants find digital activist actions on social media platforms successful

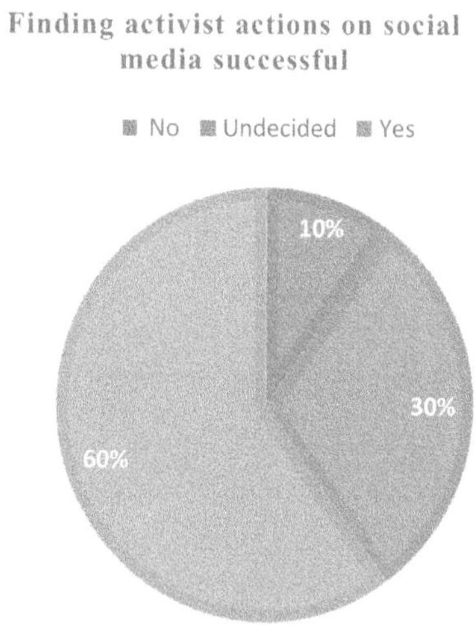

The Table 26 below shows, *according to the responses to the question "Do you think that activist actions on social media are successful?", 30 % of the 384 participants were undecided and 10 % answered "No". 60 % of the participants indicated that they consider activist actions carried out on social media to be successful.*

Table 27. Whether the participants find the use of visuals in digital activist actions conducted on social media platforms successful (left), whether the participants find the use of visuals in digital activist actions conducted on social media platforms adequate (right)

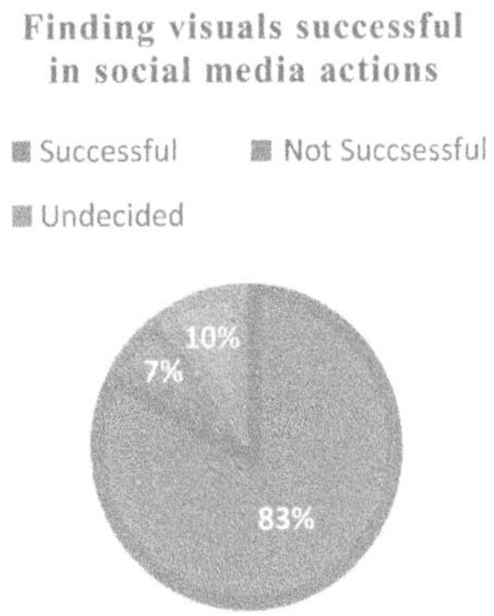

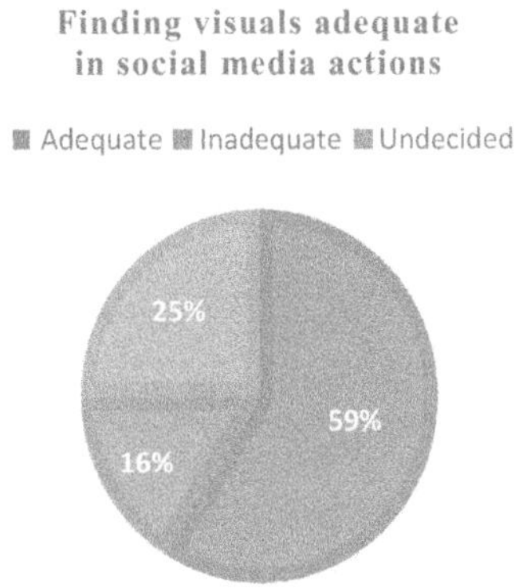

The Table 27 below shows, 83 % of participants found the content such as posters, photos, articles and videos used in activist actions on social media platforms successful. 59 % of participants stated that the content such as posters, photos, articles and videos used in activist actions carried out on social media platforms are adequate.

Table 28. Whether the participants find the content of digital activist actions conducted on social media platforms effective

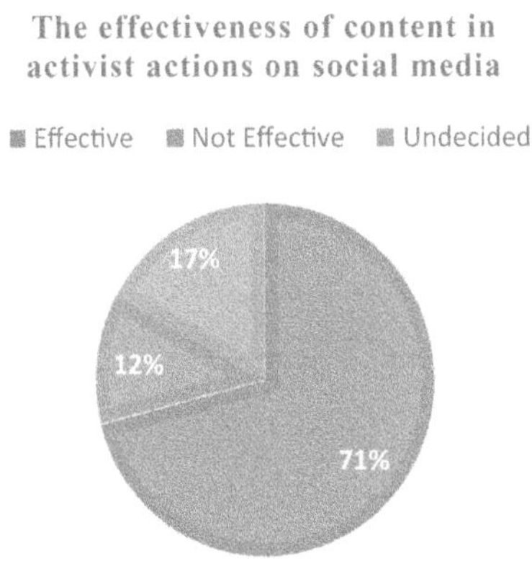

The Table 28 below shows, according to the responses of 384 participants to the question, "Do you think that content produced using techniques such as humorous tagging, drawing/illustration, caps, gifs, and video is effective in activist actions carried out on social media?", 17 % of participants said they were undecided, while 12 % thought the content was not effective. However, 71 % of respondents said these techniques were effective.

Table 29. *Whether participants find ınteractivity ımportant in digital activist actions on social media platforms*

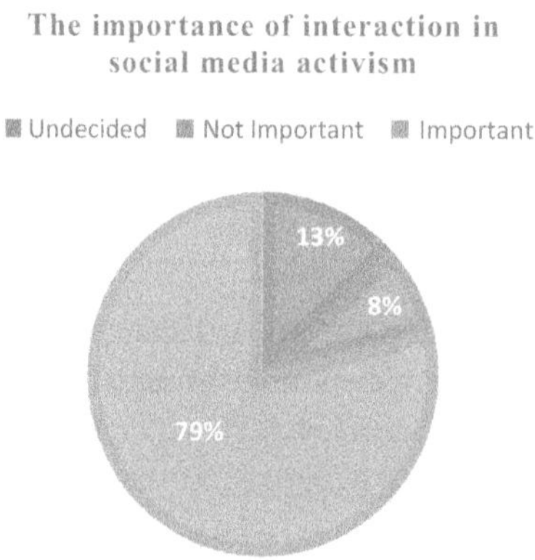

The Table 29 below shows, while 79 % of respondents found interaction important in activist actions on social media, 8 % did not find interaction important.

Table 30. Participants' participation in digital activist actions on social media platforms

What is your purpose for participating in social media activist actions?								
Base	**Total**	**Gender**		**Level of Education**				
		Female	**Male**	**Primary Education**	**High School**	**Associate Degree**	**Bachelor's Degree**	**Postgraduate Degree**
	384	**266**	**118**	**11**	**131**	**91**	**136**	**15**
Raising awareness of social or global issues	57.55	63.16	44.9	72.73	49.6	59.3	63.97	46.7
Expanding my network with others	12.24	7.89	22	0	14.5	13.2	9.56	20
Socializing	10.94	10.15	12.7	9.09	14.5	7.69	8.09	26.7
Contributing to the solution of social or global problems	19.27	18.8	20.3	18.18	21.4	19.8	18.38	6.67
Total	**100**	**100**	**100**	**100**	**100**	**100**	**100**	**100**

The Table 30 below shows, according to the answers to the question "What is your purpose for participating in social media activist actions?", 63.16 % of the 266 female participants, 44.9 % of the 118 male participants, and 57.55 % of the 384 participants participate in digital activist actions to raise awareness about social/global issues. Moreover, the highest level of this participation (63.97 %) is among those with a bachelor's degree.

Table 31. Participants' preferred methods to support digital activist actions on social media platforms (left), activist organizations known by participants (right)

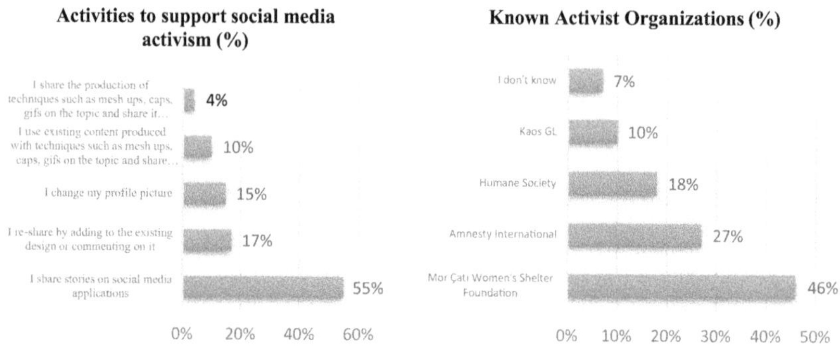

The Table 31 below shows, 384 participants were asked "Which of the following do you prefer to support activist actions on social media?", 55 % of the participants, i.e. the majority of them, share stories on social media applications, 17 % re-share by adding or commenting on the existing design, 15 % participate in the protests by changing their profile photo, 10 % use existing content produced with techniques such as mesh up, caps, gif, etc. on the relevant topic and share it with their environment, and only 4 % produce content with techniques such as mesh up, caps, gif, etc. on the relevant topic and share it with their environment. Mor Çatı Women's Shelter Foundation was identified by 46 % of the participants as the most well-known activist organization.

Table 32. Participants' top concerns on global and social issues

Which of the following global and societal issues concerns you the most?		**Gender**		**Level of Education**				
	Total	**Female**	**Male**	**Primary Education**	**High School**	**Associate Degree**	**Bachelor's Degree**	**Postgraduate Degree**
Base	**384**	**266**	**118**	**11**	**131**	**91**	**136**	**15**
Human Rights	31.25	29.32	35.59	36.36	32.82	28.57	30.15	40
Animal Rights	13.02	12.03	15.25	0	14.5	13.19	13.97	0
Women's Rights	45.83	50.38	35.59	54.55	38.93	54.95	45.59	46.67
Child Rights	7.03	5.64	10.17	9.09	9.16	3.3	6.62	13.33
LGBTI Rights	1.04	1.13	0.85	0	1.53	0	1.47	0
Environmental Rights	1.82	1.5	2.54	0	3.05	0	2.21	0
Total	100	100	100	**100**	**100**	**100**	**100**	**100**

The Table 32 below shows, according to the responses of 384 participants to the question "Which of the following global and social issues concerns you most?", 45.83 % of the participants indicated that they were very interested in women's rights, while 31.25 % indicated that they were sensitive to human rights. 266 female participants (50.38 %) were more interested in women's rights than 118 male participants (35.59 %).

Table 33. Participants' most concerned ıssues in global and social issues

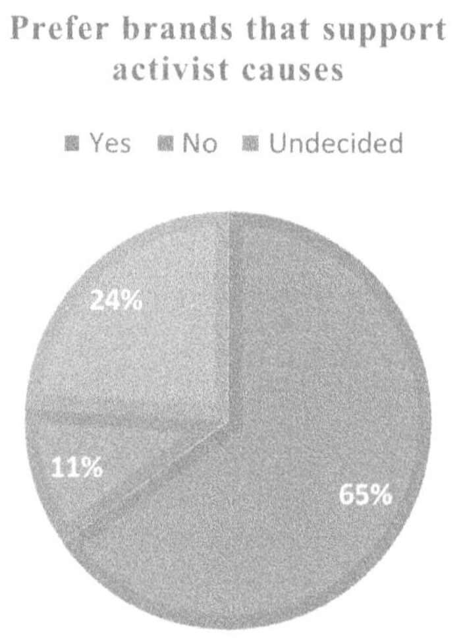

The Table 33 below shows, 384 participants were asked, "Do you prefer brands that support activist actions on social media?" According to the responses, 65 % of the participants answered "yes", 24 % answered "undecided". 11 % of respondents answered "no" and indicated that they do not consider brands' participation in activist movements in their brand preferences.

Table 34. Participants' attitudes towards brands' interactive content supporting digital activist actions on social media platforms

Would you be interested in interactive content from brands that support activist actions on social media platforms?			
		Gender	
	Total	**Female**	**Male**
Base	**384**	**266**	**118**
Yes	68.75	72.93	59.32
No	12.24	10.15	16.95
Undecided	19.01	16.92	23.73
Total	**100**	**100**	**100**

The Table 34 below shows, according to the responses to the question "Would you be interested in interactive content from brands that support activist actions on social media platforms?", 68.75 % of participants are interested in interactive content. In addition, 72.93 % of the 266 female respondents indicated that they would be interested in interactive content, compared to 59.32 % of the 118 male respondents.

Table 35. Participants' attitudes towards humor content used in digital activist actions on social media platforms

Are you interested in using humor in content produced for activist movements on social media platforms?			
Base	**Total**	**Gender**	
		Female	**Male**
	384	**266**	**118**
Yes	67.71	69.17	64.41
No	15.63	13.91	19.49
Undecided	16.67	16.92	16.1
Total	**100**	**100**	**100**

The Table 35 below shows, according to the responses to the question "Are you interested in using humor in content produced for activist movements on social media platforms?", 69.17 % of the 266 female participants and 64.41 % of the 118 male participants answered "yes". 16.67 % of the 384 participants were undecided.

Table 36. Participants' use of hastags to support digital activist actions on social media platforms

Do you share posts using relevant hashtags to support activist actions on social media platforms?			
Base	**Total**	**Gender**	
		Female	**Male**
	384	**266**	**118**
Yes	66.67	71.43	55.93
No	16.93	12.41	27.12
Undecided	16.41	16.17	16.95
Total	**100**	**100**	**100**

The Table 36 below shows, according to the answers to the question "Do you share posts using relevant hashtags to support activist actions on social media platforms?", 66.67 % of 384 participants answered yes and 16.93 % answered no to the question. While 77.43 % of the 266 female participants said they supported the posts using hashtags, only 55.93 % of the 118 male participants said they shared using hashtags.

Table 37. Participants' attitudes towards creating and sharing content to support digital activist actions on social media platforms

Do you create and share relevant content (caps, videos, photos, collages, literary content, etc.) to support activist movements on social media platforms?			
Base	**Total**	**Gender**	
		Female	**Male**
	384	**266**	**118**
Yes	66.15	68.05	61.86
No	33.85	31.95	38.14
Total	**100**	**100**	**100**

The Table 37 below shows, according to the responses to the question "Do you create and share relevant content (caps, videos, photos, collages, literary content, etc.) to support activist movements on social media platforms?", 66.15 % of 384 people answered "yes" and 33.85 % answered "no". While 68.05 % of 266 female participants answered "yes", 61.86 % of 118 male participants answered "yes".

Table 38. Participants' creation and sharing of content on global/social issues to raise awareness on social media platforms

Do you use design tools to create and share content about global and social issues?			
Base	**Total**	**Gender**	
		Female	**Male**
	254	**181**	**73**
Yes	71.26	71.82	69.86
No	20.47	20.44	20.55
Undecided	8.27	7.73	9.59
Total	**100**	**100**	**100**

The Table 38 below shows, according to the responses to the question "Do you use design tools (mobile collage applications, Canva, Photoshop, video editing tools and Adobe Illustrator, line drawing type software, sticker applications, etc.) to create and share content about global and social issues?", 71.26 % of the participants answered "yes", 20.47 % answered "no", and 8.27 % were undecided. 71.82 % of the 181 female participants and 69.86 % of the 73 male participants answered "yes".

Table 39. Participants' opinions on the attractiveness of content produced by others for global / social ıssues to raise awareness on social media platforms

Do you think that designs created by others about global and social issues should be attractive?			
Base	**Total**	**Gender**	
		Female	**Male**
	384	**266**	**118**
Yes	81.51	87.22	68.64
No	7.03	4.14	13.56
Undecided	11.46	8.65	17.8
Total	**100**	**100**	**100**

Based on the responses to the question "Do you think that designs created by others on global and social issues should be attractive?", The Table 39 below shows, 81.51 % of the participants answered "yes". The rate of those who answered "yes" was 87.22 % among 266 female participants and 68.64 % among 118 male participants.

Table 40. Participants' evaluations on the sharability of content created by others for global/social ısues to raise awareness on social media platforms

Do you think that designs created by others about global and social issues should be easy to share?			
Base	**Total**	**Gender**	
		Female	**Male**
	384	**266**	**118**
Yes	81.77	84.59	75.42
No	5.99	3.01	12.71
Undecided	12.24	12.41	11.86
Total	**100**	**100**	**100**

The Table 40 below shows, according to the answers to the question "Do you think that designs created by others on global and social issues should be easy to share?", 81.77 % of the 384 participants stated that the designs should be shareable, while 12.24 % were undecided on this issue. 5.99 % of the participants answered no. Among the 266 females, the rate of those who answered "yes" to the shareability of designs is 84.59 %.

Table 41. Participants' ratings of whether designs created by others to raise awareness of global/social ıssues on social media platforms should be compatible with technological device

Do you think that designs created by others about global and social issues should be compatible with all types of technological devices?			
Base	**Total**	**Gender**	
		Female	**Male**
	384	**266**	**118**
Yes	80.47	83.83	72.88
No	7.03	3.01	16.1
Undecided	12.5	13.16	11.02
Total	**100**	**100**	**100**

The Table 41 below shows, according to the answers to the question: "*Do you think that designs created by others on global and social issues should be compatible with all types of technological devices?*", the percentage of those who think that designs should be compatible with technological devices is 80.47 %.

Table 42. Participants' evaluations of ınstant messaging applications for communicating news transmission about global/social issues in order to raise awareness on social media platforms

Do you think that instant messaging applications (WhatsApp, Bip and Telegram) are important for communicating news about global and social issues?			
Base	**Total**	**Gender**	
		Female	**Male**
	384	**266**	**118**
Yes	82.03	84.21	77.12
No	6.77	2.63	16.1
Undecided	11.2	13.16	6.78
Total	**100**	**100**	**100**

The Table 42 below shows, according to the answers to the question "Do you think that instant messaging applications (WhatsApp, Bip and Telegram) are important for communicating news about global and social issues?", 84.21 % of 266 female participants and 77.12 % of 118 male participants answered "yes". Of all 384 participants, 82.03 % answered "yes", 6.77 % answered "no", and 11.2 % answered "undecided".

Table 43. Participants' evaluations on whether they agree with attitudes related to digital activism

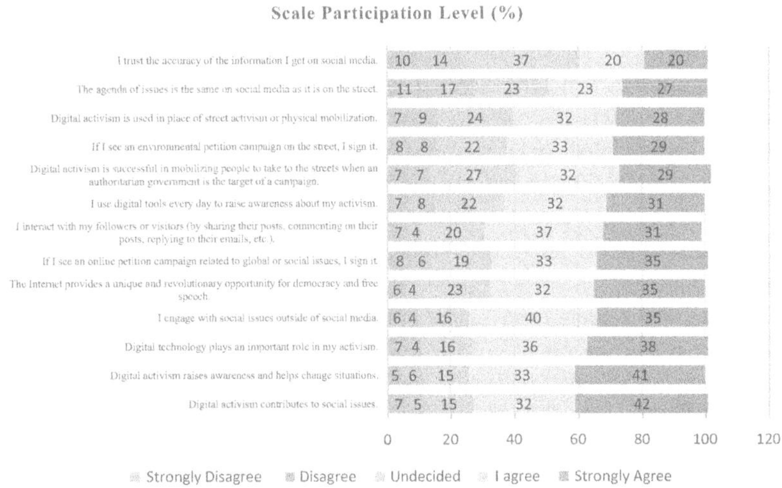

The Table 43 below shows, in terms of their level of agreement with statements related to digital activism, Generation Z participants believe that digital activism contributes the most to social issues. Although Generation Zers have the lowest level of trust in the information they get from social media, their average score is at a medium level (3.3/5).

4. Conclusion

The development of technology has changed the ownership of information and made information no longer a privilege of power. The development of technology and the individual's access to technology has affected all areas of humanity, from business models to all areas of social life and even the individual's perspective on life. The fact that information is no longer the privilege of a certain group of people, and that the daily development of technology has diversified the means of sharing it, has also affected social movements. In fact, the causality that was an actor in the industrial society has been replaced by a more flexible structure in which relative arguments have more favorable explanations with the birth of the information society and the development of technology. In this way, changing business models have transformed the habits of social life and, ultimately, the social order. The development of information technologies and the fact that they have become cheaper and more accessible have enabled individuals to share their intellectual processes with people they know or do not know in environments independent of time and space. In particular, individuals who have an opinion about a situation that makes them feel uncomfortable on a social or global scale, or about the protection of the current situation, have come together with the advantages offered by mass media and the Internet to form communities. With the development of information-sharing tools, social movements or interpersonal organizations have developed their repertoire of actions and enabled social movements to gain widespread influence. Social movements, which are particularly prevalent in times of social upheaval, allow for a regular and uninterrupted flow of information in cyberspace and facilitate the dissemination, exchange, and storage of information locally, nationally, or between countries.

The local and regional movements that emerged after the 1990s have had a widespread impact as the use of the Internet has increased over time. This has led to changes in alternative ways of organizing, acting and reacting in societies. The resulting diversity affects many areas, from people's social relations to their level of information acquisition and the way they do business. In this context, this study aims to reveal the level of awareness of Generation Z, born into the digital world as primary users of the Internet and information technologies, on social and global issues, their level of participation and whether they are activists or not. This study, which allows the evaluation of the attitudes and behaviors of Generation Z, applied the survey technique and a questionnaire form was created to reveal the impact of digital activism on Generation Z individuals. The study, which is based on voluntary participation, was conducted with a total of 384 male and female participants who are randomly selected from Generation Z individuals. The structured questionnaire, which was presented to individuals living in cities selected as highly populated from different regions of Turkey, included multiple-choice, 5-point Likert scale, and closed-ended questions. The interviews were conducted using CAWI methodology, and in the first part of the study, the participants were filtered according to the limitation of being Generation Z. According to the filtering result, the questions in the second and third sections were asked. According to the analysis, it was revealed that Generation Z individuals are quite competent in terms of using the Internet and new media tools, and their attitudes towards digital activism were measured through questions structured according to fourteen hypotheses. Based on the results, it was found that Generation Z individuals are interested in social issues, use the Internet at a rate of 69 % to obtain information about these issues, and prefer new media tools more than traditional communication tools. In this context, assumptions H1 and H5 were confirmed. The main purpose of the participants' use of social media is to spend their free time with entertainment at a rate of 62 %, and 53 % of them use these platforms to share content that interests them. In the survey form, which included questions about digital activism, 62 % of the participants stated that they had knowledge about the connotation of the concept. However, when the participants' responses to the questions about having heard of the concept of digital activism were evaluated, it was concluded that 51 % of the participants had not heard of the concept of activism, and a similar response was given when asked whether this lack of knowledge in their knowledge level defined them as activists. In fact, 44 % of participants belonging to this generation said they were undecided about defining themselves as activists. 59 % of the participants agreed that digital activism is useful in terms of raising public awareness. In this regard, the participants stated that they participate in cyberspace for an action mainly through the Instagram platform and that they benefit from news on platforms such as Instagram, X and Facebook as a source of information. 69 % of the 384 respondents follow social movements on social media platforms, while 78 % follow other digital activists or thought leaders. 58 % of respondents like or re-share content from other users who share and circulate an activism post. While 60 % of participants find digital activism campaigns or actions on social media to be successful, 83 % find the visuals used in such actions to be successful and impressive. Similarly, 71 % of the participants find the images created using techniques such as digital videos, caps, gifs, drawings, etc., effective in activist actions. Another question posed to 384 participants was whether the participants found interaction in activist movements on social media important. 79 % of respondents believe that interactivity is important. In addition, 55 % of the participants said that they support such actions by sharing stories, but only 4 % of them raise awareness of their surroundings through visual production. Due to the small number of participants who produce to support activist movements, the study's assumption that "Generation Z reproduces content using simple applications to participate in digital actions." (H6) is invalid.

One of the reasons participants prefer brands is that they believe socially conscious brands should support activist causes. In fact, 65 % of the participants stated that they prefer brands that support activist actions. In this respect, hypothesis H9 is valid. It was found that the level of interest of the participants in humorous images produced in activist actions was 67 %. 67 % of the participants support the related movements by using the hashtags used in activist actions carried out on social media platforms. Approximately the same percentage of participants indicated that they create and share content for these actions. While 81.51 % of the participants stated that the content produced in such social media activist actions should be attractive, about 80 % of the participants agreed that such content should be compatible with technological devices. The percentage of participants who believe that instant messaging applications are important for communicating news about global or social problems is 82.03 %. In the last question, which was presented to the participants using a 5-point Likert scale and measured their level of participation, it was concluded that individuals belonging to Generation Z mostly believe that activism contributes to solving social problems, but they still have a very low level of trust in the accuracy of the information they receive on social media. According to the statistical data of hypotheses H1, H2, H3, H4, H5, H7, H8, H8, H9, H10, H11, H12 and H13, the average of these statements is different from "3". In this context, although the participants are undecided in defining themselves as activists, 78 % of them support such actions and 31 % of them participate in physical actions. In general, the 384 participants in the study have a high level of awareness of social and global issues. They participate in such actions through social media platforms. Based on the results of the study, the researchers developed the following recommendations;

- In order to create a comprehensive profile of Generation Z, as evaluated in this study, more extensive research is needed. More generalizable information can be obtained through studies that are tested using different methods and techniques.
- According to the results of the research, it has been determined that Generation Z, which can evoke the concept of digital activism and participate in activist actions, is undecided in evaluating itself as an activist despite these behaviors. In this context, the definition of the concept can be clearly expressed by conducting scientific activities on what digital activism is.
- According to the findings of the study, it was revealed that Generation Z uses the Internet as a field at the level of action on social issues, turns to social media platforms more than these fields, and shares such actions with their environment. In this context, it can be suggested that activist actions carried out before the public should be presented more on social media platforms, which are intensively consumed by Generation Z individuals, with interactive and impressive images.
- Care should be taken to ensure that all types of communication developed for this generation of individuals, who experience daily life and appear as sharers, and used to raise awareness in social actions, are compatible with technology.
- Within the framework of the study conducted through the consideration of the literature, it was noted that the resources in the area are insufficient. In this context, it is considered appropriate to conduct the study on a larger sample.
- In addition to Generation Z, the relevant study can be conducted on different generations and comparative analyzes can be made between generations.
- Qualitative research, mixed methods, naturalistic observation, or experimental studies that allow in-depth analysis of smaller groups may be included.
- According to the findings of the survey study obtained from the representatives of Generation Z individuals, whose core values according to the literature include interaction, production and sharing, this generation has similarities with the characteristics mentioned in the literature.
- Replication of the research and application results in different geographical areas can contribute to the achievement of generalizable results.

Contribution of the Study to the Literature: The study has a multifaceted research content and it is believed that it will contribute to the literature due to its interdisciplinary nature, which can be used by many fields that will be carried out after it.

References

Aksoy, S. (2017). Değişen Teknolojiler ve Endüstri 4.0: Endüstri: 4.0'ı Anlamaya Dair Bir Giriş. (Electronic Version) *SAV Katkı Journal*, 4, 34–44. (7 Mayıs 2020).

Castells, M. (2003). *Enformasyon çağı: Ekonomi, toplum ve kültür. Birinci cilt: Ağ toplumunun yükselişi* (Çev. E. Kılıç; 2.baskı). İstanbul Bilgi Üniversitesi Press. (Original Pub. Date: 1996).

Drucker, P. F. (1993). *Kapitalist ötesi toplum* (Trans. Belkıs Çorakçı). İstanbul: İnkılap.

Erkan, H. (1993). *Bilgi Toplumu ve Ekonomik Gelişme*, Ankara, Türkiye İş Bankası Press, Genel Yayın No:326, *Bilim Dizisi*: 8, 2. Press.

Erkırlı, B. D., (2022). *Hipermodern Agoralarda Yeni Katılımcı Kültürler ve Değişen Aktivizm Tipolojileri: Dijital Yerliler, Dijital Göçmenler, Dijital Melezler ve Dijital Bilgeler* (Ed. A. İcil Tuncer, pp. 139–198). Dijital Aktivizm: Kavramlar ve Teoriler içinde, Konya: Literatürk Press.

Hançerlioğlu, O. (1986). Ekonomi Sözlüğü, Büyük Fikir Kitapları Dizisi: 15. *İstanbul Remzi Kitapevi*, 6.

Işık, G. (2015). *Nükleer santral karşıtı bir toplumsal hareketin analizi-sanaldan sokağa toplumsal hareketler*. Ankara: Nobel Press.

Keleş, H. N. (2011). Y kuşağı çalışanlarının motivasyon profillerinin belirlenmesine yönelik bir araştırma. *Organizasyon ve Yönetim Bilimleri Dergisi*, 3(2), 129–139. https://dergipark.org.tr/en/download/article-file/150976. 04 July 2023.

Karahasan, F. (2018). *Açılın Gençler Geliyor*, 1. Baskı, İstanbul: Doğan Egmont Press Tic. A.Ş.

Sparks ve Honey Culture Forecast. (2015). Generation Z 2025: The Final Generation. 28.03.23 tarihinde. https://www.slideshare.net/sparksandho-ney/gen-z-2025-the-final-generation-preview/99-GEN_Z_2025MET-HODOLOGYFor_Gen_Z

Şenel, A. (2004). *Siyasal Düşünceler Tarihi*. Ankara: Bilim ve Sanat Press.

Stevenson, N. (2003). *Cultural Citizenship: Cosmopolitan Questions*. Berkshire, England: Open University Press.

Önder, B. A. (2021). *Z Kuşağı: Eşitlik ve Reklam Tasarımları (Dijital Yerliler)*. Nobel: Ankara.

Taş, B. (2006). AB Uyum Sürecinde Türkiye için Yeni bir Bölge Kavramı: İstatistiki BölgeBirimleri Sınıflandırması (İBBS). *Afyon Kocatepe Üniversitesi Sosyal Bilimler Enstitüsü Journal*, VIII(2), 185–197, Aralık 2006.

Trevino, G. N. (2018). *The Arrival of Generation Z on College Campuses*. Doctoral dissertation, University of The Incarnate Word.

Toffler, A. (Tarihsiz), *Dünyayı Nasıl Bir Gelecek Bekliyor?* (Ç. M. Çiftkaya). İstanbul, İz Press.

Yıldız, A. (2018). Endüstri 4.0 ve Akıllı Fabrikalar. *Sakarya Üniversitesi Fen Bilimleri Enstitüsü Journal*, 22(2), 546–556. 15 Mart 2020.

Yücebalkan, B. (2020). Endüstri 4.0'dan Endüstri 5.0'a Geçiş Sürecine Genel Bakış. *Pearson Journal of Socıal Sciences & Humanities*, 5(9), 241–250.

Asst. Prof. Büşra T. Durmuş[1]

Women plus movement as an achievement

Abstract: The concept of post-truth has evolved since its selection as the word of 2016 by the Oxford Dictionary, defining a new era that brings its own values, identity, sociability, and interaction. The boundaries of the category of women have changed in this new era, with binary gender assumptions being challenged and emotions and personal narratives gaining importance. New media systems, such as digital activism, have played a key role in the development of post-truth identities, transforming people's judgmental worlds. In this study, an independent literature review and narrative analysis were conducted to examine the impact of digital activism on the formation of post-truth identities, with a focus on the "women+ (plus) movement" and its accrual through new media. The study found that digital activism has created an ecosystem that allows for identity construction through in-network organizations and user-derived content in spite of resistance. However, the movement's success and sustainability will depend on its ability to navigate and overcome resistance and opposition from those who oppose its goals. Overall, this study highlights the importance of digital activism in shaping post-truth identities and the role of new media in enabling activism.

Keywords: Post-truth identities, digital activism, women plus (+) movement, narrative analysis.

1. Introduction

When different periods of history are examined, it can be seen that the pace of social change and transformation was incomparably slower than that of the 21st century. Despite the revolutionary innovations that occurred over centuries, it would not be wrong to say that this change cannot compete with the 21st century. By the time the 21st century arrived, many attitudes, behavior, and norms had undergone a transformation, and a new reality had emerged. Changes in identity acceptance, especially with regards to women, have developed in connection with the feminist movement. Obviously one of the main agents of all these changes is communication systems that continuously transform themselves while transforming society with them. At this point, the question of how communication systems evolved into apparatuses that transform society along

1 Marmara University, Faculty of Communication, Journalism Department, busratosundurmus@gmail.com ORCID: 0000-0001-5158-0058.

with themselves is quite important. Then comes the question of how propaganda tools developed through new media channels, which greatly amplify the impact of making the press the fourth estate, are working, and it seems possible to find the answer to this in the concept of digital activism in digitalized media systems. Of course, it would be appropriate to explain the environment that is favorable for digital activism and the aforementioned "new reality" with the concept of "post-truth" and to use this concept as a periodizing term.

In this context, this study explores how the definition of womanhood has evolved, with a specific focus on the "women plus (+)" movement, which will be referred to as the "women plus (+) movement" for the remainder of the study. The framework of post-truth identities, as described by Baker and Chadwick (2021), will be discussed in the context of digital activism, in order to understand how the "woman plus (+) movement" developed in an environment where the fixed reality judgments have been fundamentally shaken. The historical background and conditions that led to the emergence of this movement will also be analyzed, with a focus on the feminist movement and its impact on the concept of womanhood.

At the same time, this study aims to draw a historical framework for the concept of "woman plus (+)", which represents an acceptance of identity and was only encountered in the second decade of the 2000s, in relation to the inclusive meaning of the plus (+) sign added to the name of the LGBT organization. While this framework is expected to contribute to the literature, the study also seeks to find answers to the question of which institutions this transformation took place under in Türkiye, which is also affected by the transformations related to the concept of womanhood simultaneously with the rest of the world. This study is particularly important in the context of the widespread acceptance of post-truth identity understandings through digital activist activities, facilitated by the influence of digital media systems. It provides an opportunity for evaluation, with a focus on Türkiye.

Thus the study will be divided into three sections. The first section will provide explanations about the post-truth era and the identities it creates. The following section will focus on the role of digital activism in producing and promoting post-truth identities that are based on increasingly blurred reality assumptions within the vast digital world. In the third section, a brief historical overview of feminist struggles for rights and acceptance of female identity will be presented. Following this, conceptual explanations will be provided, and the development stages of the "women plus (+) movement", as a new phase in female identity in both the Western world and Türkiye, will be illuminated. This section will also present the methodology and findings of a netnographic analysis (Kozinets,

2015) based on narrative theory (Fisher, 1984, 1985, 1989) of digital data. Lastly, the study will discuss the possibility of new identity acceptances generated by the gender revolution in Europe and America, and whether such identities have emerged in societies like Türkiye with different religious and cultural backgrounds. The study will also address how this was possible, if such identities have emerged.

1.1. Post-truth era

"Reality does not care much for how we describe it" says Colin Wight (2018: 20) unless post-truth conception came into role. But what exactly is post-truth? The term was first used in a 1992 article by Steve Tesich in The Nation titled "A Government of Lies," which discussed the Nixon administration's handling of the Watergate scandal. He notes that "We, by our actions, are saying that this is no longer necessary, that we have acquired a spiritual mechanism that can denude truth of any significance. In a very fundamental way, we, as a free people, have freely decided that we want to live in some post-truth world" (Tesich, 1992). When Tesich used the concept for the first time, he could not have imagined that this would pave the way to a new era.

Long after Tesich, the conceptualization of post-turth was used in a book named *The Post-Turth Era: Dishonesty and Deception in Contemporary Life* in 2004 by Ralph Keyes. He highlights that the post-truth era has nuances of both honesty and dishonesty, and that it expands the traditional understanding of these concepts by giving them a wider framework. Specifically, the post-truth era allows for the acceptance of emotional truths and subjective interpretations, which can sometimes conflict with objective facts (Keyes, 2004). He means that even academia has been influenced by post-truthfulness, especially in the social sciences, where academics may introduce themselves or conduct research with subjective biases, and even engage in plagiarism without consequences by explaining the situation as revealing "larger truths" (Keyes, 2004: 97–100). Keyes (2004: 109) also points out how the postmodernist approach towards truth has been replaced with a focus on "storytelling" and "narratives". It should be remembered that these two points are fundamental to the acceptance of post-truth identities that emerged after new media technologies spread all over the world.

After Keyes brought the concept of post-truth to the forefront, it gained more popularity during the election of Donald Trump as the President of the USA and the Brexit referendum in which the UK voted to leave the European Union. In 2016, the Oxford Dictionary chose "post-truth" as its Word of the Year, defining it as relating to or denoting circumstances in which objective facts are less influential in shaping public opinion than appeals to emotion and personal belief (Word of the Year 2016, n.d.). After that, the term was used 2,000% more frequently than in 2015 (McIntyre, 2018: 1). Since then post-truth became closely associated with social media, especially when the Facebook and Cambridge Analytica scandal occurred, making the manipulation of new media applications clearer. However, evaluating the concept of post-truth with just a relation to lies is obviously not enough. The addition of the prefix "post" after the word "truth" indicates not just the idea of "past truth" in a temporal sense (as in "postwar"), but also the sense that truth has been eclipse-that it is irrelevant as McIntyre (2018: 5) expresses it. While post-truth is related to lies and dishonesty, the concept has gained additional meaning as an era that follows postmodernism. In this case, even postmodernism, which rejects the idea of absolute truth, had more connection to truth than the post-truth era, which emphasizes emotional truths and subjective interpretations over objective facts. As Keyes (2004: 165) states, "Even the most ardent postmodern relativist wouldn't argue that truth-telling has no place in human discourse. No society could function on that basis. Civilization would crumble if we assumed others were as likely to lie as to tell the truth. Our social contract cannot survive lying so routine that citizens consider it normal."

Moreover, the link between the post-truth era and postmodernism is worth emphasizing, as the roots of the post-truth era lie in the sociopolitical transformations of the 1960s, the culture conflicts, and the subjectivity of the postmodern era (Cosentino, 2020: 4). After Jean-François Lyotard's book, *The Postmodern Condition: A Report on Knowledge*, was published in 1979, a rich history started to accumulate throughout the 20th century, with major contributions from Jacques Derrida, Martin Heidegger, and Michel Foucault, who created postmodernist literature. In particular, the theory of deconstructing literature gave rise to the idea of questioning everything that can be considered a text, including issues such as sexuality and religion (McIntyre, 2018: 124). Postmodern and tactical identity politics, which refers to a temporary identity adopted for a particular social, political, or cultural purpose, emerged in the late 1970s and early 1980s as a response to the metanarrative crises that arose with postmodernism (Cosentino, 2020: 18). McIntyre (2018: 124) argues that, according to postmodernists, there is no objective truth, only narrative. However, power still controls what is considered true (McIntyre, 2018: 126). From this point of view "Thus is postmodernism the godfather of post-truth" (McIntyre, 2018: 137).

As mentioned before, the conceptualization of post-truth has a relation to lies, deception, as well as bias, new identity acceptances, subjective narratives, and storytelling. It represents a new world order where emotions and subjective beliefs surpass evident-based arguments, and where the boundaries of truth and lie can be replaced and blurred (Cosentino, 2020: 3). On the other hand, as McIntyre (2018: 13) questions why feelings can matter more than facts and answers, "Someone does not dispute an obvious or easily confirmable fact for no reason; he or she does so when it is to his or her advantage. When a person's beliefs are threatened by an 'inconvenient fact,' sometimes it is preferable to challenge the fact. This can happen at either a conscious or unconscious level." He also adds that: "Thus post-truth amounts to a form of ideological supremacy, whereby its practitioners are trying to compel someone to believe in something whether there is good evidence for it or not" (McIntyre, 2018: 13). These inferences have profound implications that can be explored through the conceptualizing of "post-truth identities" by Baker and Chadwick (2021).

1.2. Post-truth identities

Post-truth as a cultural and political condition may have emerged in Western countries (Cosentino, 2020: 3), but the mentality has rapidly spread worldwide with the help of new media technologies. The rise of social media initially blurred the lines between news and opinions (McIntyre, 2018: 93), and eventually, even objective facts became subject to debate. As self-expression and identity formation occur through new technological conditions enabled by social media, the concept of truthfulness became corrupted (Cosentino, 2020: 21). Consequently, post-truth identities found their way into the mainstream, introducing a post-truth world where no identity is questioned.

From this point of view, Baker and Chadwick (2021: 312) conceptualize "post-truth identities" as a brand new phenomenon that "emerges from a confluence of individual contextual factors". They argue that in advanced democracies, individuals' confrontation and processing of information are shaped by cognitive biases, which are intensified by new media technologies, resulting in freer settings. As a technology optimist, Weinberger (2007: 170) expresses that the implicit web of relationships shapes the actual meanings of things in our world, similarly in the digitized world of meanings that helps to contextualize the information and ideas individuals encounter. He uses the term "hop over established categorizations" (Weinberger, 2007: 221) to describe the ability of digital networks to break down traditional categories and boundaries, allowing for new connections and relationships to be formed between ideas and information where that the digital world allows for a more fluid and dynamic way of categorizing and connecting information that is not limited by traditional structures or hierarchies. Thus, according to Baker and Chadwick (2021: 313), this kind of digitized "infrastructure of meaning" can both enhance group coherence and lead to the production of distorted systems of internally coherent classifications. Public connection can enable false or distorted beliefs through culture and sense of belonging as well as online post-truth communities can promote falsehood by marginalising paradoxical evidence. All those creates post-truth identities in an environment that suspect truth, science and evidence.

When social identity theories began in the 1970s with the work of Henri Tajfel, it was shown that social categorization has an obvious influence on intergroup behavior. Tajfel and his colleagues also argued that social groups needed a positive social identity to provide their members with distinctiveness. After the results of experimentation and the emergence of other ideas, two social identity theories have been accepted: "the original intergroup theory and the more recent self-categorization theory". Both theories point out that individuals define themselves in the sense of social group memberships, and their self-perception generates characteristic features in social behavior (Turner, 1998: vii). From this perspective, an individual's identity is closely linked to their sense of belonging to a group (Baker & Chadwick, 2021: 313) and this identity politics can sometimes privilege social location over truth. Loyalty in such cases lies with the group rather than with facts and reality (Wight, 2018: 20).

In the post-truth era, where every kind of identity affirmed through new media platforms has emerged and spread, the intergroup motivation behind these identities is fueled by the need for affirmation and validation within one's social group, often at the expense of truth and objective reality. As Baker and Chadwick (2021: 313) states "finally, this identity work it itself also boosted time to time by celebrity endorsements and news coverage by professional media organizations". Especially new media play a significant role in affirming these post-truth identities by using personal and emotional narratives rather than verifiable criteria. While this method doesn't always lead to a direct improvement in understanding reality, it does play a role in preserving personal well-being, which consequently affects the beliefs and actions of others. In such cases, "emotions" take center stage in shaping reality.

On the other hand, cognitive bias like motivated reasoning, confirmation bias, social conformity, and availability cascades can cause individuals to adopt beliefs that are not based on facts and objective truths. Motivated reasoning occurs when individuals selectively seek out and interpret information in a way that confirms their preexisting beliefs. Confirmation bias is the tendency to interpret new information in a way that confirms one's preexisting beliefs while discounting information that contradicts them. Social conformity is the tendency to conform to the beliefs and behaviors of the group, often at the expense of one's own judgment. Availability cascades occur when information that is initially seen as credible and widely disseminated becomes widely accepted, regardless of its veracity, due to the mental shortcut of availability. With the proliferation of new media and the impact of cognitive biases, the concept of truth has taken on a new form that can be referred to as post-truth identities (Baker & Chadwick, 2021: 315). This category includes a wide variety of groups, from anti-vaxxers and flat-earthers to vegans and those who identify with new sexual identities even definition of sex of human beings. These groups often rely on emotional appeals, cognitive biases, and personal narratives, which may not be based on objective or scientific facts and are spread through activist activities facilitated by new media systems in the post-truth era. Before exploring the new boundaries of post-truth womanhood in the context of the women plus (+) movement, it is important to have a good understanding of the phenomenon of digital activism and the role of digital media technologies in facilitating it.

2. Digital activism on post-truth online

The concept of activism emerged in the mid-70s, long before the so-called post-truth era and is focused on creating actions that have the potential to change history. Jordan (2002: 23) states that 'From many sources and in many ways, activism is generating the future of societies,' highlighting its significance in shaping the future of societies through various means and channels. Activism, as a practice of struggling for change, can lead to both progressive and reactionary aims, although it is not synonymous with direct action (Cammaerts, 2007: 217). Furthermore, activist movements often promote social change through innovative ethical ideas and moral standards (Jordan, 2002: 23), including the recognition and acceptance of fluid post-truth identities without rigid boundaries, which have gained worldwide attention.

The emergence of Web 2.0 technology enabled individuals to become active elements in the digital world, producing content and expressing their ideas on various new media platforms. This has led to the emergence of a new form of sociality. Ordinary individuals have begun to play an active role in society and have gained the opportunity to present their attitudes in daily life through digital media. Thus, a new concept of digital activism has emerged through these new channels, which will give strength to activist movements and accelerate social transformation. Media became as a medium to interact, to propagate as well as communication (Cammaerts, 2007: 220). This enables users to coordinate actions, send and receive content, create effective social and political movements, and connect with each other more easily (Joyce, 2010: 2). Of course, with the combination of digital activism activities and post-truth narratives, the emergence of new forms of sociality has become inevitable.

The main difference between digital activism and traditional social activist movements lies in their organizational structure. In traditional structures, there is a responsible administrative structure that organizes and manages the movement. However, when it comes to digital activism, the activities of digital activists are more dispersed, and the movement is leaderless (Turhan, 2017: 28). Therefore, the key feature of this new type of activist movement can be any type of organization that uses the internet interaction opportunities offered by Web 2.0 technology, as well as influencers who are effective on their followers, or ordinary people. Ultimately, it is more difficult to identify the initiator of the movement.

Of course, the basic requirement for digital activism to be conducted is to be online. Unlike traditional activism, digital activism is impossible without having internet access and tools to use this opportunity. This situation directly affects the character of the activist activity carried out, while also bringing economic limitations, it reaches the power to eliminate spatial limitations. As Joyce (2010: 3) expressed, "The whole world speaking one language – that is the power of digital code."

According to Sivitanides and Shah (2011: 4), people are divided into three groups in terms of their approach to digital activism. The first group is made up of "optimists" who attribute positive meanings to digital activism due to its potential to change the current political hierarchical situation and create stronger citizens. On the other hand, "pessimists" believe that digital activism poses a danger due to technology's moral neutrality and its both constructive and destructive effects. The third group, which consists of "persistens", is wary of digital activism specifically in terms of technology and agrees that it will not have a significant impact on effecting any change. Regardless of the general consensus as Schradie (2019: x) has expressed, "Good. Bad. Utopian. Dystopian. The impact of digital technologies on political activism has exploded into a global conversation, a furious debate over the role that platforms like Facebook, Twitter, and YouTube now play in giving voice to those previously unheard." It is an undeniable fact that social media platforms are intense areas where digital activism is displayed. However, it must be remembered that while they may define digital activist experiences, they are not necessarily more important than other factors (Joyce, 2010: 4) or channels. Ultimately, the practice of social change has already been improved and will continue to be improved (McNutt, 2018: 9–10) through the use of various media platforms.

2.1. Types of digital activism

First of all it should be remembered that digital activism depends on economic, social, and political factors which determines its users and their infrastructures as Joyce (2010: 4) expresses. As stated above, the economic situation of users has a great impact on activist practices on the internet. People who live in wealthy countries have more opportunities to access the internet and a higher possibility to purchase functional devices. Additionally, the physical location of the individual can also affect their activist practices.

Social and political norms are equally influential as economic factors in shaping digital activist practices. While any form of activism in democratic and semi democratic societies can bring about social change, undemocratic countries may view technology as a threat to their government's power. In such situations, participants are often worried about being monitored or traced by the government (Cullum, 2010: 66; Schradie, 2019: 56). However, authoritarian government intervention can lead to more impactful internet activism, as demonstrated in Iran's 'Twitter Revolution' and Egypt's 'Facebook Revolution' (Schradie, 2019: 56). Clearly, these kinds of problems occur when activist campaigns take place on social media applications that can be used on cell phones, tablets and laptops (Cullum, 2010: 67). This means that while the possibility of technology usage affects online activist movements, the geographical location is just as important as the economy, as it reflects the social and political norms of the people living there. Additionally, it is obvious that mobile tools are crucial for online activism. After all, what really matters, as Cullum (2010: 69) expresses, is 'how the tools are used in the hands of average citizens, activists, and organizational leaders.'

From this point of view, there are various types of digital activism that demonstrate their effectiveness and reasonableness. The most common form of online activism is known as advocacy or hashtag activism, which, as Devillart and Waniewski (2010: 197) state, involves "ancient activities dressed up in new methods by high-tech tools." This type of activism is often the most efficient in creating social and political change due to its dedication, sustainability, and potential for continuity. Moreover, when compared to the costs of physically present activism, digital advocacy is more reasonable and, grassroots activism could benefit from these low-cost, internet-enabled technologies (Earl & Kimport, 2011: 22). With the help of accessible tools, advocates can create an effective impact by generating hashtags, opening chat/space rooms, sharing their own thoughts and experiences, or simply sharing others' posts on social media. Thus, while social and political change may occur slowly through advocacy activism, it can lead to the emergence and acceptance of new identities that were previously unimaginable, such as the focus of this study on new women's identities.

Another type of activism is referred to as "slacktivism" or "click activism". According to Joyce (2010: 27), this is "a kind of liberal catharsis during a lunch break that gives participants the impression that they have done something about the issue when, in fact, their online action had no offline effect at all." Evgeny Morozov (2011), who authored the book *The Net Delusion: The Dark Side of Internet Freedom,* is known for his pessimistic views on technology as well as the ineffectiveness of slacktivism. He criticizes the notion that believing enough tweets can solve the world's problems as completely nonsensical. Social media platforms like Twitter and Facebook are less successful than real actions taken by individuals in generating awareness (Morozov, 2011: 190–191). Moreover, he argues that these types of "nano-activism" have zero political or social impact and are the ideal type of activism for a lazy generation (Morozov, 2009). However, on the contrary, in the long term, even these seemingly small activist actions can work as an accumulation agent in creating social or political change. This point of view will be evaluated in the following chapters.

Hacktivism is an activist approach that occurs on online platforms, and it is often referred to as "destructive activism" due to its potential to cause significant problems (Joyce, 2010: 137). The rise of hacktivism has configured hacker politics within a broader context, as stated by Jordan (2002: 121). He explains that "mass virtual direct action-based actions are always for a cause, whereas digitally correct hacktivism is its own cause (Jordan, 2002: 130)." Additionally, Jordan (2002: 130) argues that digitally correct hacktivist actions build a particular informational politics directly and do not create tools that serve other campaigns. Their main aim is to provide tools for flowing secure information. This means that while some forms of hacktivism may be peaceful and non-destructive and can be a powerful tool for effecting social or political change, it must be used responsibly and with care.

After explaining some types of digital activism and highlighting their ability to generate social transformation, it is important to focus on new identities that have post-truth features and fluid boundaries, which can be controversial. While ranking these arguments on those identities is not the main aim of this study, the focus will be on their evolution, how they emerged, and how they have become widespread, specifically in the context of the Women plus (+) movement.

3. Methodology and findings

3.1. Narrative theory

He methodological approaches in the communication field are becoming more diverse, especially when the subject has interdisciplinary elements. In this study, which exhibits interdisciplinary features involving communication, feminist studies, sociology, and even psychology, the methodology should be chosen to be suitable for all. The narrative theory (Fisher, 1984, 1985, 1989) based on digital narratives, which requires ethnographic observation, in this case, netnographic (Kozinets, 2015) investigation, makes this study a direct narrative netnographic (Allen, 2017: 75) research. While narrative netnoghraphies are storied forms of ethnographic research happens in online and shapes the study, "narrative ethnographies are stories of others that include personal experiences of the ethnographer" (Allen, 2017: 75).

According to Walter Fisher (1984), who developed the narrative theory, the presuppositions that structure the narrative paradigm are:

> (1) humans are essentially storytellers; (2) the paradigmatic mode of human decision-making and communication is "good reasons" which vary in form among communication situations, genres, and media; (3) the production and practice of good reasons is ruled by matters of history, biography, culture (4) rationality is determined by the nature of persons as narrative beings, and (5) the world is a set of stories which must be chosen among to live the good life in a process of continual recreation (1984: 7–8).

From this point of view humans, as natural storytellers, constantly generate narratives throughout their social lives, and in digital ecosystems as well. As Fisher (1989: 57) states, "all forms of human communication can be seen fundamentally as stories, as interpretations of the world occurring in time and shaped by history, culture, and character". On the other hand, the narrative paradigm seeks to understand how individuals come to believe and behave (Fisher, 1985: 357). In this study, the focus is on the Women Plus (+) movement, which is gaining more influence in social life experiences through narratives generated on new media technologies with the help of digital activism.

In this context, Fisher (1985: 347) points out that all genres, including technical communication, are episodes in the story of life. This provides an opportunity to apply this paradigm to the study, which requires a netnographic investigation and observation of the new approach that denies binary sex in the post-truth era. This opportunity also allows the study to utilize the narrative theory to answer the questions, "How have the essential boundaries of binary sex acceptance become questionable?" and "Which circumstances led to the emergence of the Women

Plus (+) movement?" by evaluating digital narratives. From this perspective, the findings of the study can be divided into two categories.

The first category focuses on the evolution of the Women Plus (+) movement in the Western world, while the second category examines how this movement emerged in a country like Turkey, where conservative societal values are still very strong.

3.2. Evolution of the women plus (+) movement

According to the Merriam-Webster dictionary (Women, n.d.) and the Oxford Wordpower Dictionary (Wehmeier, 1995: 706), the definition of women is "an adult female person". In this sense, being female is a significant basic human characteristic based on sex. This is recognized at the biochemical and cellular levels by defining the XX female genotype, as noted in a report by the Committee on Understanding the Biology of Sex and Gender Differences formed by the Institute of Medicine (Wizemann & Pardue, 2001: 4). However, the concept of womanhood has been subject to wider interpretation since the emergence of gender ideology and second wave feminist discourse.

In her influential book The Second Sex, published in 1949, Simone de Beauvoir famously wrote that "one is not born, but rather becomes, a woman" (1956: 273). This statement became a rallying cry for second wave feminism, which emerged in the 1960s and 1970s and sought to challenge traditional gender roles and expectations. One of the key questions raised by second wave feminists was who counts as a woman and who is excluded from this category. By problematizing the notion of "woman" as a fixed and essential category, second wave feminism paved the way for more inclusive and intersectional approaches to feminist theory and activism. With the publication of Judith Butler's *Gender Trouble: Feminism and the Subversion of Identity* in 1990, the challenge to the fixed and essential category of "woman" was taken to the next stage. Butler argues that sex is also a social construct, much like gender (Butler, 1999: 10). She further questions whether the exclusionary practices that underpin feminist theory's notion of "women" as a subject undermine feminist goals to extend its claims to representation (Butler, 1999: 8). And Butler adds following arguments as stated; "this effort to question 'women' as the subject of feminism, the unproblematic invocation of that category may prove to preclude the possibility of feminism as a representational politics" (Butler, 1999: 9). After the publication of Gender Trouble, the book went beyond Butler's original intention and became a provocative intervention in feminist history, cited as a foundational and basic text of queer theory (Butler, 1999: vii). Through her work, Butler deconstructed the word "queer," which then acquired a general meaning of individuals who are not heterosexual and has become a counter-identity concept (Başdaş, 2012: 343). As a result, queer theory has been critical of all forms of binary acceptance, particularly the biological essentialism associated with radical feminism's gender acceptance (Başdaş, 2012: 346). Therefore, this new wave that shares the field with queer theory, not only with women as its subject and "sisterhood" as its motto, will emerge in different contexts requiring various social formations (Durmuş, 2022: 339) to serve post-truth identities in the post-truth era through digital activism on new media platforms.

After the emergence of queer theory, feminism and the LGBT community, which are both influential activist movements, began to share similar concerns regarding fixed sexual boundaries between sexes. The concept of women has expanded its meaning as biologically born men who identify themselves as trans women, as advocated by the LGBT activist movement. Since the mid-2010s, the "plus (+)" sign was added to the acronym with the aim of expanding the group's definition to be more inclusive of individuals with gender diversity. The LGBT abbreviation falls short of encompassing all the concepts it represents, so the addition of the "plus (+)" sign reflects a commitment to inclusivity and acknowledging the diverse experiences of individuals within the community. With the increasing accessibility and popularity of the digital realm, the group's activist activities have shifted towards this area, particularly focusing on user-generated content platforms provided by new media systems.

In the meantime, a new conceptualization of "women plus (+)" has emerged to support the defense women, regardless of their ideology, race, religion, and other factors that may be associated with Western, white, middle-class women. This includes not only biological women, but also individuals with fluid genders who are close to the female spectrum. Before discussing the findings on the usage of this concept in Türkiye, it is important to consider the accumulated data from around the world available on the internet.

One of the earliest mentions of the concept "women plus (+)" before the movement gained momentum was in 2015 on a blog site (Cervantes-Altamirano, 2015) where the subject was evaluated by Eren Cervantes-Altamirano, a Brazilian-rooted woman who was one of the chief editors of Muslimah Media Watch. In her blog post titled "*Woman+: To be or not to be a feminist*," she used the term "woman+" as an inclusive term that goes beyond Western, white, bourgeois, and privileged women to encompass women who are native, Muslim, and third-world citizens. She used the contexts of "woman+colour," "woman+ThirdWorld," and "woman+religion" to highlight this inclusivity (Cervantes-Altamirano, 2015). On the other hand, Altamirano is the author of the book *Islamic Feminism and the Challenges of Gender, Sexuality and LGBTQ Rights in Contemporary Islam*, in which she writes about the LGBT-friendly interpretations of holy scriptures (Cervantes-Altamirano, 2013). Based on this information, it can be inferred that she embraces gender diversity within the concept of "women plus (+)".

The revival of the movement happened as mentioned above mid 2010s after LGBT community added plus (+) sigh to the acronym to be more inclusive. As the process continued, the LGBT+ group has focused on activism activities both in social and digital fields, carried out intense activities to create visibility and awareness, and has turned into a highly effective organization. The legal process that emerged in Ireland and the UK in 2014 and turned into the SELF ID law (Oireachtas, 2015) in 2018 has triggered debates on "Who is a woman?", causing the concept to lose its ontological meaning and opening up discussions on the acceptance of self-identified gender identity. As a result of these discussions, "women plus (+)" has rapidly become a widely accepted umbrella term to replace the concept of woman, thanks to the successful impact of digital activism.

In 2015, the term "women plus (+)" began to circulate in the context of queer theory, and one of the earliest known usages was by an education and consulting group called "She Geeks Out", which changed its name to "She+ Geeks Out" in 2018. By doing so, they expanded the concept of women in "women only" contexts to include individuals who identify as trans women or those with fluid genders who position themselves close to the female spectrum (Murray, 2019). Similarly, Ellevest, a company that provides financial coaching services to support women entrepreneurs, announced in 2021 that they would name their female category with the term "women+" (Ellevest, n.d). The founder of TC Consulting, a consultancy company based in the United States and a woman of color, Tanaisha Coleman, stated in a statement titled "Women+ Beyond The Binary" dated April 8, 2022, which she included on the company's website, that they prefer to use the "women+" concept to include cis, trans women, femmes, and individuals with fluid gender identities (Coleman, 2022). At the same time among a wide variety of women's organizations, academic groups, student organizations, and companies that have women-only concepts, many have become participants in the women plus (+) movement as an umbrella term worldwide.

The "women plus (+)" concept gained particular prominence in student spaces. For example, the Montana State University physics platform "Montana State University Women+ In Physics" started in the fall of 2017 with a focus on inclusivity for biological women and underrepresented groups in the field (Women+ in Physics, n.d.). Another example is the University of Pennsylvania graduate student group platform named "UPenn Women+ in Chemistry," which emphasizes the well-being of women as well as gender minorities in the chemical sciences (Welcome, n.d.). Additionally, the University of Chicago Women+ in Law is a student-friendly organization dedicated to advancing the success of young women and nonbinary students (Women+ in Law, 2017). Strathclyde's Women+ in Engineering Presents, is also student group focus on people who identify as female, non-binary, genderfluid, genderqueer, trans, gender nonconforming and many other gender expressions (Women+ in Engineering, n.d.).

Academic gatherings such as symposiums and conferences focused on women's issues have also embraced the "women plus (+)" concept. One example is the Women+ Data Science Symposium, which aims to provide a platform for practicing and aspiring data scientists, especially women and gender minority participants (Women+ Data Science, 2020). The Women+ in Engineering group at Strathclyde University's "Ethical Engineering" symposium also promotes diversity practices in engineering through the use of the "women plus (+)" concept (Ieer.org, n.d.).

In addition to education and academia, several companies play a significant role in spreading the "women plus (+) movement" in public spaces and online. For example, the Chamber Business Women+ (CBW+) group, which is part of the Greater Manchester Chamber of Commerce (GMCC) in the United Kingdom, aims to empower and support women and all gender identities in business by providing a platform for networking, training, and personal development (Chamber Business Women+, n.d.).

Another example of a women plus (+) group is Women+ in Geo, which aims to promote diversity, equity, and inclusion in the geospatial industry by supporting and empowering women and other underrepresented groups. The group was formed in response to the lack of diversity in the geospatial industry, particularly in leadership positions. Women+ in Geo provides a platform for networking, mentorship, and professional development opportunities for women and other underrepresented groups in the geospatial industry, and is involved in various initiatives, including organizing events and webinars, providing mentorship programs, and advocating for diversity and inclusion in the industry (Code of Conduct, 2022).

Kairos Women+ is a community-led women's organization based in Renfrewshire, Scotland, funded by The Robertson Trust. It aims to build a safe and inclusive space for women+ of all ages, ethnicities, beliefs, disabled women, trans women, queer women, and non-binary people (Our Approach, n.d.).

The list goes on in several fields and subjects in the concept of the women plus (+) movement, which is gaining more and more power as a post-truth identity example with the help of digital activist activities. However, it should be pointed out that the resistance against these new sexual identities is also growing through media and social media platforms based on Western-centered activism, which often have political motivations and implications. For example, the conservative media company Daily Wire, founded in 2015, creates intense content against the gender revolution, specifically in the USA. While women plus (+) movement gains advocators, resistence grows as well.

Now, the situation in Turkey comes into focus in this sense. How was this conceptualization accepted nearly simultaneously with the Western world, and what is the current situation?

3.3. Women plus (+) movement in Turkey

After the Pembe Hayat Association was founded in 2006 as the first transgender activist group in Turkey, feminists were urged to support and include a diverse range of women within their feminist movement. This milestone has changed the direction of the discussion in Turkey, and the question of "who is the subject of feminism?" now had a new controversial answer. From this perspective, clashes have occurred between different groups during the traditional March 8th celebrations, including radical feminists who defend biological, binary sexes and intersectional feminists who support transgender women as the subject of feminism (Durmuş, 2022: 345–346). This has led to the emergence of the women plus (+) concept in social media, which is a term used by university women's groups to include a wider range of women through digital activism.

Before discussing university women's groups, it is important to mention the Filmmor incident that occurred in February 2021. The Filmmor Women's Cooperative, established in 2003 by Melek Özman, is an initiative that defends gender equality, particularly in the media and cinema sector (Filmmor Kadın Kooperatifi, n.d.). The organization's constitution included provisions to provide employment opportunities for disadvantaged groups, including transsexuals and non-binary individuals who face struggles in their daily social and work lives. However, in 2021, a group of Filmmor workers published an announcement about leaving the organization due to the injustice, discrimination, and mobbing they experienced. In that announcement, which was made through several social media platforms, they used the term "women plus (+)" for the first time as an inclusive term for the trans gender and non-binary workers of Filmmor:

> We, 13 women+ who have worked or volunteered for the Filmmor Women's Cooperative at various times between 2016–2020, and who have experienced discrimination and violence, are writing this text in solidarity. We are doing so due to the continuation of discourse and actions that include violence and discrimination, as well as the possibility that the exploitation and violence patterns that have been ongoing within

> the institution for years may be applied to new employees and volunteers in the future. (Cumhuriyet, 2021)

The incident at Filmmor served as a catalyst for the emergence of the "women plus (+)" conceptualization in Türkiye. Following the formation of the women's group at Boğaziçi University in February 2021, the "Boğaziçi Women+'s Rights Solidarity (Boğaziçi Kadın+ Hakları Dayanışması)" account was established on social media platforms such as Twitter and Instagram. The group's statement emphasized the importance of inclusivity in both name and attitudes, drawing on cis-normative, queer feminism, and transfeminism. Additionally, the group clarified that their aim is to focus on women and non-binary individuals when using the term "women plus (+)" (Balmumcu, 2020). The emergence of this online group and the explanation of their aims through both conventional and new media channels have encouraged other universities to establish similar student formations focused on women + individuals.

Similarly, in February 2021, İstanbul Teknik University founded the "ITU Women+ Solidarity (İTÜ Kadın+ Dayanışması)," and Bilgi University established the "Bilgi Women+ Union (Bilgi Kadın+ Topluluğu)" on the same date. Consecutively in March 2021, the "7Tepe Women+ Solidarity (7Tepe Kadın+ Dayanışması)" was formed at Yeditepe University, and the "Gelişim Women+ Solidarity (Gelişim Kadın+ Dayanışması)" was established at Gelişim University (Durmuş, 2022: 351).

The formation of student groups has had a significant impact on the growth of the women plus (+) movement in Türkiye, and this has been followed by contributions from several other initiatives though activism. One of the contributions came in an article written by the Istanbul Chamber of Commerce Women's Commission in Hekim Sözü Magazine in April 2021 after Turkey resiled from the Istanbul Convention (The Council of Europe Convention on Preventing and Combating Violence Against Women and Domestic Violence) in March 2021. In the article, the following statements are made in the context of women plus (+):

> We, as women+, are diverse, whether we are accepted or not… The Istanbul Convention is the most progressive legal text written so far regarding the prevention of all forms of violence against women+ and domestic violence… We now know that violence and discrimination against women+ are being justified by reasons such as honor, public morality, culture, tradition, and religion (İTO Kadın Komisyonu, 2021: 38–39).

From the same perspective, İstanbul City Theatres and the Contemporary Performing Arts Center's (ÇGSM) YouTube channel prepared by a series of programs on "the issue of gender equality and representation in theater" under the name of "Theater and Women+" in May 2021. This series was created by Emre Koyuncuoğlu and contains three different videos, each with different guests on May 15th, 21st, and 28th. The program takes the women plus (+) concept as an inclusive term which encompasses both women and LGBT+ individuals together (Şehir Tiyatroları, 2021, 15 May, 2021, 21 May, 2021, 28 May). This demonstrates the influence and impact of digital activist activities in social media, particularly YouTube in this example.

At the end of 2021, a project titled "Speech Time: Equipping the City with the Words and Art of Women+" was launched as part of the International Day for the Elimination of Violence against Women on November 25. The project, implemented by 46 "women+" in reaction to Türkiye's withdrawal from the Istanbul Convention, included a billboard campaign, virtual exhibition, and a book. The event aimed to convey the message of the importance of the Istanbul Convention for "women+" and LGBT+ individuals (Yılmaz, 2021; 8). This project was a significant contribution to the "women plus (+) movement" as a post-truth identity example in Türkiye through digital activism in the internet ecosystem.

In October 2021, a trans activist who is a member of the Pembe Hayat Association uploaded a video discussing the conceptualization of the "women plus (+)" term. The video explained that the "women plus (+)" term is inclusive of nonbinary individuals but not necessarily transgender women, who are already considered women, according to the activist (Miss Zencefil, 2021, October 3). While this approach of defining the term as only including women and non-binary individuals may not be the worldwide approach, it is similar to the statement made by the "Boğaziçi Women+'s Rights Solidarity" group, which played a key role in starting this movement.

In December 2021, the Green Thought Association organized an online conference titled "Women+ in Power Conference" (Green Thoughts, 2022, 4 January), which focused on the struggles of women and LGBT+ individuals in the areas of ecology, climate, and gender issues. The conference aimed to highlight diversity and inclusivity on issues related to the "women plus (+)" conceptualization, with a special focus on the experiences and perspectives of LGBT+ groups. Participants from various countries discussed the challenges faced by women and LGBT+ individuals in areas such as climate change, ecology, and gender equality. However, a similar conference held in October 2020 did not explicitly use the term "women plus (+)", which suggests that the "women plus (+)" movement was not yet widespread throughout the world. Nevertheless, the topics and discussions presented were in line with the inclusive and intersectional approach promoted by the movement.

Starting from March 2022, the Lambdaistanbul LGBTI+ Solidarity Association began organizing an online event in which stories from the Women to Women Story Contest, organized by the Kaos GL (Kaos Gay and Lesbian Cultural Research and Solidarity Association), are read every week for a certain period of time. Kaos GL, founded in 1993, is one of the oldest and largest LGBT rights organizations in Türkiye, and the Women to Women Story Contest aims to promote the visibility of lesbian and bisexual women in Türkiye and provide a platform for their stories to be shared (Yunus, 2022). The event organized by Lambdaistanbul highlights the importance of intersectionality and inclusivity within "the women plus (+) movement" by amplifying the voices and experiences of LGBT+ individuals. Yunus (2022), a volunteer of Uni Quir and member of Lambdaistanbul Association's Women+ Commission, states that "new stories are emerging beyond binary genders now", emphasizing the need to recognize and include the experiences of non-binary individuals within the movement.

The progress of the "women plus (+) movement" has become visible during 8 March celebrations, which is one of the most important dates for women's rights and struggles worldwide. In Türkiye, discussions about the involvement of transgender people on 8 March celebrations began after the 2013 Traditional Feminist Night March, when LGBT groups insisted on joining. This led to a debate between trans-intersectional feminists and radical-essentialist feminists regarding the subject of feminism. In 2019, the discussions turned into a quarrel through social media. Since then, a new radical feminist group has emerged on social media under the name of @kadinizvariz, defending women's rights based on binary sex. Meanwhile, the term "women plus (+)" has become available as an inclusive celebration option for March 8th (Durmuş, 2022: 346). In an interview with Evrim Demirtaş, former coordinator of the Red Umbrella Association and a freelance lawyer, the term 'women plus (+)' was used as a new, all-encompassing term for diverse women in the context of March 8th celebrations. Demirtaş emphasized that "March 8th is a collective struggle of all women and women+ against the fate assigned to them" (Kap, 2022). This highlights the role of the "women plus (+) movement" as a new context in Türkiye.

Moreover, the rise of post-truth identities and online activism has complicated the situation even further. While online activism can be a powerful tool for social change and identity activism processes, it can also be used to spread misinformation and fuel counter-activist movements. For example, the formation of the "@fitrathareketi" account, which generates and spreads counter information about LGBT+ groups and gender revolution on social media applications such as Twitter and Instagram (Dikmen, 2022), and the march against LGBT+ group activism held under the slogan "big family gathering" at the end of 2022 (Haber Türk, 2022, 9 October), show that counter activist movements are also using online channels and get wide range support. Despite the emergence of "the women plus (+)" conceptualization spreading all around the world through social media and online ecosystems, traditional social realities still exist widely in Türkiye, especially among older generations. However, it is important to emphasize that the growing online activism and identity processes, including post-truth identities, indicate a shift towards a more diverse society. It can be emphasized that "the women plus (+) movement" plays a crucial role in this transformation by challenging traditional gender roles and stereotypes. As more individuals engage in online activism and advocacy for marginalized groups, it may be possible to see a gradual shift in attitudes towards gender and sexuality in Türkiye, although there are still many challenges that need to be addressed.

4. Conclusion

The concept of post-truth identities is explored, where truthfulness has become corrupted in the digital age, leading to the emergence of identities that prioritize social group memberships over objective reality. The rise of new media technologies and the influence of cognitive biases have enabled the spread of post-truth identities, which rely on emotional appeals, personal narratives, and often lack verifiable criteria. As a result, groups such as anti-vaxxers, flat-earthers, vegans, and those identifying with new sexual identities have emerged, promoting distorted beliefs through culture and a sense of belonging. In this post-truth world, emotions take center stage in shaping reality, and digital media technologies play a significant role in affirming post-truth identities.

In connection with post truth era, digital activism is a form of social activism that utilizes digital technologies and platforms to promote social, political, and cultural changes. With the emergence of Web 2.0 technology, individuals gained the opportunity to become active elements in the digital world and present their attitudes and ideas on various media platforms. This led to the emergence of a new form of sociality and digital activism, which gives strength to activist movements and accelerates social transformation. As a result, social and political norms are influential on shaping digital activist practices. From this point of view, the emergence of post-truth identities and online activism has brought about significant changes in the way identity-based movements are organized and sustained. The rise of the "women plus (+) movement" is a prime example of this.

This movement has become a global phenomenon that aims to promote inclusivity and diversity within the broader feminist movement. Through the use of social media and other online platforms, the "women plus (+) movement" has been able to spread its message and connect with like-minded individuals across the world. This has allowed for the creation of a community of individuals who are working towards achieving common goals related to gender equality and the recognition of diverse gender identities.

However, the cases of conservative Americans and Turkey show that the acceptance of the "women plus (+) movement" is not universal, and traditional social norms and values still need to be addressed. Despite the significant impact of new media systems, transforming societal attitudes and beliefs requires time and concerted effort. Moreover, the rise of "the women plus (+) movement" has also triggered counter-activism and resistance from those who oppose the recognition of diverse gender identities.

In conclusion, "the women plus (+) movement" represents a significant development in the broader feminist movement. Its emergence through online activism and social media channels highlights the potential for these platforms to facilitate social change. However, the movement's success and sustainability will depend on its ability to navigate and overcome resistance and opposition from those who oppose its goals.

References

Allen, M. (Ed.). (2017). *The SAGE Encyclopedia of Communication Research Methods: Volume 1.* London-New York: SAGE Reference.

Baker, C. R., & Chadwick, A. (2021). Corrupted Infrastructures of Meanings: Post-truth Identities Online. In Howard Tumber & Silvio Waisbord (Eds.), *The Routledge Companion to Media Disinformation and Populism* (pp. 312–322). London & New York: Routledge.

Balmumcu, S. (2020, 26 Aralık). Bir Mücadele Deneyimi: Boğaziçi Üniversitesi Kadın+ Dayanışması. *Birgün.* Retrieved from https://www.birgun.net/haber/bir-mucadele-deneyimi-bogazici-universitesi-kadin-dayanismasi-328035

Başdaş, B. (2012). Feminizme Farklı Yaklaşımlar ve Üçüncü Dalga. In Esen Özdemir, & Sevi Bayraktar (Eds.), *Feminizm Tartışmaları* (pp. 333–366). İstanbul: Kumbara Sanat Atölyesi ve Toplumsal Dayanışma Derneği.

Beauvoir, S. de. (1956). *The Second Sex* (Ed. & Trans. H. M. Parshley). London: Jonathan Cape.

Butler, J. (1999). *Gender Trouble: Feminism and the Subversion of İdentity.* New York-London: Routledge.

Cammaerts, B. (2007). Activism and Media. In B. Cammaerts & N. Carpentier (Eds.), *Reclaiming The Media* (pp. 217-224). Intellect Ltd.

Cervantes-Altamirano, E. (2013, 8 July). The Downfalls of Feminism and Why I Am Still a Feminist. *The Feminist Wire.* Retrieved from https://www.thefeministwire.com/2013/07/the-downfalls-of-feminism-and-why-i-am-still-a-feminist/

Cervantes-Altamirano, E. (2015, 2 April). Women+: To Be or Not to Be a Feminist [Blog post]. Retrieved from https://erenarruna.com/2015/04/02/woman-to-be-or-not-to-be-a-feminist/

Chamber Business Women+ (n.d.). About CBW+. *Harrisburg Regional Chamber.* Retrieved from https://www.harrisburgregionalchamber.org/membership/affinity-groups/chamber-business-women/

Code of Conduct. (2022, 17 January). Women+ in Geo. Retrieved from https://womeningeospatial.org/mission-vision-and-values/code-of-conduct/

Coleman, T. (2022, 8 April). Women+ Beyond The Binary. *Tanaisha Coleman Consulting.* Retrieved from https://www.tanaishacolemanconsulting.com/diversity-inclusion-blog/womxnhood-beyond-the-binary

Cosentino, G. (2020). *Social Media and the Post-Truth World Order the Global Dynamics of Disinformation.* Cham: Springer Nature.

Cullum, B. (2010). Devices: The Power of Mobile Phones. In M. Joyce (Ed.), *Digital Activism Decoded: The New Mechanics of Change* (pp. 47–70). New York: Idebate Press.

Cumhuriyet. (2021, 11 February). Filmmor'dan Ayrılan Kadın+lar: 'Tüm kurumları, feminist ve LGBTİ+ hareketi istismar etmemeye davet ediyoruz' Retrieved from https://www.cumhuriyet.com.tr/haber/filmmordan-ayrilan-kadinlar-tum-kurumlari-feminist-ve-lgbti-hareketi-istismar-etmemeye-davet-ediyoruz-1812894

Devillart, S., & Waniewski, B. (2010). The Future of Advocacy in a Networked Age. In M. Joyce (Ed.), *Digital Activism Decoded: The New Mechanics of Change* (pp. 197–208). New York: İdebate Press.

Dikmen, E. (2022, 25 November). Anormal Cinsiyet Dataymasına Meydan Okuyanlar, Fıtratı Savunanlar. *Lacivert.* Retrieved from https://www.lacivertdergi.com/dosya/2022/11/25/anormal-cinsiyet-dayatmasina-meydan-okuyanlar-fitrati-savunanlar

Durmuş, B. T. (2022). Kim Daha Fazla Özne?: Bir Netnografi Çalışması Olarak Feminizmin Halet-i Ruhiyesi. In M. Dinç & A. T. Türk (Eds.), *Çağdaş Yaklaşımlar Odağında Toplum ve Kültür Araştırmaları-III* (pp. 333–364). Çanakkale-Türkiye: Paradigma Academy.

Earl, J., & Kimport, K. (2011). *Digitally Enabled Social Change: Activism in the Internet Age.* Cambridge, Massachusetts: The MIT Press Publications.

Elevest.(n.d.).WhatDoYouMeanbyWomen+?Retrievedfromhttps://support.ellevest.com/hc/en-us/articles/1500005156622-What-do-you-mean-by-women-

Filmmor Kadın Kooperatifi. (n.d.). Retrieved from https://filmmor.org/hakkimizda/

Fisher, W. (1984). Narration as a Human Communication Paradigm: The Case of Public Moral Argument. *Communication Monographs,* 51, 1–22. http://dx.doi.org/10.1080/03637758409390180.

Fisher, W. (1985). The Narrative Paradigm: An Elaboration. *Communication Monographs,* 52, 347–367. http://dx.doi.org/10.1080/03637758509376117

Fisher, W. (1989). Clarifying the Narrative Paradigm. *Communication Monographs,* 56, 55–58. http://dx.doi.org/10.1080/03637758909390249

Green Thoughts Association. (2020, 22 October). 'Harekete Geçen Kadınlar' Konferansı / 'Women in Power' Conference [Video file]. Retrieved from https://youtu.be/bGk-rUGfMqU?si=rCfRZBGZZNNlLYI1

Green Thoughts Association. (2022, 4 January). 'Harekete Geçen Kadın+lar' Konferansı / 'Women+ in Power' Conference [Video file]. Retrieved from https://youtu.be/bSB-h0w4bRw?si=hSKJW9I8IIqojUzD

Haber Türk. (2022, 9 October). Saraçhane'de "Büyük Aile Buluşması" adıyla LGBT karşıtı yürüyüş. Retrieved from https://www.haberturk.com/sarachane-de-buyuk-aile-bulusmasi-adiyla-lgbt-karsiti-yuruyus-3521449

Ieer.org. (n.d.). Strathclyde's Women+ in Engineering Presents, Ethical Engineering – A Series of Events. Retrieved from https://ieeer8.org/member-activities/women-in-engineering/news-women-in-engineering/strathclydes-women-in-engineering-presents-ethical-engineering-a-series-of-events/

İTO Kadın Komisyonu. (2021 Mart–Nisan). Kadın+ların İstanbul Sözleşmesi'nden vazgeçilmesine değil, uygulanmasına ihtiyacı var. *Hekim Sözü,* 38–39. Retrieved from https://www.istabip.org.tr/6537-kadin-larin-istanbul-sozlesmesi-nden-vazgecilmesine-degil-uygulanmasina-ihtiyaci-var.html

Jordan, T. (2002). *Activism! Direct Action, Hacktivism and the Future of Society.* London: Reaktion Books.

Joyce, M. (2010). Introduction: How to Think about Digital Activism. In M. Joyce (Ed.), *Digital Activism Decoded: The New Mechanics of Change* (pp. 1–14). New York: İdebate Press.

Kammaerts, B. (2007). Activism and Media. In B. Cammaerts & N. Carpentier (Eds.), *Reclaiming the Media: Communication Rights and Democratic Media Roles* (pp. 217–224). Bristol, UK: İntellect.

Kap, D. (2022, 8 March). Kadın+'ların 8 Mart'ı: 'Farklı Kadınlık Deneyimleri ve Kadın Kimliğimizle Mücadelenin İçindeyiz'. *Sivil Sayfalar.* Retrieved from https://www.sivilsayfalar.org/2022/03/08/kadinlarin-8-marti-farkli-kadinlik-deneyimleri-ve-kadin-kimligimizle-mucadelenin-icindeyiz/

Keyes, R. (2004). *The Post-Turth Era: Dishonesty and Deception in Contemporary Life.* New York: St. Martin's Press.

Kozinets, R. V. (2015). *Netnogrphy: Redefined.* London: SAGE.

Mcintyre, L. (2018). *Post-truth.* Cambridge, Massachusetts: The MIT Press Publications.

McNutt, J. G. (2018). Advocacy, Social Change, and Activism: Perspectives on Traditional and Electronic Practice in a Digital World. In J. G. McNutt (Ed.), *Technology, Activism, and Social Justice in a Digital Age* (pp. 9–21). New York: Oxford University Press.

Miss Zencefil. (2021, 3 October). Duyarlı Forum #1 Kadın "+" Nedir? Ne ki Bu Kadın+? (Duyar Kastığımız Sohbetler) [Video file]. Retrieved from https://www.youtube.com/live/HpMOicQPFS0?si=uEZEfKvGHMCSoH_g

Morozov, E. (2009, May 19). The Brave New World of Slacktivism. Retrieved from https://foreignpolicy.com/2009/05/19/the-brave-new-world-of-slac ktivism/

Morozov, E. (2011). *The Net Delusion: The Dark Side of Internet Freedom.* New York: Public Affairs.

Murray, R. (2019, 18 December). Why Women+ Events Are İmportant. *She+ Geeks Out.* Retrieved from https://www.shegeeksout.com/blog/why-women-focused-events-are-important/

Oireachtas. (2015). Gender Reconition Act 2015. Retrieved from https://www.oireachtas.ie/en/bills/bill/2014/116/

Our Approach. (n.d.). Kairos Women+. Retrieved from https://kairoswomen.org/our-approach/

Schradie, J. (2019). *Revolution That Wasn't: How Digital Activism Favors Conservatives.* Cambridge, Massachusetts: Harward University Press.

Şehir Tiyatroları. (2021, 15 May). ÇGSM Atölye, Tiyatro & Kadın+ Ebru Nihan Celkan [Video file]. Retrieved from https://youtu.be/p0nJCdYPjTI?si=6HEM2RS6TwEKW52Z

Şehir Tiyatroları. (2021, 21 May). ÇGSM Atölye, Tiyatro & Kadın+ Matin Soofipour [Video file]. Retrieved from https://youtu.be/E_pQX89C-Co?si=pSMO7afdVzAdCZon

Şehir Tiyatroları. (2021, 28 May). ÇGSM Atölye, Tiyatro & Kadın+ Viola Hasselberg [Video file]. Retrieved from https://youtu.be/9XttYzFdODY?si=HzpT4BCI4ReEr6DX

Sivitanides, M., & Shah, V. (2011). The era of digital activism. Paper presented at the Conference for Information Systems Applied Research, Wilmington, North Carolina, USA.

Tesich, S. (1992). A Government of Lies. *The Nation*. Retrieved from https://www.thenation.com/archive/

Turhan, D. G. (2017). Digital Aktivizm. *Journal of Süleyman Demirel University Institute of Social Sciences*, 1(26), 26–44.

Turner, J. C. (1998). Foreword. In: A. Hogg & D. Abrams (Eds.), *Social Identifications: Social Psychology of Intergroup Relations and Group Processes* (pp. vii–viii). London and New York: Routledge.

Wehmeier, S. (Ed.). (1995). Women. In *Oxford Wordpower Dictionary* (8th ed.). Oxford: Oxford University Press.

Weinberger, D. (2007). *Everything Is Miscellaneous: The Power of the New Digital Disorder*. New York: Holt Paperbacks.

Welcome. (n.d.). Women+ in Chemistry. Retrieved from https://women.chem.upenn.edu/

Wizemann, T. M., & Pardue, M. (Eds.). (2001). *Exploring the Biological Contributions to Human Health: Does Sex Matter?*. Washington, D.C.: National Academy Press. Retrievedfrom https://nap.nationalacademies.org/catalog/10028/exploring-the-biological-contributions-to-human-health-does-sex-matter

Wight, C. (2018). Post-Truth, Postmodernism and Alternative Facts. *New Perspectives*, 26(3), 17–30.

Women. (n.d). In *Merriam-Webster Online Dictionary*. Retrieved from https://www.merriam-webster.com/dictionary/women

Women+ Data Science [Brochure]. (2020). Retrieved from https://inclusion.msu.edu/R-Ladies%20symposium.pdf

Women+ in Engineering. (n.d.). Retrieved from https://www.strathunion.com/groups/find-a-society/society/15137/

Women+ in Law. (2017). Retrieved from https://blueprint.uchicago.edu/organization/uchicagowil

Women+ in Physics. (n.d.). Retrieved from https://physics.montana.edu/research/wip/index.html

Word of the Year 2016. (n.d.). Retrieved from https://languages.oup.com/word-of-the-year/2016/

Yılmaz, B. (Ed.). (2021). *Konuşma Zamanı-Kenti Kadın+'ların Sözü ve Sanatıyla Kenti Donatmak*. İstanbul: Aramızda Toplumsal Cinsiyet Araştırmaları Derneği.

Yunus. (2022, 26 March). *Kadın+ lubunyanın hikayelerine girmek için cesaretiniz var mı?* Uni Kuir. Retrieved from https://www.unikuir.org/haberler/kadin-lubunyanin-hikayelerine-girmek-icin-cesaretiniz-var-mi-26-03-2022

Res. Asst. Hatice Öksüz[1]

Eco-criticism in "I Am Greta" documentary film design

Abstract: Humans, a small part of the ecosystem, have lived in harmony with nature for years. This harmonious relationship between man and nature has experienced a major rupture with industrialization. Increasing urbanization with industrialization has rapidly increased the alienation between man and nature. This alienation and the desire to dominate nature has led to the uncontrolled exploitation of nature and ecological problems on a global scale. With the anthropocentric approach that puts man at the center and asserts that everything in the universe is at the service of man, the devastating effects of ecological disasters and the destructive effects of all kinds of human activities on the ecosystem have brought about the rupture of the relationship between man and nature. In a changing world with the rise of capitalism, human activities have caused the answers to many questions about nature to become increasingly complex. Through Greta Thunberg's biographical documentary, it is explained that climate change is seen as an anthropocentric crisis and the necessity of taking action to combat this crisis and the inaction of countries in the face of the steps determined in the international arena. This study focuses on the human-centered ecological destruction caused by the capitalist order, the climate crisis and the role of cinema from the perspective of eco-criticism in raising the level of consciousness of activist actions towards it. The documentary film I Am Greta about Greta Thunberg, who has made a global impact with her activist actions on the climate crisis, is discussed from an eco-critical perspective.

Keywords: Eco-criticism, climate crisis, Greta Thunberg, documentary cinema, film design, activism

1. Introduction

Humans, a small part of the ecosystem, have lived in harmony with nature for years. This harmonious relationship between man and nature has caused a major rupture with industrialization. As a matter of fact, urbanization, which is a result of the industrial revolution, has rapidly increased the alienation between man and nature. The most important factor in the deterioration of this relationship

---

1 Istanbul University Social Sciences Institute, Radio Tv Cinema Department PhD Student, hatice.oksuz@ogr.iu.edu.tr; Istanbul Aydın University, Faculty of Communication, Visual Communication Design Department, haticeoksuz@aydin.edu.tr, ORCID: 0000-0002-1848-108X.

is man's desire to dominate nature. In the process that continues with glorifying man and carrying him beyond being a living being, man has become alienated from nature. This alienation and the desire to dominate nature has led to the uncontrolled exploitation of nature and ecological problems on a global scale. With the anthropocentric approach, which puts man at the center and asserts that everything in the universe is at his service, the devastating effects of ecological disasters and the destructive effects of all kinds of human activities on the ecosystem have brought about the weakening of the relationship between man and nature. Instead of solving the problem, human beings have exacerbated ecological problems, threatening the future of the planet we live in. When we look at the historical process, we clearly see the high walls that humans have built between them and other species and their domination and exploitation of nature. Again, when we continue to look at history from this perspective, it is seen that the break of the bond between the modernized human being and nature with the industrialization period is more than ever before. It can be said that the basis of this change between man and nature is the view of nature as a place dedicated to man and the drive for profit that comes with capitalism. In the changing world with the rise of capitalism, human activities have caused the answers to many questions about nature to become increasingly complex. It is seen that many innovative studies have been carried out in the international public opinion to raise awareness and solve these problems. For example, the *"United Nations Framework Convention on Climate Change"*, the *"Kyoto Protocol"* and the *"Paris Agreement"* can be counted among these efforts to combat climate change. These agreements can be characterized as concrete and decisive steps taken in the international arena to combat climate change. This study examines Greta Thunberg's biographical documentary on climate change as a human-centered crisis and the necessity of taking action to combat this crisis and the inaction of countries in the face of these steps determined in the international arena. As it is known, television and cinema, which have functions such as informing and directing the society, have always played an important role among mass media in terms of presenting both visual and auditory materials together. Cinema, in particular, has a special importance among art forms with its depiction of the past, present and future. Moreover, cinema, which is a huge industry that includes the recording and reproduction of moving images, distribution and screening stages, is also a means of creating meaning with its political economy and social functions. In addition to being an art with the films that cinema puts on the screen with visual – auditory codes, it is also an important mass communication tool with the aspect of mobilizing the audience in a mass sense by influencing them. In addition to creating a fictional world of meaning, cinema is a magical world that manages to influence the audience with its document quality. Since the world we live in has started to be destroyed, this destruction has been reflected on the silver screen thanks to the visual and auditory power of cinema, thus contributing to the formation of a consciousness that guides the society by large masses. In this context, the study examines the role of cinema from the perspective of eco-criticism in the human-centered ecological destruction caused by the capitalist order, the climate crisis and the activist actions against it to reach a level of consciousness. The documentary film design I Am Greta, about Greta Thunberg, who has made a global impact with her activist actions on the climate crisis, is analyzed from an eco-critical perspective.

1.1. Documentary cinema from an eco-critical perspective

Eco-criticism is a field of study that has gained importance in parallel with the development of ecocentrism. Lawrence Buell, one of the first names that comes to mind in the field of eco-criticism, defines eco-criticism as an interdisciplinary movement that focuses on how literature and other forms of media express environmental awareness and concerns. Buell gives a more general definition as the study of literature with an environmental focus (Fiedorczuk, 2011: 7–8). Eco-criticism, which has principles that examine the relationship between human and nature by focusing on the text, is an eco-centered theory that does not see human and non-human nature as independent from each other (İgit, 2016: 959). Eco-criticism treats nature in a position that glorifies its interconnected structure and diversity.

In fact, the social, political and philosophical agenda of environmental problems does not go back very far. In the 1960s, it is seen that studies on environmental problems gained great importance. Although some studies were carried out in previous years, it is not possible to talk about a period as organized and determined as the process that started in the 60s. Ecocriticism, which is concerned with human domination over nature, seeing nature as inferior to oneself and destroying nature, is considered a new discipline.

Although the origins of eco-criticism can be traced back to the 1970s, it is only in the 1990s that it created a new field as an academic discipline. In its most general definition, ecocriticism offers a human-oriented critical perspective on the relationship between human beings and nature. This idea, which is translated into Turkish as eco-criticism or environmental criticism, is known as a young revisionist movement that, according to Hannes Bergthaler, has deeply influenced human history in recent years. Eco-critical thought started in the 1990s by developing a problematic on how literature can be utilized in addressing environmental crises, especially in the United States of America (USA) and England (Güngör, 2015: 5). Although the origins of literary studies in the field of ecology date back to the 1960s, it became a recognized critical school in the early 1990s. Today, literary ecocriticism as a genre involves the study of nature writing. It is concerned with the role of the physical environment in literary productions, the values expressed in relation to the environment, and what a culture says about the environment and how it treats it. It also looks for similarities between gender, class, ethnicity and nature; asks how culturally produced texts affect the relationship with the natural world; traces changes in a culture's concept of the environment over time; and examines representations of the environmental crisis in literature. In sum, ecocriticism argues that the world is composed of the social sphere and the ecosphere, that the two are interrelated, and that neither can be thought outside the context of the other (Willoquet-Maricondi, 2010: 3). In the 21st century, the study of literary works on nature has been extended to a wider field, including cultural works.

Ecocriticism in the contemporary sense first emerged in the 19th century as nature writing. Henry David Thoreau's works can be said to be the first examples of eco-critical studies. Eco-criticism aims to return all beings in nature to the subject position by questioning the advantageous position of humans in cultural products. At the same time, ecocriticism addresses the mutual bond between nature and human relations by revealing the missing or problematic aspects of these representations by focusing on the representations of nature in cultural texts (Şen, 2018: 34). According to Oppermann, eco-criticism is to examine the sociocultural consequences of the deteriorating structure of ecological balances. Oppermann draws attention to how the relationship between living and non-living inorganic substances is reflected in literary texts, and emphasizes features such as description, discourse and use of language in literary and cultural texts (Oppermann, 2012: 9). Eco-criticism emphasizes that the world we live in does not consist of human beings and their endless greed for profit. According to Garrard, ecocriticism makes the concept of "human" the subject of criticism by examining the link between human and non-human throughout human history (Garrard, 2016: 17). When the human-nature relationship is analyzed, human beings, who try to enter the mysterious world of nature, have become ambitious to dominate nature in the process. Accepting nature as an unlimited resource that serves him and offers everything for his needs, man has caused the balance of nature to deteriorate over time. Social transformations in the modernizing world have brought environmental problems such as air and water pollution. The most discussed of these problems is undoubtedly climate change.

When we look at the studies on climate change, some studies accept the Industrial Revolution that emerged in 18th century England and Western Europe as a milestone as a result of the change in social life and new production practices, while others accept World War II, which centers on the devastating impact of the atomic bomb on the world (Normand, 2015: 64). It is known that there are many steps taken at the international level to combat climate change, which has become an important problem for the whole world. In the 1990s, the climate crisis started to be discussed in the international arena as a security issue. In 1992, the United Nations Framework Convention on Climate Change (UNFCCC) and the Conference of Parties (COP) in 1995 are among the activities at the international level that include measures taken against the climate crisis. At the same time, steps such as the UNFCCC, the Kyoto Protocol and the Paris Agreement are considered to be the basic steps that determine the scope of globally accepted climate policies (Cerit Mazlum, 2019: 7). Even if some of these steps have not been implemented, they have made the issue of climate crisis worth discussing on an international scale and paved the way for the formation of various social organizations and movements.

As mentioned earlier, ecocriticism is generally used to analyze written texts. Today, ecocriticism has a wide range of fields, from politics to economics and even artistic forms. Among artistic forms, cinema, which appeals to the visual and auditory senses, has a unique language and a unique potential to mobilize the masses, is also used quite effectively. From the invention of cinema to the present day, the world has been viewed from different windows. The power of cinema, which is basically fed by visual codes, in the context of visual communication has always maintained its importance in the historical process and has penetrated our lives in a wide range. This effect of cinema on the masses stems from the fact that it has a structure that is experienced as a group and that it can successfully blend many tools (music, effects, visuals) that can manipulate human emotions. It is highly likely that the viewing experience of a group of people with similar sensitivities will mobilize this audience depending on the power of the movie.

When we look at eco-critical thought in cinema, we see that it is a field of study that examines the way nature is treated in documentary, fiction and experimental films. The concept of documentary was first used in 1926 by John Grierson in a review article in a New York newspaper about Robert Flaherty's film Moana (Corner, 1996: 191). Expressing his opinion on Robert Flaherty's "*Moana*", John Grierson argued that it was a document in the sense that it presented the scenes from the daily life of a Polynesian teenager as a visual narrative (Grierson, 1979: 25–27). With this view, he defined documentary cinema. In later processes, he further clarified this view and characterized the concept of documentary as a creative form of reality (Adalı, 1986: 13). Ünsal Oskay, on the other hand, gave the following words while defining documentary film: "Documentary film is an art form, a field of art that resists against forgetting, cruelty and unhappiness arising from a certain form of human relationship with nature and other people" (Oskay, 1997: 148). From the moment cinema entered our lives, it is accepted that the first films we watched belonged to the documentary film genre. The first images recorded by the brothers Auguste and Louis Lumiere, whom we know with the invention of cinema, belong to documentary reality. The first films consist of images from everyday life. Therefore, these films have documentary quality and take their place in the literature as the first examples of the documentary film genre. Documentary cinema has brought many debates from the beginning to the present day. The most important of these debates is related to the definition of documentary cinema, which arises from the relationship between documentary cinema and reality. The aim of documentary film is to present stories from life to the audience. "The documentary should be the voice of what people talk about in their fields and factories and homes" (Rotha, 2000: 87). Documentary films can be expressed as an interpretation of reality in which messages are encoded for the benefit of society.

Documentary films impose a distinct mission on their directors in terms of creating a sociological and cultural consciousness. Documentary film directors can address issues that concern a large segment of society through a particular life or lives (Nichols, 2017: 261). According to Sözen, the documentary film director processes the real, not the imaginary, and brings it to the audience. The same characteristics that cause fiction films to be art are also valid for documentary films. What makes documentary films not just ordinary recorded images that are pleasing to the eye is the same as what makes fiction films art. The director's artistic competence, his/her perspective on life and the way he/she makes sense of life are at the forefront of this. Like a photographer or a painter, the documentary film director makes choices according to his/her own artistic horizon (Sözen, 2010: 243).

With the exception of all kinds of films that center on nature, it is possible to analyze every film with an ecocritical approach, regardless of its subject and genre. Lawrence Buell has developed a set of criteria that analyze different narratives such as fiction, documentaries and novels from an eco-critical perspective. According to Lawrence, these criteria show whether there is environmental awareness in the analyzed work. The first of these criteria refers to works in which the non-human world does not only constitute a basis for human action and presents human history in an integrated structure with nature. The second criterion is defined as works that do not present only human interests as important. The third and final criterion includes works that present a moral perspective that encompasses responsibilities towards the non-human environment. (Willoquet-Maricondi, 2010: 3). As it can be understood from these criteria, what is important in any work's perspective on nature is to make sense of nature not as an object but as a subject.

The way the human-nature relationship is represented in films is analyzed with an ecological approach. As a result of this analysis, its positive and negative effects are investigated (Şen, 2018: 45). According to Bozak, in his book "*The Cinematic Footprint*", ecology cannot be limited conceptually. Because, according to him, it is impossible to say where nature ends and culture begins, and vice versa, emphasizing that ecocriticism has no clear boundaries (Rust & Monani, 2013: 1). Therefore, documentary cinema as a genre differs from other film genres in terms of its narrative form and its presentation of real-world scenes. When documentary cinema works are analyzed from an eco-critical perspective, it is possible to read that themes such as climate crisis, environmental problems, and human-nature relationship are frequently included. In this context, it can be accepted that the argument that the eco-critical approach has no sharp boundaries is valid.

The first stage of creating a movie is the world of imagination. The next stage is design. The transformation of the story created in the dream world into a concrete form constitutes the design part of the work. According to Tuncer, "subject", "form" and "word" must complement each other in the art of cinema. It is not possible for one to be added to the other. At the design stage, content and form must be compatible with each other in order to present the meaning to the audience without interruption. The music used in the film should be designed and implemented effectively as a means of emotional transmission of the narrative. A documentary film that is designed may not be fully implemented, but the documentary films with the highest success rate are the ones that have achieved the implementation stage to a great extent (Tuncer, 2003). As a matter of fact, the design stage covers the processes that start in the mind and then are transferred to practice as a concrete form. As it is known, visual language is the basis of the movie. In this context, it is possible to give a complete picture of the subject by capturing the features of the subject that can be visualized (Cereci, 1997: 54). In documentary films, while the subject and message are important, it is also important to use the formal features successfully for the purpose of the documentary. Because the stories of ordinary people in documentary films and the absence of star actors draw attention to how the story is constructed. Stylistic features such as unsuccessful editing, weak visual materials, improper use of sound are factors that will negatively affect the watchability of the documentary and the transmission of the message. The stories of documentary films, on the other hand, deal with all kinds of issues related to the universe. In fact, documentaries provide a unique opportunity to bring issues such as the climate crisis and environmental problems to a wider audience and have become a field that prepares a suitable ground for eco-critical analysis. When we look at the documentary genre among eco-critical films, it is seen that visual and auditory narrative techniques are generally used effectively to evoke a sense of urgency and to motivate action. For example, the documentary film *"An Inconvenient Truth"*, directed by Davis Guggenheim in 2006, emphasizes the urgent need to take measures against climate change. At this point, it is observed that a personal narrative is dominant and striking visual images are used together with scientific data. Images of former US Vice President Al Gore's conference on the science behind global warming and images of the effects of climate change on the world are used together. Another eco-critical documentary film is *"Blackfish"* directed by Gabriela Cowperthwaite in 2013. The documentary film explores the treatment of captive killer whales. It uses a combination of archival footage, personal narratives and expert interviews to reveal the dark side of the marine park entertainment industry. The film has caused a public outcry that has led to the introduction of legislation for the protection of animals. As can be seen in both documentaries, visual and audio elements are used to create a sense of urgency and emphasize the importance of issues such as climate change and environmental problems. At the same time, these films utilize personal narratives to create an emotional connection between the audience and the subject matter. This evokes a sense of responsibility within the framework of the subject matter and simultaneously the urge to take action. Eco-critical documentary films can also challenge dominant cultural narratives about the natural world. Werner Herzog's 2005 film *"Grizzly Man"* is about Timothy Treadwell's life story with grizzly bears and the character's death by a bear attack. This film presents the cultural narrative structures of the dominance of nature in an optimistic way, and at the same time conveys to the audience that the natural world is full of unpredictable dangers even against this optimism. The 2012 documentary film *"Chasing Ice"* by Jeff Orlowski is a challenge to communities that deny climate change. This film, which presents the melting of glaciers in Greenland using time-lapse photography, sets an example for the preparation of emergency action plans against climate change on a global scale. The documentary film *"I Am Greta"*, about the life of Greta Thunberg, a 15-year-old activist who took action against the climate crisis alone in front of the Swedish Parliament, and her struggle against the climate crisis, is one of the exemplary film studies for similar action plans. In this context, the study will examine the role of eco-critical documentary films in taking measures against the climate crisis, promoting environmental awareness, and inspiring action. How they use visual language, sound and narrative techniques to explore environmental issues, raise awareness and criticize the climate crisis will be examined from an eco-critical perspective.

1.2. Who is global climate activist Greta Thunberg?

Greta Tintin Eleonora Ernman Thunberg was born on January 3, 2003 in Stockholm, Sweden. Her mother Malena Ernman is a famous opera singer. Her father Svante Thunberg is an actor. In 2006, her sister Beata was born. While mother Ernman continued her world tour, father Thunberg took a break from his work to take care of his daughters. Greta was diagnosed with Asperger's Syndrome when she was eleven years old. While this condition does not pose a problem in Greta's ability to learn and think, it makes it difficult for her to interact with others. Because of this characteristic, Greta is able to quickly focus on a topic of interest and master it easily. Greta's focus on the climate crisis led her to learn everything she could about climate change (Doeden, 2021: 9–10). On August 20, 2018, Greta Thunberg, a fifteen-year-old ninth grader, went on strike against the climate crisis in front of the Houses of Parliament in Stockholm, Sweden, expressing her deep concern about climate change and the dire consequences if people do not change the way they produce and use energy. On her first day of action, Greta distributed leaflets about the dangers of climate change. She held a handmade banner reading *"Skolstrejk för klimatet"*, which means *"School strike for climate"* in Swedish (Doeden, 2021, pp. 7–8). Greta, whose vigil that she started alone became more and more crowded day by day, started her silent action before the elections to be held in Sweden in September and continued these actions after the elections. After the election, Greta continued to lead strikes every Friday. Thunberg, who carried out her action with a banner reading *"School strike for climate"*, managed to become an agenda in a short time through social media. As a matter of fact, as it is known, social media is digital, interaction, hypertext, hypertext, networked and virtual and is an effective tool of today in terms of bringing global and social issues to the agenda regardless of time and space (Yengin & Bayrak, 2022: 41). Thanks to social media, social issues create a domino effect and resonate all over the world in a short time (Toktay, 2022: 22). We see a similar effect in the movement initiated by Greta. Greta Thunberg, who is also on the agenda of the international media, has become popular in the fight against climate change. As Önder states, Greta's medium is the digital medium, which reached children all over the world. In this movement, the child sat in front of the Parliament with a backpack and a cardboard sign and physically triggered the movement that day (Önder, 2021: 212). The *"School Strike for Climate"* themed actions, which started under Greta's leadership, spread around the world with the participation of students in high school and pre-secondary schools within a year and a half (Doeden, 2021: 8–9). Greta Thunberg was named *"Person of the Year"* by Time Magazine in 2019 (URL-1). In 2019, she was awarded the *"Human Rights Award"* and the *"Right Livelihood Award"* by Amnesty International. She has also been nominated for many prestigious awards, including the Nobel Peace Prize.

1.3. "I Am Greta" documentary film analysis

"I Am Greta", the biographical documentary of Greta Thunberg, a young activist who made the climate crisis a global agenda item and became a symbol of the fight against the climate crisis with her actions to mobilize the masses, premiered at the Venice Film Festival on September 4, 2020 (URL-2). Nathan Grossman directed the documentary film about Greta Thunberg's climate strike in front of the Swedish Parliament, which soon became a symbol of many climate actions on a global scale. It is a biographical documentary about the life of 15-year-old Greta, who is known for her school strikes for the climate in front of the Swedish Parliament, leading a movement that will resonate all over the world. The operant analysis of the documentary *"I Am Greta"* is as given in the table below.

Table 1. Operant analysis of the documentary "I Am Greta"

Operant Analysis of the Documentary *"I Am Greta"*	
Director	Nathan Grossman
Writers	Hanna Lejonqvist Per K. Kirkegaard Olof Berglind
Genres	Biography Documentary
Running Times	1 hr 37 min
Release Date	Sept. 2020

Synopsis: The first shot of the movie shows Greta Thunberg crossing the ocean in her sailboat. In the following shots, we see Greta Thunberg starting her protests in front of the Swedish Parliament with a banner reading *"Skolstrejk För Klimatet"* after watching images of different types of disasters from all over the world. When we read these successive frames in their entirety, we realize that we are going to watch a true story of Greta Thunberg's activist actions against climate disasters and her life story shaped by this. The fact that the plans used for environmental problems are document visuals causes the problems in today's world to be revealed with all their nakedness. The film tells the story of Greta Thunberg, a young Swedish activist who started her individual struggle against the climate crisis until it turned into a global struggle. From an eco-critical perspective, the film focuses on environmental themes and the depiction of the relationship between humans and nature. Focusing on the adventure of Greta, a pioneering voice in the fight against climate change, the story frequently includes themes such as environmental themes, the relationship between humans and nature, raising awareness against the climate crisis and climate activism. The film tells the story of Thunberg's protest in front of the Swedish Parliament, leading to a global climate activism. Throughout the film, the audience is presented with the destructive impact of human-related problems such as pollution, climate change, loss of biodiversity and deforestation on the environment, including forests, oceans and wildlife. Thunberg argues that the deteriorating relationship between humans and nature must change and that we must learn to live in harmony with the natural world. On her way to the United Nations Climate Action Summit in New York, Greta crossed the ocean in a wind-powered sailboat instead of an airplane to reduce her carbon footprint. Another striking aspect of the movie is that youth activism is at the forefront. Thunberg's story has inspired young people around the world to take action to address climate change. The film also covers issues ranging from the climate policies of governments to the role of corporations in addressing climate change. While criticizing the silence of world leaders on climate change, the film also draws attention to the power of global powers over environmental policies.

Balance: It has been observed that the proportional differences of the figures and objects in the images in the documentary film design analyzed are formally harmonious in a way to complement the frame. It is seen that this balance created is effective in all scenes throughout the movie. Thanks to the symmetrical and asymmetrical images captured by the film's shooting scales, perspectives, rhythmic editing, the film design is saved from being boring and static. In this way, Greta's story is told in a fluid way. The rational and emotional aspects of the subject, namely the need for an urgent action plan against the climate crisis and the activist action initiated by Greta Thunberg in the fight against this crisis, have been revealed with a holistic perspective of features such as the arrangement of images, camera position, clarity, light, color. Emotions such as enthusiasm, awareness and mobilization, which are stimulated in the viewer, are reinforced with the harmony of visual and linguistic messages.

Emphasis on Attractiveness: Since the film is about a harsh stance against the global climate crisis, the cold color scale dominated by gray and blue tones, which are used intensively and support the message it gives, is skillfully processed. The use of light and color in cold tones is thought to be effective in conveying the seriousness of the climate crisis to the audience. When we look at the film design, all visual and auditory arguments used in terms of thematic are presented in a certain rhythm. Thanks to the harmony created between the visual messages used and the linguistic messages that follow each other, an aesthetic harmony has been achieved. All visual and auditory messages used in the documentary film design from a thematic perspective are presented in a certain rhythm. Especially when the linguistic messages are analyzed, it is determined that the phrases used create a meaning beyond what is said in terms of semantics and the audience is intended to raise awareness on concepts such as climate crisis, environmental pollution and emergency action plan.
Visual Hierarchy: In the analyzed documentary film design, in addition to aesthetics and functionality, there are disaster scenarios created by the climate crisis on a global scale and the desire to take action to solve this crisis. When considered in this context, the emotion desired to be created should be supported in terms of design. Looking at the documentary film narrative from a design perspective, the desire to create a dramatic effect, especially in the scenes where activist actions are presented to the audience, and the associations created by the cold colors in blue and gray tones to capture the visual hierarchy bring the message to the forefront with the support of visual messages. While the identities of ordinary people are in the foreground in the visually created universe, it is seen that cold colors dominate from the beginning to the end of the film in order to support semantic integrity due to their importance. The visual language used is placed in accordance with the basic design rules (size, smallness, clarity, blur, completeness, simplicity, density, distance, proximity, etc.) and is free from elements that create semantic confusion. It can be said that the general plans used are important in terms of creating an objective perspective on the world on the brink of disaster and having the effect of mobilizing the masses to take measures against this situation. The cold tones of color and lighting also support the subject in terms of showing the gravity of the situation.

2. Conclusion

Eco-critical films are a powerful tool for raising awareness and mobilizing audiences on environmental issues. Through a harmonious blend of visual and audio narrative techniques, filmmakers can create a sense of urgency around the climate crisis and environmental issues, and challenge the cultural narratives of the dominant capitalist system, which has devastating effects. The documentary film "I Am Greta" is a powerful combination of cinematic elements and rhetoric that effectively presents the voice of the young climate activist Greta and her message to the world, addressing the issues of today. Considering the design of the documentary film, the current state of the climate crisis is effectively conveyed within the framework of urgent themes such as ecological destruction, climate change, global warming, and the continuity of species. The emotional and personal dimensions of Thunberg's story are addressed. It is thought that this film has a significant impact on issues such as climate crisis, environmental communication and activism, supporting awareness-raising processes and contributing to a global conversation on climate change. Considering the meaning-making power of the film by taking into account the design principles of the film, it brings together the idea that the film may have the potential to mobilize audiences on critical issues. As a matter of fact, when documentary film design is read within the framework of eco-criticism, it is tried to explain how such films shape the perspective towards the natural world and how they inspire the masses to act on issues such as climate and environment. This study attempts to evaluate documentary film design from an eco-critical film perspective by addressing the theoretical and practical aspects of cinema in relation to the efforts of climate activists to emphasize ecological awareness. As a result, when the documentary film *"I Am Greta"* is analyzed from an eco-critical perspective by considering the principles of design, it is observed that the narrative effectively uses all the necessary techniques in terms of details that strengthen the meaning such as clarity, size, smallness, visual hierarchy, proportioning. Moreover, it was observed that the film examines the relationship between humans and nature and is designed to emphasize the role of governments and capital owners in climate change. Ecocritical studies, which were first addressed in the field of literature, emphasize that the multifaceted ecology of the moving image can only gain meaning by coming together with elements such as production, distribution, media, text, space, experience and interpretation. Such an approach also reveals the existence of conceptual and methodological choices that lie between the lines, beyond the boundaries of this study, waiting to be posed as a problem. When film productions are analyzed from an ecocritical perspective, it is seen that reception studies and ethnographic research are lacking. In terms of exceeding the scope and limitations of this study, it is important in terms of inspiring future research and contributing to the literature, although no conclusion is drawn from a reception or ethnographic research.

References

Adalı, B. (1986). *Belgesel Sinema/Belgesel Sinemanın Doğuşu, İngiliz Belgesel Okulu ve Türk Belgesel Sineması.* Istanbul: Hil Publications.

Cereci, S. (1997). *Belgesel Film.* Istanbul: Şule Publications.

Cerit Mazlum, S. (2019). Küresel İklim Politikaları. *İklim Değişikliği Eğitim Modülleri Serisi 2.* Ankara: WEglobal Danışmanlık A.Ş.

Corner, J. (1996). *The Art of Record: A Critical Introduction to Documentary.* Manchester: Manchester University Press.

Doeden, M. (2021). *Greta Thunberg : Climate Crisis Activist. Minneapolis*: Lerner Publications Company.

Fiedorczuk, J. (2011). The Problems of Environmental Criticism: An Interview with Lawrence Buell. *Polish Journal for American Studies*, 7–13.

Garrard, G. (2016). *Ekoeleştiri* (Trans. E. Genç). İstanbul: Kolektif Kitap Publications.

Grierson, J. (1979). *Flaherty's Poetic Moana. L. Jacobs içinde, The Documentary Tradition*. Newyork: W.W. Norton&Company.Inc.

Güngör, A. C. (2015). Animasyon Sinemasına Eleştirel Yaklaşım: Wall-E Filminin İncelemesi. *The Turkish Online Journal of Design, Art and Communication – TOJDAC*, 5(1), 1–16.

İgit, A. (2016). Animasyon Filmlerinde İnsan-Doğa İlişkisi. *Gümüşhane University e-Journal of Faculty of Communication*, 951–980.

Nichols, B. (2017). *Belgesel Sinemaya Giriş* (Trans. D. Eruçman). Istanbul: Boğaziçi University Publications.

Normand, V. (2015). In the Planetarium: The Modern Museum on the Anthropocenic Stage. In H. M. Davis, & E. Turpin (Org.), *Art in the Anthropocene: Encounters among Aesthetics, Politics, Environments and Epistemologies*. Londan: Open Humanities Press.

Oppermann, S. (2012). Ekoeleştiri: Çevre ve Edebiyat Çalışmalarının Dünü ve Bugünü. In S. Oppermann, & S. Oppermann (Org.), *Ekoeleştiri: Çevre ve Edebiyat* (pp. 9–57). Ankara: Phoenix.

Oskay, Ü. (1997). Belgesel Sinema, Ampirik Algılama ve Büyük Balık Küçük Balığı Yer Dedirten Globalleşmenin Kültürü. In *Belgesel Sinema Üzerine, Belgesel Sinemacılar Birliği I. Ulusal Konferansı Bildirileri* (p. 148). İstanbul: Tayf Publications.

Önder, B. A. (2021). *Z Kuşağı: Eşitlik ve Reklam Tasarımları (Dijital Yerliler).* Ankara: Nobel Akademik Publications.

Rotha, P. (2000). *Belgesel Sinema* (Trans. İ. Şener) Istanbul: İzdüşüm Publications.

Rust, S., & Monani, S. (2013). Introduction: Cuts to Dissolves-Defining and Situating Ecocinema Studies. In S. Rust, S. Monani, & S. Cubitt (Eds.), *Ecocinema Theory and Practice* (p. 1–13). Routledge.

Sözen, M. (2010). Belgesel Filmin Tasarım Boyutu ve Türk Belgesel Sinemasından Örnek Uygulamalar. *ZKU Journal of Social Sciences*, 6(11), 241–266.

Şen, A. (2018). Bilimkurgu Sinemasında Ekolojik Adalet ve Ekoeleştiri. *İlef*, 5(1), 31–60.

Toktay, Y. (2022). *Terörün Sosyal Medyası*. Çanakkale: Paradigma Akademi Publications.

Tuncer, Ö. (2003). http://www.kameraarkasi.org/makaleler/makaleler/belgeselsinemadakaliplarimiz.html

Willoquet-Maricondi, P. (2010). *Framing the World: Explorations in Ecocriticism and Film*. University of Virginia Press.

Yengin, D., & Bayrak, T. (2022). *İletişim Kuramları 101*. Istanbul: Der Publications.

URL-1: https://time.com/person-of-the-year-2019-greta-thunberg/. Date of Access: 30 March 2022

URL- 2: Bantmag: https://bantmag.com/i-am-greta-ile-dunyayi-gretanin-perspektifinden-gorme-zamani/. Date of Access: 30 March 2022

PhD. Erdem Koç[1]

New Media and Digital Activism in the Framework

Abstract: The means of communication used by individuals to convey their feelings and thoughts have differentiated with the advancing technology and this differentiation has also been reflected in the forms of communication. The concept of new media, which started to take shape after the 1970s, and the developments in communication technologies have also transformed social movements. The spread of social media has begun to play a leading role in social movements. The most concrete example of this is the Arab Spring protests that started in Tunisia at the end of 2010 and spread to other Arab countries in waves. With the introduction of digital tools such as Facebook and Twitter, the rapid communication opportunity between activist groups has turned into anti-government protests, riots and even armed rebellions in the Arab world.

The aim of this study is to reveal how the new media environments shape the media agenda within the framework of the views put forward by the Agenda Setting Theory, which emerged as a result of the studies on the effects of mass media and the transformation created by the social movements. In this study, the concept of digital activism, which is considered as a form of social mobilization in new media, is included. In this context, the events of the Arab Spring, which started in Tunisia in December 2010 and spread to other Arab countries, which is accepted as the first example of digital activism in the world, were analyzed by content analysis method.

Keywords: New media, digital activism, agenda setting, social movements.

1. Introduction

New virtual media environments that lay the groundwork for the evolution of web technologies and that offer users the opportunity to interact are described as "new media technologies". There is a one-way communication in the environment we call traditional media, which includes the written and visual media. With the development of computer and internet technologies, the environments where two-way communication and interaction take place are now called "new media". The change and development in communication technologies started with the invention of the telegraph in the 1800s, and with

1 Maltepe University, Faculty of Communication, Communication Studies, erdemkoch@hotmail.com. ORCID: 0000-0003-3164-9796

the spread of computer technologies and the internet in the 90s, these changes and developments gained momentum and became a natural extension of daily life. Today, the tools used as a way of transmitting information have changed and turned into information technologies called "new" independent of time and space. Especially with the adoption of internet technologies in our daily lives, the concept of online media, digital media and new media, which includes all of them, has also gained popularity. In the 1970s, new media emerged as a concept created by researchers dealing with social, psychological, economic, political and cultural research and research, reaching different dimensions with computer and internet technology, which gained momentum in the 90s. (Dilmen, 2007). In the information society we live in, globalization and innovations in communication technologies have paved the way for the creation of new communication policies. The transformations brought about by the developments in communication technologies have given birth to the concept of new media. The new media began to take shape after the 1970s, especially in the fields of computer and information processing, by adapting the developments to the field of communication. Therefore, new media, also defined as information and communication technologies, is a two-way "mixed" media, some specific to computer operations and some specific to communication tools such as communications, telecommunications and broadcasting. Thus, the concept of new media is used to characterize a wider variety of communication tools. Unlike traditional communication tools, new media technologies such as digital television, internet, GSM, WA, GPRS, CD, VCD, DVD, interactive CD and similar media are produced with technologies different from mass media in quantitative terms (Törenli, 2005). Communication tools and technologies that reach the masses are characterized by the concept of "media". When media is mentioned, mass media and media such as radio, television, cinema, books and magazines come to mind and are still used today, and their existence is strengthened by new communication technologies (Manovich, 2001).

2. Purpose of the research

In today's world, where the internet is becoming more and more widespread and an indispensable part of daily life, the changes created by new communication technologies and the tools supported by these technologies in society are increasing day by day. Research indicates that new communication tools shed light on social change. New social movements aiming to create social changes and the activist events that occur in this context are taking place with the new media tools in which the Internet acts as a catalyst. This approach, which deals with the transformation of mass media in the 20th century, when the new media sets the agenda, from the perspective of the new media, is also important in terms of presenting a digital activism research framework.

Social movements that started in Europe at the end of the 18th century and spread all over the world, have experienced changes in the formation of the action and the place of organization with the developing technology in the new world order. Developments in communication technologies have transformed social movements in this sense. People have started to use new media channels to express their problems in the order. In this study, the social and political movement called the Arab Spring, which started in Tunisia in 2010 and spread to other Arab countries with a domino effect, was examined as the first digital activism originating from social media.

2.1. Research method

When internet researches are examined within the framework of agenda setting theory, it is seen that content analysis and discourse analysis methods are frequently used methods. The method in this research is discourse analysis, which is a quantitative and quantitative method used to analyze new media tools and texts. There are two main types of approaches used in the literature to analyze Internet-based applications; It is a user-based approach mostly used by research companies such as internet usage habits, duration, and opinions. The second approach is a content-based approach to analyze the text used and the content created by internet users. In this study, discourse analysis method, which is a qualitative research method from different theoretical sources, approaches and methods, will be used.

2.2. Social media and social networks as new media environment

Today, the concepts of "social media" and social networks, which internet-based applications add to our lives, have brought new dimensions to interpersonal communication. With the evolution of web technologies, one-way communication has left its place to a new formation where interaction takes place instantly and users are active. This internet-based concept, called social media, which entered our lives in the 2000s, offers a new communication world in which interaction, instant sharing and ideas are freely expressed, affecting and changing from social life to daily life and news habits.

It is thought that the history of social media started with the "world wide web" (www) going public in 1991. With the emergence of forums and blogs towards the end of the 1990s, social networks began to become widespread as individuals actively shared their ideas with other users. In order to evaluate the social networks made possible by Web 2.0 applications in the context of new media, first of all, the definitions of the concept of social media in the literature should be mentioned. Firstly, Boyd and Ellison (2007) define social media as "virtual environments where users can create a fully or partially open profile, prepare a list of people they are in contact with, display, share and observe the profiles and relationships of other users".

According to another definition, social media is a common term for online tools and websites that create mutual interaction by providing users with the opportunity to share information, thoughts, interests and information (Sayımer, 2014). Based on the definition of "social media, which explains the content, opinions, thoughts, experiences, approaches and environment as online technologies and applications where individuals share", wikis or online dictionaries that allow the user to contribute to the content, blogs where individual interests are shared, and social media where users share their own lives with images. Applications such as Facebook are applications that form the core of social media (Koç, 2020: 908).

In a narrow sense, social media is defined as "web-based services that bring individuals together with different individuals in virtual space with the development of the internet, defined as an electronic communication network that connects computer networks and corporate computer systems around the world", while social media in a broad sense. It can be expressed as "web-based services that allow individuals to create open and partially open profiles on an unspecified level and display the list of people who share links with different people". The use of the word "web-based" in the two definitions in the literature points to the Web 2.0 application that forms the basis of social media.

There are various definitions on the concept of social media. According to Bruns and Bahnisch's definition, social media is; It is expressed as websites that are built on internet technology and that allow social interaction and sharing. It is possible to list the common features that can be characterized as characteristic in social media environments that differ in terms of content, functioning and form, which are also prominent in the definitions in the literature (Kırık, 2013a, 2013b).

- Participation: Social media is a medium that encourages everyone with an interest in the subject to contribute to the content. Visitors enrich the site content through wiki applications, links or comments and interact with other members, including the site owner. The social network structure allows this process to develop naturally.

- Openness: Social media, in general, openness to participation mentioned above structured on the principle. Setting limits on sharing or accessing content with encryption methods or interfering with what participants write with moderation method are not acceptable features in social media environments.
- Bidirectionality/Chat: While analog media is based on the understanding of broadcasting that provides one-sided message flow, there is interaction in social media environments. Communication takes place in a conversational atmosphere where mutual views and interests are shared.
- Community: Social media environments allow the formation of groups gathered around common topics in a short time. In these online communities, communication and interaction takes place effectively.
- Connection: Another feature that enriches the content of social media and turns it into open-ended information or communication resources is the links in the environment. Links are one of the keys to accessing different resources or communities related to the topic of that medium.
- Danah Boyd, another researcher who studies social media, has gathered social media features under five main headings;
- Continuity: Social networks show contextual differences, but continuity is at the forefront in all of them. The accounts created are not interrupted unless they violate the rules.
- Repeatability: Content shared on social media can be used over and over again as it is inexpensive and easy to store content.
- Searchability: Most of the social networks have their own search function and it is very easy for users to search on these social networks.
- Scalability: It is possible to collect and measure the data obtained as a result of the previous feature, the research feature. In this context, social media offers the opportunity to develop different strategies with the data obtained.
- Positionlessness: It is possible to access to social media where there is an internet connection. Social networks can also be used without borders, which is the characteristic of the Internet.

It is seen that various forms of social media are capable of responding to different needs in different fields. It is the users who are the producers and consumers of the information in the social media content, which is apparently different in the distinction between traditional and new media but has similar characteristics in practice.

The most important factor in social media becoming so active is undoubtedly the interaction and sharing opportunity of Web 2.0. Social networks are one of the environments where sharing between individuals is the highest. Social networks can also be expressed as web-based environments where photos, videos, texts and all kinds of data are shared. Social networks are interactive environments where communication is established with words, images and sound files. Social networking within the scope of social media does not only aim to chat and share. Users are individuals and institutions through social networks, they can have information about the company, establish friendships, be aware of new products and services, and buy online, thus social media meets also their shopping needs. Social media with a wide variety of channels is not just about social networks. forums, blogs, micro-blogging sites, e-mail groups established by individuals and wikis are also new media applications within the scope of social media (Kırık, 2013a, 2013b).

Although it has started to be used primarily among young people in terms of technology use, it is seen that individuals of all ages actively use social networks today. The most popular and widely used social media networks that offer a virtual environment to a large number of individuals are sharing sites such as Facebook, Twitter, Yahoo, Linkedin, Youtube, Instagram, Snapchatt, people share their feelings, thoughts and opinions on many similar platforms.

2.3. Basic theoretical approaches in new media

Communication begins with the existence of humanity, and every new technology that people produce to meet their needs leads to changes in the functioning of societies. With the emergence of mass newspapers at the end of the 18th century, communication theories began to take shape. In this context, every new mass media has fed the theories and caused theorists to come up with new ideas. The internet, which is the most important communication tool of the 21st century, and social media and similar new communication channels enabled by the internet lead the social changes predicted by communication theorists. In this section, the relational link between mass communication theory and research and new media technologies will be evaluated. In this context, the theories of Marshall McLuhan and Jürgen Habermas are discussed.

2.4. Marshall Mcluhan's global village concept

In the theory of technological determinism, which sees technology as optimistic as the determinant of human and social relations, the view that media technologies affect how individuals think and act in society is dominant. McLuhan, one of the most important representatives of technological determinism, explains how communication technologies transform people's senses and the impact of technology on society, with an approach that focuses on the quantitative diversity of tool use by turning the world into a global village. McLuhan's basic assumptions about communication technologies pioneered communication studies. The concept of "Global Village", which was expressed by McLuhan in the 1960s from these basic assumptions, is that the rapid spread of the use of mass media by the society as a result of developing communication technologies will transform the world into a global village.

The Vietnam War is seen as an indication that the effect of globalization is due to electronic technology. The Vietnam War, called the first television war, is a war that every American home directly witnesses but becomes a "participant" rather than a spectator. With this war, the civil/military separation disappears. In peacetime, electronic media drives all non-industrialized regions to progress. Television affects the masses in both war and peace, and technical necessity drives social change. This brings about the communication revolution. Marshall McLuhan's concept of global village begins to live in the imagination of the entire planet with the spread of capitalism, which has been connected to each other by satellites since the 1970s (Armand & Mattelart, 1998).

The development of mass media is likened to a global village. McLuhan associates the fact that people living in a village have instant news about every event regardless of time and place, with the power of mass media. McLuhan bases her theory of the global village on the idea that the world will become a single consciousness, and that electronic media will become a global village where humanity will reunite and become a global village (Rigel et al., 2005). Today, this statement proves its correctness day by day. Thanks to the new communication tools that surround our lives with the effect of technological developments, it makes the distance close and makes information as easy as a click. Based on McLuhan's idea of global village in the 1960s, the idea that communication tools, especially television, made the world a global village where similar feelings and thoughts were shared. Today, the idea of a global village continues with the technologies made possible by the internet, which we call interactive media, which has replaced television and mass media.

Mc Luhan, one of the representatives of the technological determinism theory, which came to the fore with the spread of new communication technologies, discussed the effect of technology on the individual in an instrumental context. According to Mc Luhan, the tool is an extension of the human being. All structures created by human hands; language, laws, ideas, assumptions, tools, clothes, computers, all these are extensions of the human body (Mc Luhan, 2001). In this context, Technology is in a way like an object attributed to people. The view of the whole of the media as an extension of some physical and mental abilities of people, considering the new media context enabled by new communication technologies, the effects of the technological determinism theory appear as an undeniable fact today (Mc Luhan, 2012). McLuhan that with the phrase "the tool is the message", what the word is written is more important than the words. He emphasizes that;

- It is necessary to focus on form rather than content because communication doesn't only change the content.
- The content is always there, but if the medium is unknown, the message is also unknown. So the common message is the tool.
- The tool makes changes in people's perceptual habits.
- The tools are not neutral, so they affect the audience. They have effects on senses. For example, television sends messages to unused lazy senses.

McLuhan divided human history into three periods by focusing on technology. The first period is the tribal period before the 1500s, in which face-to-face and spoken communication takes place. The second period is the founding of the printing press which is also called the mechanical period covering the years 1500 to 1900. It is a period in which written communication flourished with the invention of the printing press, the printing of newspapers, magazines and books. The third period is the period after 1900, which is called the electronic age. In this period, oral culture began to dominate again with the presence of developing new communication technologies such as radio and television. According to McLuhan, world societies have returned to their essence with the electronic era. McLuhan deals with all these arguments from a positive perspective on this technological process that the world is entering (Güngör, 2011).

Emphasizing the importance of the tool in communication, McLuhan's classification of mass media as hot and cold tools is a distinction he uses in his technological analysis. He described the communication tools that appeal to a single sense, in which the individual has less opportunity to participate, as hot tools, and he puts the tools that appeal only to the sense of hearing or sight, such as photography, cinema, and radio, into this class. On the other hand, cold communication tools are the tools in which individuals appeal to more than one sense at the same time and the participation of the individual is in question. According to Mc Luhan, the telephone is an example of a cold communication tool (Yaylagül, 2012). Based on this idea, the internet, which is today's most important communication tool and where the participation of the individual is high, can be described as a cold communication tool.

It can be said that in the approaches of "the tool is the extension of the human being", the "the tool is the message", in which Mc Luhan deals with the effects of technology optimistically, each new technological development destroys the old one and emphasizes that technologies affect individuals positively and are the driving force of social change.

2.5. Jürgen Habermas' public space model

The concept of public space, which was tried to be conceptualized and discussed in the late 1980s and early 1990s, is now being tried to be explained in order to understand social developments and changes. In this context, one of the leading thinkers in the conceptualization of the public sphere is Jurgen Habermas (Hasdemir & Coşkun, 2008).

Jurgen Habermas is regarded as the second generation representative of the Frankfurt School, which sees communication tools as cultural and ideological devices. Habermas, a student of Adorno, who continues the tradition of critical thinking, criticizes the ideological functioning of technique and science in modern society. Although the discussions on the concept of public sphere increased in the 1980s, it was first elaborated by theorists in the 1960s. The Structural Transformation of the Public Space is Habermas's doctoral thesis written in the 1960s (Smith, 2005). Habermas explains that one of the ways of controlling the capitalist system by "improving" depends on the creation of what he calls the "public sphere". According to Habermas, the public sphere creates the environment for the establishment of democracy, which will bring freedoms, and is defined in a principle that is ensured by the participation of all individuals in the society (Karagöz, 2013). Habermas sees the public sphere as social life; It is defined as a discussion area where information is circulated around the question of common interests, and information is exchanged, and as a result, the public is formed. Habermas defines the concept of public sphere as follows; "The public sphere is a forum in which public societies gather as public society to legitimize public opinion" (Timisi, 2003).

Habermas calls meetings "public", as in closed societies, when open to the public, as indicated in the same public spaces or public buildings. The state is a "public power" and earns its title because it has a duty to ensure the common social welfare of those subject to its law. The public presents itself as a separate sphere from the private sector and media elements such as the media, sometimes state organs and sometimes public communication services are seen as "public organs" (Habermas, 2003). On the other hand, public societies point to public power in opposition to private assets. It means being outside the private state apparatus (71). The concept of public sphere emerges in the context of the relationship between freedom of thought and the triangle of ruler-administered, which is the biggest problematic of our day. With Habermas' public space, the visibility of ideas and thoughts without recognizing a place makes it possible in the new communication environment that today's information age offers to individuals. According to Habermas, who argues that real democracy can be realized in a public space that will create the consensus of the society, all others must make a consistent effort and create a public space. At this point, the function and effect of the mass media that make up the modern communication media come into play.

The function of the media created by the new communication technology is extremely important in the creation of a public space of the kind idealized by Habermas. In this context, although the media is expected to create a discussion ground for democracy, commercial concerns are an obstacle. Today, it can be said that the new social sharing environments enabled by the internet allow the public space where free thoughts in Habermas's ideal are expressed. According to Habermas, early modern capitalism was autonomously structured within the private sector, which operated with the rules of classical liberalism in the press. Thus, besides printed mass media such as newspapers, magazines and books, activity areas such as coffee shops, sports events, theater, music and entertainment also supported the formation of public opinion. In particular, the way the press conveys, narrates and perceives has a significant impact on forming the public opinion process (Karagöz, 2013).

It can be thought that the function of creating public opinion of the traditional press continues with the developing technologies and increases its effect in terms of creating public space. In particular, the virtual environments created by the new media, how it affects the concept of social movements is discussed and its power in creating social movements is thought. On the other hand, Habermas states that internet technologies do not have the feature of being a public space. Habermas states that identities are invisible in the internet environment and that identities are selected and produced virtual in the internet environment. Therefore, according to Habermas, this ambiguity between the co-speaker and the word maker prevents the internet public space from being a genuine public space (Timisi, 2003).

2.6. Social mobility in new media: Digital activism

With the internet, which is called the invention of the 20th century, the changing communication technologies have also shown their effect in the media, and the sources of journalism and citizens' news have diversified. With the evolution of the web, new media platforms have gained popularity and citizens have begun to express their rights and law on these new media platforms, and at one point to create their own public spaces. It can be said that this change caused the collective social movements that emerged in the 1960s to change shape and formed the starting point of the activist actions, which are the extension of the new social movements that are frequently used today and where the new media platforms are used as the place of organization.

Downing discussed its role in building, supporting and mobilizing communities to understand the concept of new media, called alternative media. In this context, social movements are characterized by three main classifications: The first is popular uprising, which is a reaction to oppression and violence by the state or economic institutions. Based on strategically organized groups targeting governmental institutions to initiate economic and social change, the rational actor model that defines actions is the second classification. This model includes strikes, sit-ins, boycotts and demonstrations. Third and lastly, it is the theory of "new social movements" that examines these movements in terms of cultural changes in a given society, and its focus is on building subcultures independent of the constraints of the status quo by establishing relationships between individual members of an oppressed group. Downing's examples include activist movements related to the concept of identity construction and identity politics, such as the awareness-raising tactics of the feminist movement in the 1960s and 70s (Sayımer & Çetinkaya, 2015).

The values that came to the fore in the "New Social Movements" in the expanding literature in the 70s are not new and show similarities with the old. For example, social activism movements that were against slavery and child labor in the 19th century, changed into modern campaigns such as feminism, anti-war movements and environmental movements in the early 20th century and turned into structures organized with the help of new media tools. Rather than advancing under the leadership of a hero, the new social movements emerged as voluntary associations with equal management rights called "activists". New social movements, which bring new forms of discourse and action, mostly overlap with activism in the literature, and the actors of this movement overlap with the concepts of activist (Sert, 2015).

According to J. N. Kim and K. Sriramesh, activism; It describes the coordinated effort of a group of people organized voluntarily to solve a problem that threatens common interests. Activism is the struggle to create change, and those who struggle in this context are called activists. Therefore, activism includes two elements, both action and action. The activism movement in a society is linked to the concept of democracy, which is a matter of social consensus. To the extent that participatory democracy develops, social organizations will emerge (Kim,

2009: 16). In the definitions given, it can be said that the starting point of activism is social movements. Social life and communication tools, which have changed with global changes and technology, have also transformed activist movements. The concept of digital activism, which is described as one of the tools or types of activism, has also been the driving force of new social movements.

The concept of digital activism, which is associated with activism and the internet, and which has emerged by integrating with the internet in recent years, is discussed. It is thought that especially the rate of internet usage in Arab revolts and sharing networks such as Facebook and Twitter made internet revolutions possible (Tosuner, 2015). As a concept, Digital Activism includes the use of offline tools, such as "cyber activism" and "online organization", beyond just posting on the Internet, including mobile phones and the distribution of digital content via portable memory sticks. Digital activism means mobilizing activist actions in digital environments using communication technologies. Slativism, Klicktivism, hacktivism etc. Individuals can perform their activist activities in a very fast, effective, polyphonic, simultaneous and accessible way thanks to new communication technologies. The rapid development of communication and internet Technologies, at the same time, the concept of activism has also changed and the target audience's transition from real media to digital media has made it possible for activists to reach actions to be taken on a topic simultaneously and quickly (Yeğen, 2014).

The aim of both new social movements and digital activism, which is seen as social mobilization in the new media, is to create social change on a subject axis. The struggle that came together to create this social change while people who act as activists are described as activists in social movements, they have turned into "activists" in digital activism.

2.7. Conceptual framework of agenda setting theory

Agenda setting theory, which is used to explain the effect of the media on the audience and is included in the literature with the names of creating the agenda and creating public opinion, is an approach that also meets the virtual agenda created in the new media. Since its existence, mass media has aimed to inform the audience, inform and determine the agenda of the society. Although human beings satisfy their sense of curiosity by means of mass media and synthesize the presented information according to their own thoughts, it is assumed that the way the information is presented affects the thinking of the recipient. From this point of view, it is considered as a theory in the literature. The agenda-setting approach taken aims to reveal the impact of the media on society.

People become aware of media content by reading, watching or following the news published in the media every day, or by following them on social networks. The first link in the chain of media effects that begins with exposure to media messages is the stage of being informed. Afterwards, when more information is started to be obtained about the realized subject, the stage of "cognitive effects" is started. Afterwards, the chain is completed with the "attitude change" ring along with the "behavior change" stages. At this point, the starting point of the agenda setting approach is the dimension of "informing and informing the media", which is the first stage of media effects (Yüksel, 2014). The idea that the media determines the topics that the public thinks and talks about with the way it presents the news while informing and informing the masses, and that the media decides the importance of the agenda are the issues put forward by the agenda setting approach.

The English equivalent of "agenda-setting" and our language is often "agenda-setting", the concept translated as "determination" has different equivalents in some studies. Although it is widely used with the name of "setting the agenda" in Turkish literature, in some places, "agenda formation", in some places "agenda setting", "agenda preparation", equivalents are also seen (Yüksel, 2014: 354).

Table 1. Internet usage and Facebook user ınformation

Country	Population	Internet Usage Rate	Number of Users	Facebook User Rate	Facebook Age Range 25–34		Distribution by Gender	
					18–24	25–34	Male	Female
Tunus	10.549.100	34.0 %	3.586.000	22.73 %	42 %	28 %	58 %	42 %
Mısır	81.121.077	21.2 %	17.200.000	8.29 %	50 %	28 %	64 %	36 %
Libya	6.355.112	5.5 %	350.000	0.51 %	34 %	36 %	79 %	21 %

The reason that popularized agenda-setting studies was that in the 1970s, the approach had an alternative quality to previous approaches. One of the pioneering researches that can be considered as the starting point of the agenda-setting approach is the approach of Robert E. Park, one of the first scientists working in the field of mass communication from 1915 to 1930, in which he refers to the news elimination of the media, which is now called the agenda-setting process. As seen in Table 1, the first study in the literature that inspired scientists belongs to Walter Lippmann. Lippmann's 1922 "Public Opinion" is based on the view that viewer-dominated elements of the media also predominate or take precedence over the mind's image of the media's audience. Then, in 1963,

Bernard Cohen's 1963 statement explains a similar sentiment: "The press is often not good at telling people what to think, but it's pretty good at telling readers what to think" (Dearing & Rogers, 1996).

According to the agenda-setting approach introduced by Maxwell McCombs and Donald L. Shaw (1972), the media draws attention to specific issues and constantly presents topics that tell individuals what to think about and what to know about, so the media sets the agenda. Studies conducted within the framework of the traditional agenda-setting approach were conducted to test hypotheses that suggest that the agenda-setting effect of the media weakens or strengthens at different times and on different issues. These researches are also the main purpose of most of the researches to determine whether the order of topics on the media agenda and the order of topics on the public agenda overlap and to find the reasons for this.

The view that the media may not be good at saying what to think, but very good at telling us what to think about"" reflects the basic idea of the agenda setting approach. The theory has been discussed from different angles in the literature and interpreted with other theories. These are Rogers and Dearing's different agenda setting model. Rogers and Dearing distinguished three different agendas. The first of these is the mass media agenda, which means the attention directed to the issues and events that are the priority of the mass media content. The second is the public agenda, meaning a different emphasis on issues of public opinion and knowledge. Finally, it is the political agenda, in which politicians define the issue and political proposals and influence voters in the way they react to what they want (McQuail & Windahl, 2010). Based on these three agenda assumptions, it can be said that the agenda, which concerns the public and is concerned with politics, directly affects the mass media and the mass media authority.

According to Manheim (Cereci, 2001), who conceptualizes the interaction of the three agendas in a way that includes three important dimensions, in agenda setting;

- Dimensions for the media agenda; the visibility of the scope given to the subject is the importance and value of the audience.
- Dimensions for the public agenda; awareness (level of awareness about the issue), personal significance and favoritism, (positive or negative judgments about the issue).
- Dimensions for the policy-policy agenda; the possibility of action of support in favor of the issue (the probability of an action by the official body) and freedom of action.

Agenda setting approaches put forward in the 1970s reveal the influence of the media, which has the power to even affect the way we perceive the world today. Media is a source of information for people. The media determines the agenda of the society by including a subject or event that it wants. In doing so, the media creates a control mechanism over information, controlling information that is crucial to maintaining social power. They also have the power to exercise power over people who have the power to control the flow of communication. This is called threshold guardians, who influence the agenda of what people think by deciding which messages are featured in the media.

The question and the factors affecting the media contents are the subjects that the theory researchers work on. Among them, Shoemaker and Reese (2014) explained the classification comprehensively at five different levels. The five categories ranging from the micro level that can be seen in the sense of media workers to the macro level created by the ideology are also called the "hierarchy of influences". These categories;

- It is the effects that originate from media workers, covering roles such as the values, beliefs, personal attitudes and professional backgrounds of media workers.
- Media routines are the effects that result from the working order. Broadcast period, time and place constraints, news value can be explained as the effects arising from commitment to the news source.
- They are the effects of mass media for their institutional purposes. At this point, the main factor affecting media content is the economic interests and ownership structures of media institutions. Attention is drawn to the monopolization in the media and the power of media owners in setting the agenda.
- It is the effects coming from outside the institution, which is caused by government pressures or which includes lobbying activities carried out by certain pressure groups for a content.
- The last item is the effects of ideological tendencies, which are the main determinants on media contents.

People satisfy their curiosity to learn about what is going on in the environment by applying to the mass media. Mass media often prefer not to inform the society but to give information about the issues that should be on the agenda in the society. In summary, the priorities of the powers, not the priorities of the society, play the guiding force. Whatever the powers (political and commercial) want the society to think about, they set the agenda of the media accordingly.

While television, radio and newspapers, which we call traditional media, have the power to influence the masses, it is seen that the masses have the power to set the agenda in the traditional media, with the emergence of the new media today. Despite the one-way media audience dominance in the past, the audience has become active with the opportunities offered by the internet and especially web 2.0 technology, and there has been two-way communication. Thanks to the new media, instant access to information without time and place limits has also been reflected in the change in the speed of the agenda. The new media agenda, which was parallel to the agenda of the traditional media in the first years of the internet, has changed with the reactions to social events on social networks in recent years, this process has changed with instant sharing from the scene and it has been seen that alternative media are effective in determining the agenda. Thanks to the interaction feature of the new media, users can share and interpret the news and topics they want, and thus create their own agenda. In this process, the actions that took place in the society constitute the agenda in social media environments, and social networks, whose interface is suitable for organizations, create a public space most of the time. Twitter has become an effective tool at this point.

2.8. The effect of new media on organization in social movements: The example of the Arab Spring

The events of the Arab Spring, which is called the Internet or social media revolution in the literature, can be called a great social and political movement that started in Tunisia in 2010 and affected the whole world by showing a domino effect. Arab Spring is an anonymous concept used to express popular movements of different scales, which stand out against oppressive attitudes and authoritarian governments in the Arab world and positively define the democratization process. The popular movements first started in Tunisia when the peddler Mohammed Bouzazi set himself on fire.

The people, fed up with the social injustice in the country, revolted, and on January 16, 2011, Tunisian Prime Minister Zine El Abidine Ben Ali fled the country and people declared their victory. The rebellion, which started in Tunisia, set an example for other Arab countries and a domino effect was seen in North Africa and the Middle East in a short time. The main countries affected by the Arab Spring Revolution are; It has been effective in Tunisia, Algeria, Egypt, Libya, Bahrain, Jordan and Yemen, as well as in Mauritania, Saudi Arabia, Oman, Syria, Iraq, Lebanon and Morocco. Although it is thought that Arab countries are rich due to oil refineries in the perception, this revolt of the people has shown that there is an unjust economic order in reality and has announced the chaos created by poverty to the whole world.

In the 21st century, the idea that revolutions will be tweeted, blogged and shared on Facebook has occurred without the need for television and radio. In a scientific study of the latest revolutions, more than 3 million tweets, thousands of blog posts and hundreds of gigabytes of YouTube videos were examined. As a result, social media played a central role in shaping political debate in the Arab Spring, and online conversations about the revolution have often proven to occur before major events. Especially in this Tunisia and Egypt survey, Facebook, Twitter and Youtube were collected, political websites in Egypt, political dialogue on the whole Tunisian blog, and 3 million tweets were collected and filtered. In conclusion, the critical role of social media in the Arab Spring proven (Korkmaz, 2013).

The events of the Arab Spring include Manuel Castells' concept of the politics of rebellion. Castells (2000) defines politics as a politics of insurrection that aims at a political change in the sense of institutional change with its logic embedded in political institutions. What is meant by the politics of revolt is the cooperative mobilization of issues for political or cultural change that are not, for various reasons, a primary part of a political system. At this point, Arab youth, who could not find their expectations in the current political system, showed resistance against unemployment, poverty and administrative corruption. Arab youth, who entered into a policy of revolt that will force political change against their unfair rule based on human rights violations, from unjustified arrests, took action with the experience of years. The common point of these revolts spreading in Arab countries stems from the people's desire for a democratic and equal order. As Castells said, with the developments in the internet and information technologies, the world's becoming a global village has played a key role in organizing the youth against the oppressive regime in Arab countries to rebel against the political order. The Arab Spring has also added a new dimension to the debates on the importance of social media in the realization of activist movements; whether it determines the agenda in traditional media or not.

Another remarkable aspect of the Arab Spring was the new means of communication that the young activist group used to organize in this process. These tools were the internet, social networking system and mobile phones brought by the "Information Age" in which they lived. In the Arab Spring, young people used social media tools in a way similar to the silent street politics they seized as cultural heritage. The lack of internet control in Tunisia and Egypt, and the lack of tracking systems in Russia and China have enabled young activists to listen to voices in the virtual world with very large networks and not be caught by the security forces. As a result, social networking sites were implemented as a digital version of street politics in the Arab Spring. While street politics continued in the form of cyber activism, internet environments functioned like the back streets of the Arab Spring. In this respect, social networks have kept activists out of sight and protected from the wrath of the government, while at the same time, they have been able to rally behind the government and mobilize the public. The reason why the Arab uprisings cannot be called a social media revolution in the full sense is that the restrictions on Facebook and internet usage and internet speed differ according to the countries (Akbıyık & Öztürk, 2012). Based on Table 1, it can be said that the internet is widely used in Tunisia, and it is used relatively effectively in Egypt compared to other Arab countries. According to this table, it can be concluded that the use of social media is predominantly by young people and that social media plays a key role in organizing.

3. Conclusion

This study aims to investigate the effect of digital activist actions, which are seen as a new form of social mobilization for which new communication technologies pave the way, on agenda setting. One of the most important effects of the digital revolution has been on social movements. In this new structure, unlike the past, there is a virtual public space where individuals can make their voices heard against inequalities. This new platform, called social media, has added a new dimension to individuals' organizing and taking action. Digital activism in new media environments; It is effective in social movements with its low cost and fast and easy communication to large masses.

In the context of Arab Spring actions, it has been seen that new media tools facilitate the organization of activist movements and play an important role in transforming the actions into practice. It can be said that the heaviest results occurred in the Arab Spring and that Libya, Egypt and Tunisia were listed consecutively, compared to the others and these countries show a reverse structure in terms of internet access opportunities and the tendency to establish a community in a social network. Especially in the case of Libya, activist, blogger, mainstream media profiles that can be considered as journalists raise the rate considerably for this country. For this reason, it can be thought that international intervention in Libya is also provided on social media, in other words, Libya was subjected to pressure during the intervention on Twitter with an effort to emphasize the justification of the operation. In the 21st century, the new order that began to be experienced under the influence of capitalism, which Mc Luhan called the "global village", is now the scene of the challenges of political, economic, social and environmental problems in digital environments. These challenges are seen all over the world under the name of "new social movements". The examples of these movements, in which the new media is the driving force, in the world, especially the Arab Spring, point to the social media revolution.

When the findings related to internet usage purposes are examined, followers mostly connect to the Internet for information, social media, research, and being informed. People use social media to be aware of current news and events, to communicate with others, to support an ideology or social movement. In terms of digital activism, the internet is used to call for action, follow current news and events, and interact with other activists. One of the main reasons for this is anonymity. Facebook does not require people's real names and surnames to use an account, rather than family or friendship networks, networks established for activism can be used. On the other hand, content flowing in reverse chronological order on Twitter – with the absence of tabs such as games or detailed profiles – offers an easy-to-use and follow-up structure. When the hashtags that facilitate the classification of content and raise issues are added to this, the role of Twitter becomes more important in activism.

In terms of digital activism, it is "necessary" to gain new supporters and connect with different networks, to disseminate information, to create public opinion – often international – and to exert pressure on the formed public opinion and political actors. The conceptual evaluation reflects an activist-centered perspective, based on the interviewees' own experiences in the digital environment – and often even online. Through digital activism, physical boundaries are crossed, the activities of the activism are announced, new supporters are reached, and the agenda is set. The digital activism movement, the first example of which was seen in the world with the Arab Spring, is expected to continue to increase its influence in different ideological reflections in the following periods, as well as agenda setting and related social consequences.

References

Akbıyık, A, Öztürk. (2012). M. Sivil Toplum ve Sosyal Medya Perspektifinde "Arap Baharı" ve "Wall Street'i İşgal Et" Eylemleri. *Turgut Özal Uluslararası Ekonomi ve Siyaset Congress*, II, 1003–1025.

Boyd, Danah M., & Ellison, Nicole B. (2007). Social Networks Sites: Definition, History and Scholarship. *Journal of Computer-Mediated Communication*, 13(1).

Castells, M. (2000). *The Information Age: Economy, Society and Culture Volume 1 The Rise of The Network Society*. United Kıngdom: John Wiley & Sons Ltd. Publication, 2e.

Cereci, S. (2001). Gündem Oluşturmada Medyanın Rolü. *İzmir: Dokuz Eylül University Sosyal Bilimler Enstitute Journal*, III, S.3, 2001, 22.

Dearing, J. W., & Rogers, E. M. (1996). *Communication, Concepts 6: Agenda-Setting*. Thousand Oaks, CA: Sage: .

Dilmen, N. E. (2007). Yeni Medya Kavramı Çerçevesinde İnternet Günlükleri-Bloglar ve Gazeteciliğe Yansımaları. *Marmara Communication Journal*.

Güngör, N. (2011). *İletişim Kuramlar ve Yaklaşımlar* (pp. 159–160). Ankara: Siyasal Publishing.

Hasdemir, T. A., & Çoşkun, M. K. (2008). Kamusal Alan ve Toplumsal Hareketler, Ankara University. *SBF Journal*. https://dspace.ankara.edu.tr/xmlui/handle/20.500.12575/65979. Accessed Date: 06 July 2022, 176 Yaylagül,, a.g.e., p. 106.

Kırık, Ali Murat. (2013a). *Gelişen Web Teknolojileri ve Sosyal Medya Bağımlılığı, Sosyalleşen Birey, Sosyal Medya Araştırmaları 1*. Konya: Çizgi Publishing.

Kırık, Ali Murat. (2013b). *Yeni Medya Çağı Çerçevesinde Türkiye'de Televizyondan İnternete Dönüşüm ve Sosyal Paylaşım Ağlarında Gençlerin Konumu*, PhD Thesis, Marmara University.

Kim, J.-N., & Sriramesh, K. (2009). A Descriptive Model of Activism in Global Public Relations Research and Practice. In K. Sriramesh & D. Vercic (Eds.), *The Global Public Relations Handbook* (Revised edition). New York, NY: Routledge.

Koç, N. E. (2020). Sosyal medya, katılımcı kültür ve kitle çevirisi. *RumeliDE Dil ve Edebiyat Araştırmaları Dergisi* (Ö8), 905–927. https://doi.org/10.29000/rumelide.822087.

Korkmaz, A. (2013). Arap Baharı Sürecinde Ġnternet ve Sosyal Medyanın Rolü. *International Symposium on Language and Communication: Research Trends and Challenges* (ISLC), İzmir, 17–19 July 2013, pp. 2147–2153.

Manovich, L. (2001). *The Language of New Media*. Cambridge. Gülşah Başlar, Yeni Medyanın Gelişimi ve Dijitalleşen Kapitalizm, Akademik Bilişim 2013 Conference, http://ab.org.tr/ab13/kitap/AB2013_Bildiri_Kitap.pdf. Accessed Date: 09 July 2022.

McCombs, M. E., & Shaw, D. L. (1972). The Agenda-Setting Function of Mass Media. *The Public Opinion Quarterly*, *36*(2), 176–187. https://www.researchgate.net/publication/209410047_The_Agenda-Setting_Function_of_Mass_Media.

McLuhan, M. (2001). *The Global Viilage* (Trans. Bahar Öcal Düzgören, p. 123). Scala Publishing.

McQuail, D., & Windahl, S. (2010). *İletişim Modelleri-Kitle İletişim Çalışmaları* (Trans. Konca Yumlu, p. 136). Ankara: İmge Publishing.

Michele, Armand ve Mattelart. (1998). *İletişim Kuramları Tarihi* (Trans. Merih Zıllıoğlu). İstanbul: İletişim Publishing.

Rigel, Nurdoğan. (2005). *21.Yüzyıl İletişim Çağını Aydınlatan Kuramcılar Kadife Karanlık*. İstanbul: Su Publishing.

Sayımer, İ. (2014). Yeni Medya Ortamlarında Ağlar Oluşturan Toplumsal Hareket Deneyimleri. *Elektronik Mesleki Gelişim ve Araştırma Journal* (EJOIR).

Sayımer, İ., & Çetinkaya, A. (2015). Alternatif Medyanın Twitter'da Gündem OluÇturma Süreci: Berkin Elvan Olayı Üzerine Bir inceleme. In Selva Ersöz Karakulakoğlu & Özge Uğurlu (Eds.), *İletişim Çalışmalarında Dijital Yaklaşımlar* (pp. 236–237). Ankara: Heretik Publishing.

Sert, N. Y. (2015). *Aktivizm Toplumsal Değişimin Yeni Yüzü*. İstanbul: Değişim Publishing.

Shoemaker, P., & Reese, S. D. (2014). *Mediating the Message in the 21st Century: A Media Sociology Perspective*. New York, NY: Routledge

Timisi, N. (2003). *Yeni İletişim Teknolojileri ve Demokrasi*. Ankara: Dost Publishing.

Tosuner, A. (2015). *İnternet Aktivizminde Twitter'in Stratejik Konumu, İletişim Çalışmalarında Dijital Yaklaşımlar* (Eds. Selva Ersöz Karakulakoğlu, & Özge Uğurlu). Ankara: Heretik Publishing.

Törenli, N. (2005). *Yeni Medya Yeni İletişim Ortamı* (pp. 87–88). Ankara: Bilim ve Sanat Publishing.

Yaylagül, L. (2012). *Kitle İletişim Kuramları* (p. 71). Ankara: Dipnot Publishing.

Yeğen, C. (2014). Dijital Aktivizmin Bir Türü Olarak Hacktivizm ve "Redhack". *E-Journal of Intermedia*, 1(1), 118–132.

Yüksel, O. (2014). *İnternet Gazeteciliği ve Blog Yazarlığı* (p. 95). Ankara: Sinemis Publishing.

Dr. Yakup Toktay[1]

Reading hacktivism over the Russia-Ukraine war: The case of Anonymous

Abstract: The war between Russia and Ukraine is not only a traditional clash of military power, but also an asymmetric war involving cyber-attacks. The aim of this study is to explore how asymmetric warfare is seen in the Russia-Ukraine tension and to reveal the effects of asymmetric warfare on the course of events, the cyber warfare strategies used, the formation of volunteer hacktivist groups and the attacks carried out. For this purpose, the study was designed according to the qualitative research method, internal case study, and the reflections of the conflicts between Russia and Ukraine in cyberspace were examined through critical case sampling. As a result of the research, computer and digital technologies have opened a new front to warfare, making it not only a tension on the hot frontlines. Although digital transformation brings many advantages for the government and the military, it also carries great risks. The use of AI-supported computer systems for government and military purposes increases the possibility of cyber-attacks against these systems.

The launch of a cyber attack against Russia by Anonymous, the most well-known global face of the hacktivism movement used as an asymmetric warfare tactic, paved the way for the formation of a collective movement, leading hackers from different parts of the world to launch anti-Russian cyber attacks. Consequently, the war has ceased to be a frontal struggle and the conflict has moved online. On the other hand, the Ukrainian government's call for the formation of a volunteer IT army against Russian aggression, which garnered global support, was reciprocated by the international community, turning the war into a world war in a sense, and a great example of mobilization was observed. However, although the anti-Russian hacktivist movements had a weak impact on the course of the war, they had a significant impact on slowing down operations, manipulating information and opening a separate front in the war. In addition, asymmetric warfare against Russia did not ultimately deter Russia from its goal. Moreover, in terms of cyber and electronic warfare strategy, Russia has succeeded in damaging the Ukrainian logistics and communication infrastructure by using advanced electronic warfare equipment in the region and has exhibited counter-hacktivist actions in cyber space as well as in the field. Ukraine, on the other hand, seems to have learned lessons from Russia's cyber attacks in 2014 and 2016. In this context, the national cybersecurity strategy report prepared by Ukraine mainly includes a defense and offensive action plan against the Russian cyber threat.

Keywords: Russian- Ukraine, war, activism, hacktivism, Anonymous.

1 Bandırma Onyedi Eylül University, Media and Communication Department, ORCID: 0000-0003-3253-9898.

1. Introduction:

The conflict between Russia and Ukraine, which erupted in 2022, has a centuries-old history. While the common cultural and political ties between the two countries also go back a long way, they have also been rivals for power and influence in the region. In 2014, Russia's annexation of Crimea escalated the conflict. Moreover, Russia's autonomous recognition of the Ukrainian cities of Donetsk and Luhansk in the Dosbas region as the Donetsk People's Republic (DPR) and the Luhansk People's Republic (LPR) escalated tensions. On February 24, 2022, Putin launched a full-scale invasion of Ukraine in what he described as a "de-Nazification" of Ukraine. As a result, the Western world imposed severe international sanctions on Russia. The sanctions led to a contraction of the Russian economy, the withdrawal of Western companies from the Russian market, and the isolation of Russia in the international arena.

After Ukrainian leader Zelensky announced in his address to the nation that Ukraine would respond to Russian aggression, Mykhailo Fedorov, Ukraine's deputy prime minister for digital transformation, called for the creation of Ukraine's volunteer IT army to fight against Russian aggression. This call was answered both nationally and internationally, with Anonymous, one of the world's most popular hactivist groups, declaring "cyber war" on Vladimir Putin in response to the invasion of Ukraine. This situation has transformed the war from conflicts based on military power to asymmetric warfare using the war tactics of the new century. Strategies such as information warfare, cyber-attacks, psychological warfare and propaganda, which are defined as asymmetric warfare, have transformed the Russia-Ukraine war from a traditional clash of military power into an asymmetric war with cyber-attacks behind the frontline.

The main problem of this study is to focus on this point and to reveal how asymmetric warfare is seen in the Russia-Ukraine conflict. For this purpose, the methodology of this study is qualitative research, which allows us to understand the "why" and "how" of social events and phenomena in order to understand how the war between the two countries has transformed from a mere frontline to a war between networks, its effects on the course of the war, the strategies used, the formation of voluntary hactivist groups and the attacks carried out. In the study designed with qualitative method, case study design, the interpretation of the data was based on descriptive analysis.

In the related literature review, many studies on hactivism and cyber warfare were found (Jordan, 2004; Coleman, 2011; Denning, 2001; Hunsinger & Schrock, 2016; Green, 2016; George & Leidner, 2019; Johnson & Robinson, 2014; Dahan, 2013; Sauter, 2013). However, studies on the impact of hactivism on the Russia-Ukraine war are limited. On the other hand, this war is one of the clearest incidents in which the conceptualization of hactivism is embodied, and such a hactivist collectivism has never been witnessed before. Therefore, investigating the phenomenon of hactivism in the Russian-Ukrainian war will make a significant contribution to the literature.

1.1. Method

This study is a qualitative research and was designed according to an intrinsic case study. In intrinsic case studies, a topic is selected and the internal situation related to that topic is tried to be revealed (Merriam, 2018: 8). The internal situation in this study is the reflections of the conflicts between Russia and Ukraine in cyberspace. The events or phenomena that develop within the subject addressed by critical situation sampling constitute the findings of the study. Critical case sampling is one of the types of purposive sampling and is an in-depth examination of a situation identified in relation to the research problem. The interpretation of the research findings was based on descriptive analysis. Although description is the first step of a scientific research process, it involves observing, recording and interpreting events or phenomena (Gökçe, 2022: 42).

The population of Ukraine, located in the west of Russia, decreased by 0.59 % compared to 2020, and the population of Ukraine was recorded as 41,319,838 in the 2021 census. Kiev, the capital of Ukraine, is the oldest known Russian city and the center of the Orthodox faith. Came under the rule of Moscow in 1654 due to the rise of the Ukrainian identity in the region and its geography (Önder, 2022: 101). In Ukraine, which declared its independence following the collapse of the Soviet Union, Russian language predominates in addition to about 18 different languages. With the close environment doctrine, it can be stated that Russia aims to take the countries that gained independence after the collapse of the Soviet Union and which were previously under the roof of the Soviet Union under its control again (Keskin, 2015: 45). Putin's desire for Ukraine's return to Russian domination has its origins primarily in an effort to gain prestige for the Russians and at the same time to limit the influence of Western imperialism in Eastern Europe. The inclusion of eight countries that left the Soviet Union after 1949 is extremely important to Putin, because Ukraine's accession to NATO means that Russia's international influence may be at stake. The origin of the tension between Russia and Ukraine goes back to the early 1990s. Russia, which initially followed some policies that would affect Ukraine economically, implemented a policy of economic pressure in the region by applying various embargoes in areas such as natural gas and electricity. In 2005, Putin described the collapse of the Soviet Union as "the great geopolitical disaster of the century" and emphasized that thousands of Russians were stranded outside their own country. Putin's nostalgia for the Soviet Union has helped him legitimize different conflicts, such as the 2008 invasion of Georgia (Önder, 2022: 102).

After the 2010 elections in Ukraine, internal turmoil occurred in the country and the people were polarized as "pro-eastern and pro-western". A similar situation was observed in the Crimea in the same period. By 2010, after the Ukrainian elections, internal turmoil arose in the country, and the people were polarized as "pro-eastern and pro-western" ones. Putin supported the idea of reunification with Russia, advocating the forcible annexation of Crimea from Ukraine. Finally, on February 27, 2014, with the occupation of Crimea by Russian soldiers, Crimea was separated from Ukraine and passed under the control of Russia. Later, Putin also annexed Ukraine's Sevastopol. However, although the Ukraine-Russia conflict seems to have started with the Crimea incident, its real origin is based on the fact that the Association Agreement, which was intended to be signed with the European Union on November 21, 2013, could not be realized because of Russia's oppressive regime. This issue has led to protests in Kiev, the capital of Ukraine. These protests, which were initially thought to be easily suppressed, soon crossed the borders of Kiev. Tensions arose between the protesters and the then-president Viktor Yanukovych administration, and these protests were suppressed by the police. Despite Yanukovych's moderate policies in the parliament in this period, he could not get any results, on February 22, 2014, after the president had to leave the country and the new government was formed, he issued an arrest warrant for Yanukovych (Önder, 2022: 103; Özdal, 2015: 70–71; Bingöl, 2014: 16–17). In 2014, Petro Poroshenko, who was known for his Western-oriented policies, came to power in Ukraine. As a result of the failure of the temporary government's policies aimed at the nation-state, Russia proposed a referendum on Crimea's sovereignty. In response, armed groups known as the "Green Men," who were considered pro-Russian and appeared in unmarked uniforms, confronted protesters in the Crimean capital of Simferopol and exerted pressure on Ukraine and Crimean Tatars to leave the island. Following the referendum, Crimea joined Russia on March 16, 2014, with an approval rate of approximately 96 %.

April 6, 2014, marked the escalation of the crisis between Russia and Ukraine. Donetsk, a city in Ukraine with a significant Russian population, is also a region of economic and strategic importance, housing the production of aerospace and defense industries.

This region, located in eastern Ukraine, is of significant importance due to its coal deposits. Although Russia fulfills many of its needs (such as natural gas and electricity) for this high-value area, the two countries are economically and commercially interdependent. When pro-Russian separatists in Ukraine began to take action similar to what happened in Crimea, the Ukrainian people joined a volunteer army in their struggle for independence.

During this period, the Russian government claimed it had no connection to the events, but this assertion was not considered credible by the international community. Eventually, Russian separatists in Donetsk and Luhansk regions held referendums on May 11, 2014. As a result, the Donetsk People's Republic (DPR) and the Luhansk People's Republic (LPR) were established, largely due to Ukraine's vulnerability for various reasons. Aleksandr Zakharchenko was elected president in Donetsk and Igor Plotnsky in Luhansk (Özdemir & Eminoğlu, 2022). Although Ukraine declared that it does not recognize these Republics, Russia displayed a positive attitude towards the issue. When it came to May 24, 2014, the two people's republics announced that they formed a confederal structure and called this structure "Novorossiya", that is, "New Russia" (Uyaniker, 2018: 151–152).

On July 17, 2014, the shooting down of a Malaysian Airlines passenger plane by a Russian-made rocket near Donbas garnered significant international attention. Russia claimed that the voice recordings from the incident, which were captured and said to belong to separatists, were manipulative in nature, and they asserted that Ukraine was responsible for the incident. However, despite Russia's denial, it could not clear itself of blame in the eyes of the international community, resulting in a series of sanctions imposed by many countries. By July 31, 2014, Russia, Ukraine, the Donetsk People's Republic (DPR), the Luhansk People's Republic (LPR), and the Organization for Security and Cooperation in Europe (OSCE) initiated talks for the First Minsk Agreement, and the parties reached an agreement on September 5, 2014. The agreement led to a ceasefire for only five days, and the conflicts resumed afterward. On February 12, 2015, the Second Minsk Agreement was reached, this time with the involvement of France and Germany, along with the OSCE as a mediator. However, despite the agreement, conflicts resumed shortly thereafter, and approximately 4,000 ceasefires were violated within roughly three months (Koçak, 2015: 20–21). In 2016, there was some partial rapprochement within the Normandy Quartet, but no agreement could be reached among the parties. Furthermore, during this period, changes occurred in the Ukrainian leadership. Russia accused Ukraine of violating its borders due to military exercises conducted in Crimea, leading to mutual investigations between Russia and Ukraine.

By 2017, separatist forces bombed a train station near the city of Donbas, resulting in the loss of many civilian lives. In February 2018, Russia announced its decision to issue Russian passports to residents of Donbas and provide full support in economic, social, and military aspects. Ukraine's relatively tolerant response to this announcement marked one of the stages of annexation between the two countries.

A brief ceasefire, declared on July 1, 2018, was formally achieved on August 29. However, just two days after this event, the leader of the Donetsk People's Republic (DPR), Aleksandr Zakharçenko, lost his life in a bombing. On October 1, 2019, Vladimir Zelensky, the Ukrainian president, developed a formula for achieving peace with the separatists, which included granting autonomy to Donbas with the condition that the region would not separate from Ukraine. However, within 24 hours of this announcement, widespread protests erupted in Ukraine, and the formula was shelved. In the 2018 crisis in Ukraine, Russia accused Ukrainian ships of illegally entering Russian waters in the Crimea Peninsula and seized them (Soydan, 2019: 84).

In the 2019 Ukrainian elections, Vladimir Zelensky came to power and displayed a pro-Western stance, expressing a desire for Ukraine to be a part of NATO. This orientation towards the West is not entirely new, as Ukraine had previously demonstrated its Western-leaning policies through various actions, notably during the Orange Revolution in 2004. These complex political relations eventually led to a military operation against Ukraine. According to Russia's announcement on February 24, 2022, they deployed over 100,000 troops along the Ukraine-Belarus border and launched a military operation against Ukraine (Alkanalka et al., 2022: 27).

Upon the occupation of Donbas, Putin addressed the nation, declaring the Minsk Agreement null and void and characterizing the operation in Donbas as solely a military operation. Despite repeated ceasefires, Minsk agreements, and diplomatic negotiations, the Donbas crisis has escalated day by day over the past seven years. In fact, "Ukraine has not abandoned its pro-Western stance since the annexation of Crimea, while Russia has continued to support separatist movements in eastern Ukraine, alleging Ukraine's violations of the Minsk Agreement" (Çelik, 2022). Putin's announcement of the military operation raised rumors of war in the public opinion. Ultimately, images that reached the world portrayed significant losses, including not only in the Ukrainian economy, industry, and military but also among civilians who voluntarily joined the army. The conflicts have resulted in numerous casualties among both Russian and Ukrainian citizens, and as of September 2023, they continue unabated. Ukrainian leader Zelensky declared in his address to the nation that they would respond to Russia's attack. While Ukraine receives support from the European Union and gains strength at times, Russian artillery continues relentless air and ground attacks. Putin, who referred to the military operation as a purification of Ukraine from the military and Nazism, as of September 2023, has not led to a ceasefire, surrender, or withdrawal from the conflict by either side.

Certainly, this war is not just a conflict based solely on military power; it is a conflict where both sides employ the tactics of 21st-century new-generation warfare, including various forms of manipulation. In this war, we observe the utilization of asymmetric warfare methods, which fundamentally encompass both conventional and irregular methodologies. Asymmetric warfare is a type of conflict that can occur between states with unequal power balances, minority groups, or different entities, and it can take on various forms that may evolve over time (Önder, 2022: 104). The term "asymmetric warfare" has been used, particularly in the post-Cold War era, to describe the struggles against global powers where different means are employed beyond traditional military weapons and methods (Varlık, 2013). Such wars can involve a range of strategies, including information warfare, cyberattacks, propaganda, psychological operations, and may lead to complex conflicts where not only military power but also soft power and information warfare are employed.

2. Cyber warfare with hacktivism

Developments in Internet technology that started in the 90s and the use of the Internet for military purposes have transformed the cyber space into a new propaganda and war ground. It is known that especially states use the internet effectively for public diplomacy, cyber warfare and propaganda purposes (Toktay, 2022: 74). Cyberspace is an area that describes the use of electronic and electromagnetic spectrum by networked systems and related physical infrastructures to store, exchange and share data. In this sense, cyberspace can also be defined as a global area consisting of a network of information technology infrastructure by connecting networks such as the Internet, telecommunication networks and computers (Andress & Winterfeld, 2012: 18–19).

In cyberspace, information circulates from one medium to another, is processed, reproduced and stored. The realisation of all these processes depends on the communication of the tools with each other. In other words, cyberspace consists of communication systems, computers, networks, satellites and communication infrastructure, all of which use information in digital format. Wi-Fi, laser, modems, satellites, local networks, mobile phones, fibre optics, computers, storage devices, fixed or mobile equipment, including voice, text and image data that can be remotely controlled through a network are all included in cyberspace (Johnson, 2015: 157).

According to Martin Libicki, today's information wars take place in 7 ways:

- Command and control battle
- Intelligence-based warfare
- Electronic warfare
- Psychological warfare
- Hacker war
- Economic information warfare
- Cyber warfare

Cyber warfare is the area of knowledge that is particularly focussed on in times of war and encompasses everything both in the physical environment and in cyberspace. In this sense, cyber warfare uses cyberspace as a means of deliberately harming people, assets or economies. In cyber warfare, both sides seek to prevent the enemy from accessing the information space and maximise their own knowledge of the battlefield. Cyber warfare is conducted not only for offensive purposes but also for defensive purposes (Johnson, 2015: 157). One of the main targets of cyber attacks are today's critical infrastructure networks, control and command systems, logistics centres, intelligence units that manage personnel planning and operations. Most command and control systems and weapon systems today have computer chips, and this is where the importance of logistics systems becomes apparent. Computers calculate and control the forces, weapons, equipment and supplies that will deploy military forces to the area of operation. A possible cyber-attack on logistics systems by the enemy can prevent attacks by enabling the enemy to learn what is happening and change the data and discover the next moves in advance (Andress & Winterfeld, 2012: 18–19). The increase in access to the Internet towards the 2000s gave rise to one of the first forms of digital protest, namely online political demonstrations. The main reasons for dissatisfaction with the Internet at that time were restrictions on freedom of expression, monopolisation of media sources, manipulation of information or lobbying (Lakomy, 2013: 182–183).

At this point, the concept of electronic civil disobedience, which is a non-violent but electronic form of protest against individuals and institutions engaged in unethical or illegal activities, has emerged (Wray, 1999: 108). The emergence of hacktivism dates back to this point. In a broad sense, hacktivism is a phenomenon of joint and co-operative, often anonymous, political and technological activities to create opposition to actions in the political sphere (Lakomy, 2013: 183). The hacktivist collective first emerged from the 4chan website in 2003. There is no leadership in the group, which acts with the slogan "We are a legion". The most prominent group of the hacktivism movement is

Anonymous. The hacktivist group Anonymous generally opposes governments and corporations that it believes impose censorship and promote inequality. As the group is decentralised, there is no prominent leader and no hierarchy, so there are internal debates about which ideas or issues to support. In activism, anyone can hack for any purpose they want, claiming to be part of the group, but they usually attack organisations that they claim abuse power (URL-1). Anonymous was named one of the 100 most influential people in the world by Time magazine in 2012 (URL-2). Anonymous has many social accounts, but only their Twitter page has 15.5 million followers. Hacktivist groups use computers and computer networks for protest purposes as a manifestation of specific political demands. Alexander Samuel of Harvard University argues that hacktivism is a peaceful, non-military use of illegal or legally ambiguous digital tools to achieve specific political goals (Lakomy, 2013: 124–125).

On 24 February 2022, following Russia's attempted invasion of Ukraine, the hacktivist group Anonymous declared "cyber war" on Vladimir Putin in retaliation for the invasion of Ukraine. Since then, the group has carried out several cyber-attacks that have infiltrated websites and leaked data from Russian state institutions as well as state-run news organisations and companies (URL-3). The group has carried out cyberattacks by briefly blocking access to websites, including the state-controlled Russian news agency RT, the Russian oil company Gazprom, the Kremlin and other official government organisations (URL-4).

The Russian invasion of Ukraine has led to a resurgence of cyber militancy and the recruitment of new members by Anonymous. "Never before have hacktivists been so mobilised internationally in defence of the same cause," said Athina Karatzogianni, an academic in media and communication at the University of Leicester, in an interview (URL-5). On the other hand, Mykhailo Fedorov, Ukraine's deputy prime minister and minister responsible for digital transformation, called on digital talents to create Ukraine's volunteer IT army. The call was responded to in the national and international arena and it is estimated that there may be close to 400 thousand hackers fighting online for the "IT Army of Ukraine". Again, 270,000 members have gathered in the Telegram group. Viktor Zhora, deputy head of the State Special Communications Service of Ukraine, emphasised that the IT army is a "voluntary movement" and that no attacks have been made on civilian computer networks and said, "These cyber warriors are targeting military and government targets, not civilian targets." (URL-6).

The international collective hacker group Anonymous has conducted its operations against the Kremlin, the FSB (intelligence service) and the state broadcaster RT, carrying out DDoS attacks, so-called "denial of service" attacks. (URL-5). The hackers carried out their actions by claiming that innocent Ukrainians were being massacred and added that "if nothing is done to restore peace in Ukraine, we will intensify attacks against the Kremlin" (URL-1).

Ukraine's "Information Army" has continuously launched DDoS attacks against Russian targets on the Telegram channel. 2022 June Vladimir Putin's speech was postponed following a cyber attack. Other groups working in conjunction with hacktivists have launched massive hacking and leak operations against Russian government organisations, and hundreds of gigabytes of data leaked from Russia have been posted online. Hackers also defaced the website of the Russian Space Research Institute and leaked files claiming that data had been stolen from the Russian space agency Roscosmos. On the other hand, another attack was made against Putin's yacht. In the maritime tracking data, Putin's yacht was changed to "FCKPTN" (URL-7).

On the other hand, Russia has also launched a number of attacks on Ukraine under the name of cyber warfare. The three main pro-Russian hacktivist groups are Killnet, NoName 057, XakNet, and the most active hacktivist group, Killnet, has attacked approximately 650 targets since April 2022, with only 5% of these attacks being on Ukraine. The main targets of pro-Russian hacktivist groups are countries that are largely opposed to Russia, such as the European Parliament.

In early February 2022, the Russian military intelligence unit GRU launched a series of DDoS (Distributed Denial of Service) attacks against Ukrainian websites. The attacks mainly targeted Ukrainian banking and defence websites. Russian advocacy groups also used the malware-as-a-service platform "DanaBot" to launch DDOS attacks against Ukrainian Ministry of Defence websites. Belarusian state-sponsored hacker group also launched a mass phishing attack against Ukrainian military personnel and attempted to hack the e-mail accounts of military personnel by phishing. It is recorded that Russia increased the number of cyber-attacks by a large margin in this period and carried out 467 thousand attacks (URL-8). On the other hand, in addition to cyber-attacks, Russia has also used electronic warfare tactics to attack Ukraine. Electronic warfare systems called Leer 3 and Krasukha-4, which they also used in Syria, were deployed in the area of operation in an effort to locate electromagnetic systems within a 6 km radius and block wireless communication, including cell phones (McDermott, 2017).

Russia's dedicated electronic warfare (EW) brigades have carried out asymmetric warfare strategies such as disrupting enemy surveillance radars and satellite communications networks, jamming GPS lines in the VHF and UHF bands, intercepting satellite communications and cell phone networks. Russia's electronic warfare tools Krasukha-2 and -4, Leer-3, Moskva-1 and Murmansk-BN were used during the Ukrainian conflict in 2014–2022 and Russian EW brigades infiltrated the local cellular network with the Leer-3 system and sent false orders and propaganda messages to Ukrainian soldiers and civilians (McDermott, 2017).

Although Russian forces blew up several radio and television broadcasting towers in an attempt to cut the lines of communication, Ukrainian leaders continued to reach the outside world unhindered by Russian electronic warfare (Clark, 2022).

3. Conclusion and discussion

As it is known, the purpose of the emergence of computer technologies was for military purposes. Especially the bipolar world that emerged after the second world war and the cold war dragged the world into struggle and competition in every field. Computer and digital technologies have transformed wars from being fought only on hot frontlines to a new type of warfare. Although the digital transformation of the government and the military brings many advantages, it also harbours great risks. The use of artificial intelligence-supported computer systems for governmental and military purposes also raises the possibility of cyber-attacks against these systems.

Anonymous, as the most well-known global face of the hacktivist movement, launched a cyber-attack against Russia, at the same time paving the way for the formation of a collective movement, enabling hackers from different parts of the world to join the cyber war in the ranks of Ukraine. Thus, the war has ceased to be a struggle that takes place only on the frontline and has enabled the transfer of hybrid conflicts to the online environment. This situation is also important in the context of the battle of facts between the two sides of the conflict, especially in terms of information warfare (Svyrydenko & Możgin, 2022: 45). As a result, in such war environments, the spread of fake news is circulated faster than ever before. This is another evidence of the transformation of war from physical to psychological and hybrid warfare.

The Ukrainian government's call for a volunteer IT army against Russian aggression, which garnered global support, turned the war into a world war in a sense, and one of the most important examples of mobilisation emerged. Anonymous, a cyber-military hacktivist group supporting Ukraine, has proven to be an effective weapon of war by legitimising its attack activities. However, anti-Ukrainian and anti-Western Russian hacktivist groups have also damaged Ukrainian logistical and military infrastructures through cyber-attacks.

In 2015, Ukraine published a national cybersecurity strategy under the so-called "hygiene" measures. Therefore, Ukraine seems to have learned from Russia's cyberattacks in 2014 and 2016. From the Russian side, the hacktivist efforts against Russia did not change its plans. In this context, although the impact of hacktivist movements on the course of the war remains weak, their impact on slowing down operations, manipulating information and opening a separate front to the war is undeniable.

References

Alkanalka, M., Önder, E., & Bolgün, E. (2022). *Rusya-Ukrayna Savaşı.* Ülke Politikaları Vakfı İkinci Yüzyıl Serisi Haziran 2022.

Andress, J., & Winterfeld, S. (2012). *The Basics of Cyber Warfare: Understanding the Fundamentals of Cyber Warfare in Theory and Practice.* Newnes.

Bingöl, O. (2014). Ukrayna Krizinin Ulusal, Bölgesel-Küresel Bağlamı ve Gelecek Öngörüleri. *Karadeniz Araştırmaları Dergisi*, 41, 15–38.

Clark, B. (2022). The Fall and Rise of Russian Electronic Warfare. *IEEE Spectrum*, 30.

Coleman, G. (2011). Hacker Politics and Publics. *Public Culture*, 23(3–65), 511–516. https://doi.org/10.1215/08992363-1336390.

Çelik, S. (2022). 2022 Rusya'nın Ukrayna'yı İşgali: AB Entegrasyonu İçin Yeni Dönem. *Uluslararası Anadolu Sosyal Bilimler Dergisi*, 6(2), 521–533. https://doi.org/10.47525/ulasbid.1093088.

Dahan, M. (2013). Hacking for the Homeland: Patriotic Hackers Versus Hacktivists. *International Conference on Information Warfare and Security, Reading* (pp. 51–VII).Reading, United Kingdom: Academic Conferences International Limited. Retrieved from https://search-proquest-com.ezproxy.baylor.edu/docview/1549245919abstract/7E2AACB1A23147FCPQ/1.

Denning, D. E. (2001). *Activism, Hacktivism, and Cyberterrorism: The Internet as a Tool for Influencing Foreign Policy* (Vol. 239). Networks and Netwars: The Future of Terror, Crime, and Militancy.

George, J. J., & Leidner, D. E. (2019) From Clicktivism to Hacktivism: Understanding Digital Activism (2019). *Information and Organization*, 29(3).

Gökçe, E. U. (2022). *Uluslararası İlişkiler Çalışmalarında Açıklamaya veAnlamaya Dayalı Nitel Araştırma Süreci, Yöntemler ve Bilgisayar Destekli VeriAnalizi.* Pamukkale Üniversitesi Sosyal Bilimler Enstitüsü Dergisi, 2022 Sayı51: Özel sayı 1, Denizli, pp. Ö37–Ö53.

Hunsinger, J., & Schrock, A. (2016). The Democratization of Hacking and Making. *New Media & Society*, 18(4), 535–538. https://doi.org/10.1177/1461444816629466.

Johnson, P., & Robinson, P. (2014). Civic Hackathons: Innovation, Procurement, or Civic Engagement? *Review of Policy Research*, 31(4), 349–357. https://doi.org/10.1111/ropr.12074.

Johnson, T. A. (2015). Cyber Intelligence, Cyber Conflicts, and Cyber Warfare. *Cybersecurity*, 155.

Jordan, T., & Taylor, P. A. (2004). *Hacktivism and Cyberwars: Rebels with a Cause?* Psychology Press.

Keskin, M. (2015). Yakın Çevre Doktrini Bağlamında Rus Dış Politikası: Ukrayna Müdahalesi. *Barış Araştırmaları ve Çatışma Çözümleri Dergisi*, 2, 45–62. https://doi.org/10.16954/bacad.15518.

Koçak, M. (2015). *Bölgesel Çatışmadan Küresel Krize Doğu Ukrayna*. Ankara: SETA Press.

Lakomy, M. (2013). *Democracy 2.0. Political Interaction in New Media*. Cracow.

Mcdermott, R. N. (2017). *Russia's Electronic Warfare Capabilities to 2025: Challenging NATO in the Electromagnetic Spectrum*. International Centre for Defence and Security.

Merriam, S. B. (2018). *Nitel Araştırma: Desen ve Uygulama İçin Bir Rehber* (çev. Selahattin Turan, s. 48). Ankara: Nobel Akademik Yayıncılık.

Önder, B. A. (2022). *Propaganda Afiş Sanatinin İdeolojik Bir Aygit Olarak Söyleme Tezahürü*, Ankara: Siyasal Kitabevi.

Özdal, H. (2015). İç Bölgesel-Küresel Dinamikler Bağlamında Ukrayna Krizi. *Uluslararası Hukuk ve Politika Dergisi*, 11(42), 69–102.

Özdemir, Şennur, & Eminoğlu, Ayça. (2022). Yeni Nesil Savaş: Rusya'nın Donbas'ta Uyguladığı Hibrit Savaş Yöntemi. *Hitit Sosyal Bilimler Dergisi*, 15(1), 68–85.

Uyanıker, Halit. (2018). Kırım Sorunundan Donbas Savaşına Ukrayna-Rusya Uyuşmazlığı. *Karadeniz Araştırmaları Dergisi*, 59, 137–158

Sauter, M. (2013). "LOIC will tear us apart": The Impact of Tool Design and Media Portrayals in the Success of Activist DDOS Attacks. *American Behavioral Scientist*, 57(7), 983–1007. https://doi.org/10.1177/0002764213479370

Soydan, Emrah. (2014). *Ukrayna Krizi Sonrası Ukrayna-Rusya Ilişkileri* (Yayımlanmamış Yüksek lisans tezi). Aydın Adnan Menderes Üniversitesi Sosyal Bilimler Enstitüsü, Aydın, 2019.

Svyrydenko, Denys, & Wiktor Możgin. (2022). Hacktivism of the Anonymous Group as a Fighting Tool in the Context of Russia's War against Ukraine. *Future Human Image*, 17, 39–46. https://doi.org/10.29202/fhi/17/6

Toktay, Y. (2022). *Terörün Sosyal Medyası*. Paradigma Akademi. Çanakkale.

Varlik, Ali, Bilgin. (2013). Savaşı Tanımlamak: Terminolojik Bir Yaklaşım. *Avrasya Terim Dergisi*, 1(2), 114–129.

Wray, Stefan. (1999). On Electronic Civil Disobedience. *Peace Review*, Vol. 11, 107–111. https://doi.org/10.1080/10402659908426237.

URL-1: https://www.bbc.com/news/technology-60784526. Accessed Date: 07 September 2023.

URL-2: https://www.cnbc.com/2022/03/25/,07.09.2023. Accessed Date: 07 September 2023.

URL-3: https://www.cnbc.com/2022/03/25/what-is-anonymous-the-group-went-from-4chan-to-cyberattacks-on-russia.html. Accessed Date: 07 September 2023.

URL-4: https://www.wired.co.uk/article/hacktivism-russia-ukraine-ddos. Accessed Date: 07 September 2023.

URL-5: https://www.france24.com/en/europe/20220323-ukraine-conflict-presents-a-minefield-for-anonymous-and-hacktivists. Accessed Date: 05 September 2023.

URL-6: https://www.bbc.com/news/technology-60622977. Accessed Date:17 August 2023.

URL-7: https://www.wired.co.uk/. Accessed Date: 22 August 2023.

URL-8: https://www.stm.com.tr/. Accessed Date: 12 July 2023.

Asst. Prof. Buket Akdemir Dilek[1], Asst. Prof. Muhammed Dilek[2]

Digital activism in Twitter post against censorship/mobing in the cinema: "The Bergen" movie

Abstract: IV. Feminist Wave, also known as Digital Feminism, aims to highlight women's struggle in digital media and tries to legitimize the existence of women in social life within the patriarchal system. In this study, 5 tweets and comments made by other users on these tweets that was sent related to the preventing of the screening of a movie called Bergen which tells the biographical story of a woman who was murdered by her ex-husband were examined. Interesting point about this prevention is that the screening was banned in the Kozan district of Adana where her ex-husband is from. Related tweets about this incident were analyzed using the discourse analysis method. As a result of the data obtained from the tweets and comments, not showing the film was considered as a kind of censorship and mobbing in the public opinion. The common language created against censorship in tweets can be considered as a digital activist movement. With this study, which can be included in the context of digital feminism, an example has been set for the relationship between digital activist movements and cinema.

Keywords: Feminst theories, bergen movie, turkish movie, censor, digital feminism.

1. Introduction

Censor; it prevents the independent and direct delivery of the message and manipulates the message by blocking it. Censorship is the suppression of information, in general, putting barriers to the distribution of information produced by mass media (Bülbül, 46, 2001: 293). In general, censorship is divided into narrow and broad meanings. Censorship, covering film and television, is narrowly defined as the state's control of what is marked as "immoral" through mass media (Person & Simpson, 2001: 69). In its most general definition, censorship is the prevention of the expression of the views of the society or groups within the society (Elkin, 1962: 71). Censorship, in its narrow sense, is

1 Hasan Kalyoncu University, Faculty of Communication, Radio, Television and Cinema Department, buket.adilek@hku.edu.tr, ORCID: /0000-0001-7809-2935.
2 Hatay Mustafa Kemal University, Faculty of Communication, Radio, Television and Cinema Department, mdilek@mku.edu.tr, ORCID: 0000-0002-2781-0682.

the state's control over publications. In its broad sense, it is the imposition of barriers to the collection, shooting, and broadcasting of films and news (Tişvek, 1968: 6).

Censorship is implemented in 4 different ways. These forms of censorship; are state censorship, self-censorship, local censorship, and mixed censorship. State censorship is the presence of civil servants on the censorship board. In this understanding of censorship, state interests precede individual interests and the authorities apply this to the system. Self-censorship is the limitation of individuals to avoid censorship by the state. Local censorship is the censorship practiced by the central government and governorships. It is the regionally preferred censorship system due to cultural differences. Mixed censorship; is formed by the election of the censorship board from civil servants and the public. It is the censorship method preferred by the state to legitimize the practice of censorship and to avoid reactions from the public (Tatar, 1979: 53–59).

The first censorship in Turkey was in the Ottoman Period and it was included in the martial law decree of 1877 (İnuğur, 2002: 260). The first censorship practice in Turkish cinema was experienced by Ahmet Fehim Efendi with the movie Mürebbiye in 1919 (Onaran, 1968: 59). In the film, the French woman who works as a governess in a mansion in Istanbul seduces all the men in the house, and then this incident is revealed and the French woman is expelled from the mansion. The film was banned by the occupying forces in line with the conviction that Anatolia was besieged by the occupying states at the time this film was shot, and France was among them, and that the expulsion of the French woman from the house at the end of the film could be interpreted as the expulsion of the French from Anatolia (Özön, 1970: 60).

After the collapse of the Ottoman Empire and the proclamation of the Republic of Turkey, there was no article in the constitution about censorship until 1932. In 1932, by the General Police Status Law, the authority to supervise films was given to the governorships and the first censorship took place in the law in this way (Özuyar, 2004: 75).

With the Regulation on the Control of Films and Film Scripts put into effect in 1939, censorship in cinema was moved to a higher point (Öngören, 1979: 30). As can be understood from the name of this regulation, it has made the censorship type applied in Turkish Cinema two-stage. First, the film is sent to the censorship in the form of a script and it is evaluated whether it is suitable for shooting. According to the evaluation, the film script is either completely rejected or edits are made in the places specified in the scenario and filming begins. After the approval of the censorship board for the shooting of the movie, the movie is shot and presented to the censorship board in its final form. If, as a result of the inspection, it does not pose a problem in its screening, that film is put on the screen (Özgüç, 1976: 12, 13). Turkish Cinema, which has been subjected to many political and social censorship practices from past to present, as in the example of Yılmaz Güney, is still subject to certain restrictions even today. This restriction is not the problem of the movie being released in Turkey, as in the Bergen movie example, but rather the barrier to the regional screening of the movie.

In this study titled "Digital Activism in Twitter Posts Against Censorship: Bergen", the digital activist movement that emerged in social media as a result of the application of a type of censorship that we have defined before, to the Bergen film will be examined.

1.1. Feminst theories and digital feminism

The feminist movement is the basis of women's struggle to get rid of patriarchal society and social pressure from past to present. In various periods of history, women have been represented differently in public and social spaces due to the return of the patriarchal system. The feminist thought movement aims to create an equal social structure by eliminating these differences.

The idea of feminism is first encountered academically in the work "A Vindication of the Rights of Women" written by Mary Wollstonecraft in 1792 (Sevim, 2005: 7,8). In the book "Feminism is for Everybody Passionate Politics" written by Bell Hook, the author defines feminism as a movement that aims to end the abuse and oppression stemming from sexism and sexism (Hook, 2000: 1). Feminist ideology says that there are conflicts in social relations between men and women because of status. The reason for this conflict is not due to biological differences between men and women. The basis of this conflict stems from the power conflict experienced from the past to the present in human history (Mitchel, 1985: 11–12).

This movement, which was carried out for the liberation of women, is divided into certain sections such as history and work area, and this distinction is called certain waves. In the historical process, it has been tried to explain the problems that feminist movements have addressed and brought into issues from different perspectives. The primary reason for separating feminism into certain periods in this way is that women and feminist societies in different periods of history are directed to different subjects in the patriarchal order. Feminism; First Feminist Wave, Second Feminist Wave, Third Feminist Wave and Fourth. It is divided into different periods and titles in the form of the Feminist Wave.

To briefly touch on these periods chronologically, First Feminist Wave; It started to show itself at the end of the 19th century and the beginning of the 20th century. The basis of this theory was laid in the book "Vindication of the Rights of Women" by Mary Wollstonecraft (Wollstonecraft, 2012: 124, 125). The search for rights for women to exist in social life such as equal opportunities, voting rights, and property rights are the focal points of this wave. They advocate the idea that women should have basic rights with men as human rights in social life, and that women should show their presence outside of home life (Mitchel & Oakley, 1998: 44).

Second Feminist Wave; It started in the 1960s and continued until the end of the 1970s. The feminist women's movement that emerged on the specified dates, besides defending the economy and reproductive rights, focused on women who are in a secondary position due to the return of the patriarchal system and gender differences in many different fields. Even though women seem to be in an equal position with men by law, marginalization and commodification of women continue as a result of the patriarchal order (Kaiser, 2012: 11). Due to the place women are positioned in the patriarchal system, an ideological struggle has been entered. At this point, intellectual individuals defending the feminist ideology have made theoretical and cultural studies related to the patriarchal system and the position of women. He explained the basis of this theory with the phrase "sex one is not born a woman" in his work "The Second Sex" written by Simone de Beauvoir. Pioneers of feminist theory such as Simone de Beauvoir, Eva Figes, German Greer, and Late Millet were particularly interested in how women were suppressed in the patriarchal system and their position in social life in their works. As Kaiser puts it, those who took part in and thought about the Second Feminist Wave especially tried to emphasize the difference between sexuality and gender (2012: 127). Against the patriarchal view of women, which was tried to be legitimized by the increase in mass media in this period, Second Feminist Wave thinkers criticize this situation, instead of defining it as an individual problem, it is handled as a social problem. It has been argued that the emancipation of women should be in all areas.

The Third Feminist Wave; which emerged in the 1990s has brought a critical view towards the practices and the misunderstandings experienced of the Second Feminist Wave. This misunderstanding that has come to dominate the feminist movement is the idea that it includes only upper-middle-class white women (Taş, 2016: 171). According to Josephine Donovan, Feminist Wave researchers express that they are stripped of all political identities, revealing the clashes between liberal humanist theory and cultural theory, which is a woman-centered theory, in a postmodernist structure (Donovan, 2001: 351–352). This movement acts as a framework by including sexual orientation debates involving LGBT groups as well as gender (Hooks, 1981: 87). According to Budgeon, Third Feminist Wave states that women are interested in the power relations experienced among themselves, but apart from the struggle of women with men in the patriarchal system, they are also interested in this relationship because the rival of women in the patriarchal system is women (Budgeon, 2011: 249). This approach focuses on the individual rather than looking at women's problems in general and focuses on individual women's problems.

The last movement of the feminist movement, the Fourth Feminist Wave, also known as Digital Feminism; In parallel with developing technologies, it aims to make women's struggles more visible by using internet technology and digital platforms-social networks, argues that women's presence in the public sphere should be within the framework of equality, and aims to legitimize the existence of women in the still-standing patriarchal public space (Tekvar, 2017: 537). With the Fourth Feminist Wave, feminism has moved to the virtual environment (Knappe & Lang, 2014: 364). Kaya; as he stated in his study, with social networks, women can come together by getting rid of the labels of class, ethnic identity, etc. (2018: 566). The ability of social media to instantly interact with individuals and the fact that the Fourth Feminist Wave has a structure that makes it possible to come together through social networks and start a movement together makes digital activism possible. As definition and purpose, the path of action that the Fourth Feminist Wave is interested in and has chosen is digital activism.

Twitter is one of the environments that have an important place among social media and can provide the fastest interaction. With Twitter's power to disseminate data to the masses and to act massively, individuals can come together very quickly on a topic. Twitter is the most suitable application area for the Fourth Feminist Wave, that is Digital Feminism. Twitter has the ability to gather under a single title and express its opinion on a topic collectively. With hashtags, individuals can make their voices heard collectively. Using this medium to eliminate gender inequality and defending this mentality here is Digital Feminism. Individuals, under the hashtags, can address the masses by finding the opportunity to express their own problems or the problems arising from gender inequality in society. As Sandoval stated in his study, thanks to the feminist movements provided by hashtags, reconciliation and unification is achieved among women and differences that depending on the culture, economic, social, biological, class, etc. are eliminated (Sandoval, 2000: 52). Talking about events such as the victimization of women in the patriarchal system, which the mainstream media refrain from or doesn't care about, and the inability to take legal action enables activist actions to be carried out.

From past to present, feminist theories discussing the position of women in the patriarchal social structure have been shaped according to the dynamics of the time and society. With the developing mass media, the media that feminist theories are interested in has changed. Studies on feminist theories have been carried out to represent women realistically in the continuation of the struggle for existence in the patriarchal system, to make themselves visible with the developing technologies, and to make their voices heard. With the emergence of new social media networks in parallel with the developments in technology, feminist theorists have made studies on digital feminism and the struggle of women in the patriarchal system has been made more visible, especially in the medium such as Twitter, which has the power to create mass issues through individual users.

1.2. Making the self visible of women as the fourth wave feminist movement in Turkey

For many years, Turkey has been struggling for the survival of women in social life. Although they have received the right to vote at a earlier date than in many Western countries, women in Turkey are constantly struggling because they have a conservative society from past to present and the patriarchal structure is increasing its power day by day. The pressure brought by the patriarchal social structure and exerted on women comes from childhood grows progressively and exponentially and in adult life it causes gender discrimination experienced in the workplace, harassment, rape, violence against women, femicide, etc. Against this sexist approach, media organs mainly maintain the patriarchal view and reflect this in their news languages.

In the news and media platforms where domestic violence and femicide are told, women are trivialized, negated, theorized, and accused (Altun et al., 2007: 11). A language that normalizes news about violence against women, male violence and femicide is used in news channels (Dursun, 2010: 23). In television news and newspaper news, women's exposure to male violence is provided by visual elements and words. By adding masculine discourses to the texts, such as "Honor killing", "wanted to divorce", "married woman" etc. murder and violence are legitimized, and the utilization of visual elements that are blaming towards women creates an unequal representation and news coverage. Today, the sexist representation of women in the fields of mass communication and information dissemination and the masculine style have created new spaces for women to express themselves. In Turkey, Twitter is at the forefront of this field. Women who cannot make themselves visible fully and objectively in traditional media tools make themselves visible with social media and can stand against the patriarchal system by coming together. This attitude of women on digital platforms is digital activism. For example; The European Council on the Prevention and Combating of Domestic Violence and Violence Against Women and Domestic Violence, which entered into force on May 11, 2011, was withdrawn from the Istanbul Convention on March 20, 2021 and as a result of this withdrawal mass reaction has shown in Twitter and mandy other social media platform.

Violence against women started to be talked about more, as Turkey's separation from the Istanbul Convention in 2021 created sensitivity in the general public and the social media. In 2021, 280 women were murdered by men in Turkey and the murder of 217 women is suspicious (Kadın Cinayetlerini Durduracağız Platformu, 2021; Yıllik Veri Raporu, 2022). The movie *Bergen*, in which the life of the famous female artist Bergen, who was exposed to violence and brutally murdered by her ex-husband was released, was released in 2022 when the women's issue was talked about a lot, but after a short time the screening of the film was banned in the Kozan district of Adana, the hometown of her ex-husband. The censorship of the film in this way was met with a reaction on many social media networks. These reactions soon became a proliferating digital activist movement.

2. Digital activist moment on twitter on Bergen film century

Belgin Sarmışer, the singer who became famous by the name Bergen, was born on July 19, 1959, in Mersin. She started her education at the Ankara State Conservatory but had to stop her education due to financial difficulties and started to work. She was discovered by chance while she was working, and started singing by fabricating her age as if she was older. She married a man she met named Halis in the pavilion where she worked. The famous artist, who was subjected to violence during her marriage, took a break from the stage as a result of her husband's imposition. After a while, Bergen, who fled due to her experiences, started performing again. One day when she was performing, her husband poured vitriol on her face. While Bergen was performing with a severely injured and partially deformed face, Halis was imprisoned. After this incident, Bergen continued her relationship with her husband instead of severing her ties, and the fame of the singer spread abroad day by day, and the singer began to be known as the "woman of pain". After Halis was released from prison, the violence between the two, whose relationship continued, started again, so Bergen divorced her husband. Returning to work after the divorce, Bergen was shot dead by her husband in her car while returning home after a night scene (Bergen kimdir? Acıların Kadını Bergen'in trajik hayat hikayesi, 2022). The dramatic story of a famous Turkish artist Bergen was adapted into a feature film in 2022.

Bergen was shot in March 2022 under the direction of Mehmet Binay and Caner Alper. Sema Kaygusuz and Yıldırım Beyazıt wrote the screenplay of the film, which tells the real-life story of singer Bergen. Farah Zeynep Abdullah with the character of Bergen and Erdal Beşikçioğlu with the character of Halis, Tilbe Saran as the mother took place in the leading roles in the movie. The movie made a huge impact in Turkey and was watched by 718,043 people in the first week of its release and earned 22,678,859 TL at the box office. It was screened for 21 weeks and as a result of this screening, it was watched by a total of 5,462,753 people and earned 159,713,879 TL (Bergen, 2022).

The *Bergen* film made a big splash after its release and broke the box office record in a short time. The film, which was met with great interest by the audience, was removed shortly after it was released in the Kozan district of Adana, where Halis Serbest, the murderer of Bergen, currently lives. This news spread in a short time on social media and news channels, and reactions related to the subject emerged. After these reactions, the Mayor of Kozan stated that the movie was not released in the region, but a reservation was made, and that the movie would not be shown in the region because it contained violence. The fact that the film was banned in Kozan and it was censored in a way caused a stir on Twitter. Many Twitter users met under hashtags against the censorship of the film, and many Twitter users, as a digital activist movement, criticized the censorship.

3. Research

In the research part of the study, the *Bergen* movie mentioned in the previous paragraphs and the tweets that has been sent as digital activist movement after movie's censor in Kozan district of Adana will be analyzed according to the discourse analysis method of van Djik.

3.1. Data collection process

Within the scope of the research, tweets posted by 2 personal and 3 corporate accounts and comments of other Twitter users under these tweets were evaluated. The tweets and comments made on these tweets were examined in the context of digital activism and censorship. Data were collected by taking screenshots. The detected 602 tweets were classified according to individual and corporate accounts.

3.2. Analysis of data

In the first stage of the research, the tweets of the Mayor of Kozan and the tweets from 1 journalist and 3 corporate accounts about the banning of the *Bergen* movie in Kozan Municipality were analyzed using discourse analysis, and then the comments under the tweets were examined. Tweets sent about the cancellation of the Bergen movie from Kozan Mayor Kazım Özgan's account, NTV Culture and Art's account, Sözcü Newspaper's account, BBC News Turkey's account, Journalist Candaş Tolga Işık's account were analyzed using discourse analysis method. While grouping to obtain data; tweets were separated into categories those who support the movie's cancellation, those who react to the movie's cancellation, those who are unresponsive, and those who make off-topic comments. Van Dijk's discourse analysis method that he has applied to news texts is used in this study to examine the production of digital activist discourse by analyzing the language used in the relevant tweets posted on the Twitter platform.

Table 1. The distribution of tweets sent from 2 personal and 3 corporate accounts regarding the censorship of the Bergen film in terms of content

Account	Number of Followers	Support for Censorship	Criticism of Censorship	Unbiased	Irrelevant	Like
Kazım Özgan	4,071	10	119	1	3	180
NTV Kültür Sanat	5,06,813	0	85	4	4	438
Sözcü	42,22,582	0	84	3	6	178
BBC New Türkiye	34,60,946	0	72	0	2	1266
Candaş Tolga Işık	3,08,985	6	180	9	14	56,043

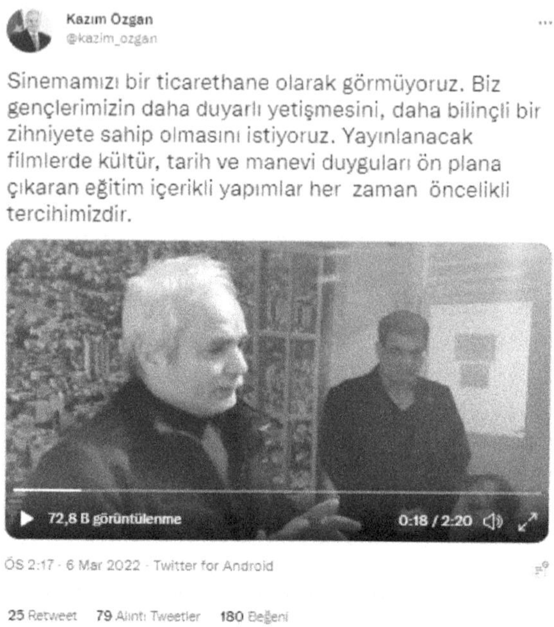

Figure 1. We do not see our cinema as a business. We want our young people to grow up more sensitive and have a more conscious mindset. Educational productions that emphasize culture, history and spiritual feelings in the films to be broadcast are always our priority.

After the Bergen movie barred from screening by Kozan Municipality and Kozan Mayor Kazım Özgan tweeted the video in Figure 1 from his official Twitter account, which has 4086 followers. This tweet by Özkan is related to the statement that the censorship applied to the *Bergen* film is necessary. On video; "*We have a strategy in cinema. We took children from our rural villages and made them watch the movie Eren Bülbül. We talked to the Ministry of National Education and we are bringing movies with social content about our youth… Our primary goal here is not making money. Our first aim is to give a vision to young people. We do not charge the poor and primary school children… When I asked those who are interested in cinema about the subject, I learned that there was violence in it. Why should I tell my children about this violence?… We play movies that will protect their homeland, nation, state and spiritual values. I don't find it right for children to learn such a thing, there is no other reason. They said the movie was screened, they lied. It was never released… Are they advertising it to get more views?"* When we look briefly at the discourses in the video, the reason why the film was not screened is violence, and reporting of the ban was deliberately preferred to increase the box office revenues of the film. Özkan emphasizes the justification of the censorship in his video statement and uses the topics of education of children and being an example to society to explain his justification. He does not characterize the film's failure to be screened as censorship, emphasizing that the film has never been released. Considering the interaction of Kazım Özgan's tweet, a total of 133 comments were made. 10 support, 119 criticism, and 1 neutral and 3 non-related comments were made under the tweet. The tweet received 180 likes, 79 quoted tweets, and 25 retweet interactions. The majority of users who commented critically on the tweet attribute the reason of the censorship to the fact that the person who killed Bergen lives in Kozan. Some users who criticized the tweet posted by Özkan, mocked the situation.

For instance, user @Aygiz2 responded in a tweet dated March 6, 2022:

"Viewers aren't buying empty rhetoric. There was violence in the movie. Is this the reason? A woman was subjected to violence and the film focuses on her life. It wasn't enough to throw misery at her face, she was killed. Your censorship justification doesn't convince anyone. (see Figure 2.)"

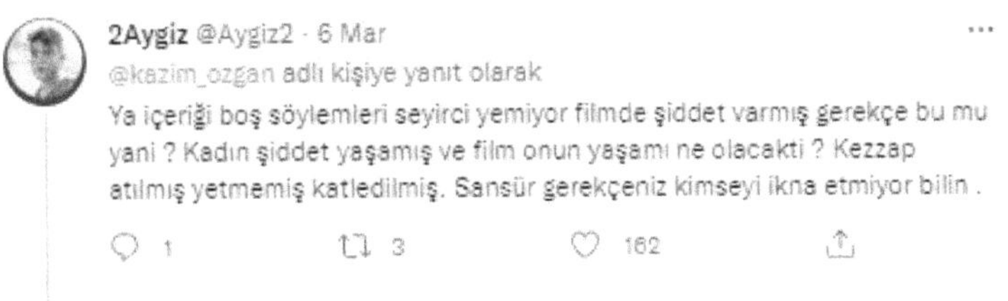

Figure 2. Screenshot showing @Aygiz2's answer to @kazim_ozgan. (Twitter, Accessed on March 12, 2023).

User @oktay_levent, on the same date, stated:

"Is Venom a movie for educating children? Is 'Uncle' film highlighting spiritual feelings? Don't act with a reflex of defense without researching, without knowing. There is censorship plain as day for the Bergen film. (see Figure 3.)"

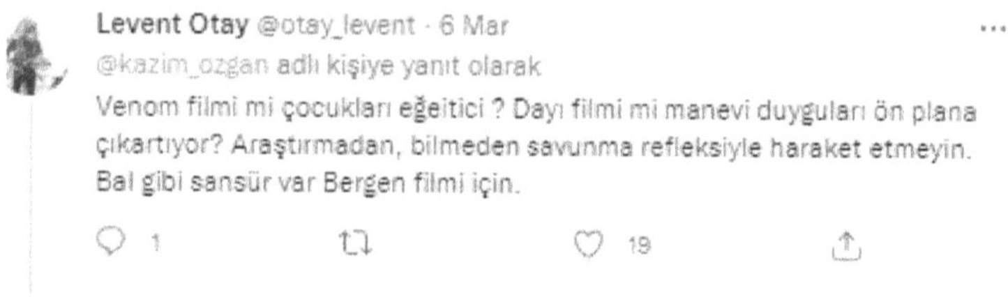

Figure 3. Screenshot showing @otay_levent's answer to (Twitter, Accessed on March 12, 2023).

In the comments made under Kazım Özgan's tweet, it is emphasized that this action is a kind of censorship, contrary to the tweet. Violence against women is highlighted in the comments. This situation, the justification of censorship is met with surprise and anger in the critical comments of the tweet. Another remarkable thing among these comments is the likes that come to these comments. In particular, the response given to Özkan by the user named 2Aygiz was liked by 162 users, which means that the critical comments were read and agreed by the audience. Although the number of likes of Özkan's tweet is 180, it is noteworthy that the number of tweets agreeing with the censorship applied to the film is 10. The difference in the number of comments between the two opposing views can be read as the users support the existing tweet by liking, but they do not have anything to say or comment on the subject. The majority of the comments supporting the tweet agrees with the Özkan's comment on the news of this banning being an advertising campaign to increase the box office of the movie.

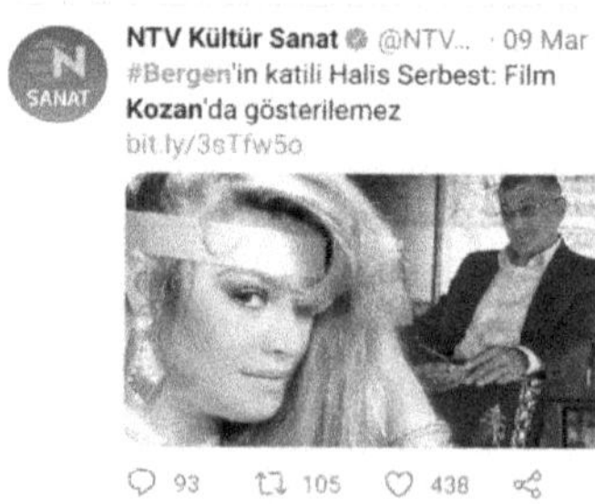

Figure 4. Bergen's murderer Halisl Serbest: The movie cannot be screened in Kozan

NTV Culture and Arts Twitter account, which has 506,813 followers, tweeted about this censorship using hashtags that directing the users to the news page. A total of 93 comments were made on the tweet. Of these comments, 85 are critical of censorship, 4 are neutral, and 4 are not relevant to the topic. In this tweet by NTV Culture and Arts regarding the Bergen film, no comments were made to support the censorship. The tweet received 438 likes, 74 quoted tweets, and 31 retweet interactions. The tweet posted by the corporate account acts as a sort of news headline. The tweet includes the comment of Halis Serbest, who is Bergen's murderer, and directs the reader to the related news link. The most striking point in the tweet is that the title of "the murderer" is placed in front of Halis Serbest. The news text reflects the hashtag and the word "killer" is used again in the text.

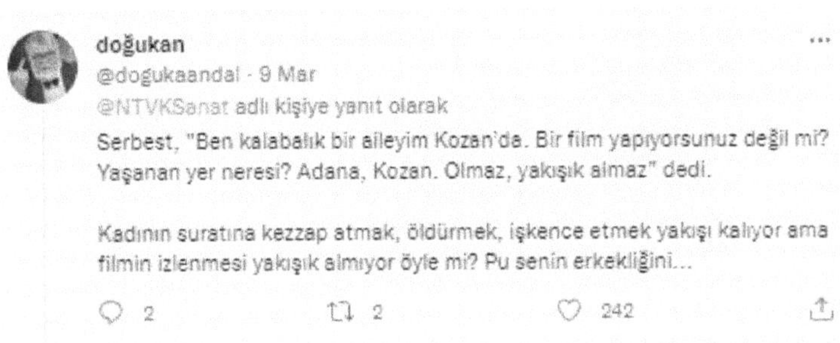

Figure 5. Screenshot showing @dogukaandal answer to NTV Culture and Art Twitter Account. (Twitter, Accessed on March 12, 2023).

Among the comments under the tweet in Figure 4 that is posted by the NTV Culture and Art Twitter account, the tweet with the most interaction is the tweet shown in Figure 5. On March 9, 2022, user @dogukaandal expressed his reaction as follows; "Serbest; ""I am a large family in Kozan. You're making a movie, right? Where is the subject covered? Adana, Kozan. No, it doesn't look good," he said. Serbest; ""I am a large family in Kozan. You're making a movie, right? Where is the subject covered? Adana, Kozan. No, it doesn't look good," he said. It is appropriate to smack and torture a woman's face, but isn't it appropriate to watch the movie? Shame on your manhood..." When the tweet text is analyzed in terms of discourse, the first sentence formed is the sentence made by Halis Serbest in the previous tweet. After this sentence, the user responds to the sentence that Serbest has formed. The torture inflicted on Bergen by Serbest in real life has been reiterated. Serbest's comments that screening of such a topic that takes places in Kozan where he has a large family wouldn't be befitting is criticized. The user reminds that Serbest found torture and murder befitting but the screening of a movie and then the user criticizes the patriarchal mindset of Serbest by saying "I spit on your manhood". The fact that this comment received 242 likes shows that the majority of the followers agree with this comment. Considering the number of likes received by this comment that came under the original tweet, it is seen that the followers follow the comments closely.

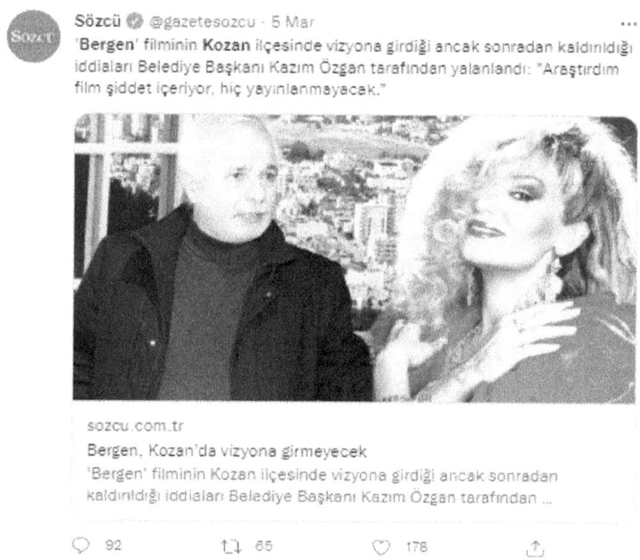

Figure 6. Screenshot of @gazetesozcu's post with mayor Kazım Özgan's statement. (Twitter, Accessed on March 12, 2023).

A total of 92 comments were made on the tweet that was sent by Sözcü's Twitter account, which has 3,406,946 followers. Sözcü's tweet was sent without using hashtags and it redirects the user to the news page. 72 of these comments are criticism of the applied censorship, 2 of them are not related to the subject and the rest are the comments on other user's comments. In this tweet by Sözcü regarding the *Bergen* movie, no comments supporting the censorship were made. The tweet received 178 likes, 44 quoted tweets, and 21 retweet interactions. Instead of using real characters to emphasize the censorship of the movie, the visual preferred in Sözcü's tweet was, unlike the tweet posted by NTV Culture and Art, the poster of the leading actress in the movie and the image of the mayor who banned the movie in the region. In the newspaper's tweet dated March 5, 2022, Kazım Özgan's statements were presented as follows: "The claims that the Bergen movie was released in Kozan district but was later removed were denied by Mayor Kazım Özgan: 'I researched, the movie contains violence, it will never be released.'" User In the tweet, the name Bergen was shown in bold and in quotation marks, and it was repeated that the subject was the movie, and the word Kozan was used in bold to emphasize the place. The use of the sentence "the movie contains violence, it will never be broadcast" in the text makes it visible that the movie was censored.

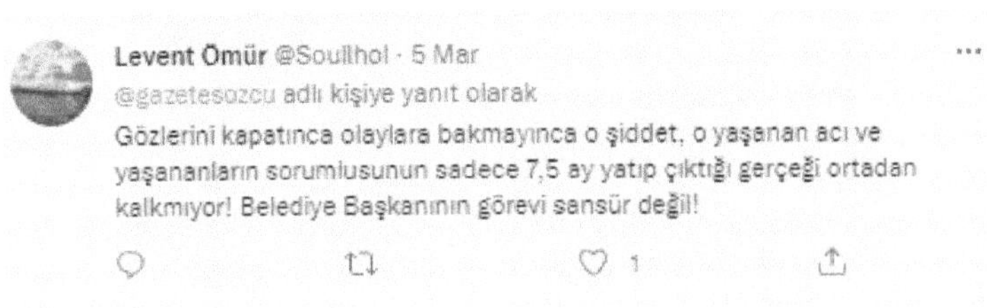

Figure 7. Screenshot showing the response of user @soullhoul to @gazetesozcu's post containing Mayor Kazım Özgan's statement.

Among the comments made under the tweet posted by Sözcü, some tweets claim that this treatment of the film is censorship. In the example of Figure 7, it is the individual account that responded to the tweet of the Sözcü newspaper and clearly expresses his personal opinion on this issue. Indeed, on March 5, 2022, user @soullhoul stated in their post: "When you close your eyes and do not look at the events, the violence, the pain, and the fact that the person who committed these acts only received a 7.5-month sentence does not disappear. The mayor's job is not censorship!" Indeed, as seen, the language he used in his tweet indicates that he is angry. To make this anger visible, he uses an exclamation point while finishing both of his two sentences. The exclamation mark means happiness, anger, anxiety, etc. It is a sign used to increase emotions and empathy. While it is said in the tweet that the censorship applied to the film is carried out by the mayor, the tweet also criticizes the response of the justice system in the country on the crimes of femicide and violence. This tweet, posted by the official Twitter account of a newspaper that can be described as opposition in Turkey, again shows an oppositional stance.

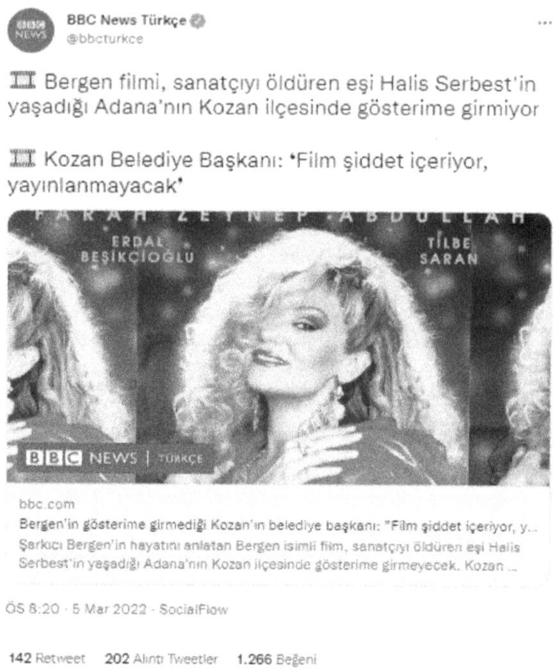

Figure 8. Screenshot of the news shared by BBC English News on its Twitter account.

The tweet sent by the BBC News Turkey Twitter account, which has 4,222,582 followers, without using a hashtag, stated: "The movie Bergen is not being screened in the Kozan district of Adana, where Halis Serbes lives, who killed the artist. Mayor of Kozan: 'The movie contains violence, it will not be broadcast. (see Figure 8.)" A total of 93 comments were made on the tweet dated March 5, 2022. This tweet also directs the users to the news page. Of these 93 comments, 84 were criticisms of the censorship, 3 were neutral, and 6 were non-related tweets. There was no comment supporting censorship in this tweet by BBC News Turkey about the *Bergen* movie. The tweet received 1.226 likes, 202 quoted tweets, and 142 retweet interactions. The poster featuring the movie's leading role was used in the news tweet. Unlike the tweets from other corporate accounts, emojis were used in BBC's tweet. It is possible to read the reason for using such emojis in the tweet as attracting attention and reaching to the audience who actively uses emojis. No personal comments were made to the tweet, which was posted as a news text. Although the main tweet did not contain any positive or negative remarks, the censorship was heavily criticized in the main tweet's comments made by other users.

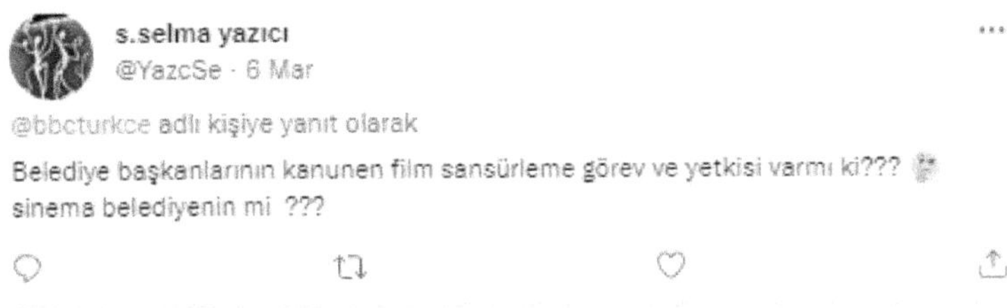

Figure 9. Screenshot of user @YazcShe, who commented on the news on BBC News Türkiye Twitter account.

Although the word censorship is rarely used among the comments made on the tweet posted by the BBC News Turkey Twitter account, certain issues such as the ban on the film and its illegality were frequently discussed. In the example of Figure 9, the user especially preferred to ask questions while criticizing. Twitter user's @YazcShe stated the following in their tweet dated March 6, 2022: "Does the mayor have the duty and authority to censor movies by law? Does the movie theater belong to the municipality?" Inseed that, she made her critical attitude visible with three question marks at the end of both sentences. In addition to the tweet in Figure 9, many users displayed a skeptical attitude under this tweet by BBC News Turkey, especially asking the question of whether the mayor has the authority to ban movies.

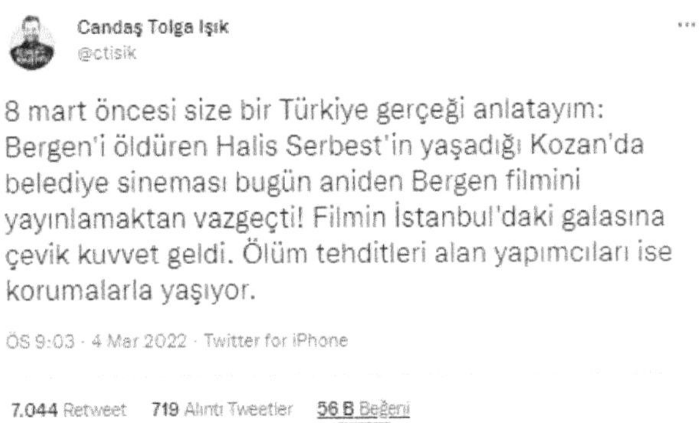

Figure 10. Screenshot showing the comment made by Candaş Tolga Işık from his account under the username @cisik on March 4, 2022.

Candaş Tolga Işık, who has 308,958 followers, received a total of 209 comments on his tweet, which he tweeted about the incident without using hashtags. On

March 4, 2022, Twitter user with the username @ctisik, Candaş Tolga Işık, stated the following in their tweet: “Let me tell you a fact about Turkey before March 8: The municipal cinema in Kozan, where Halis Serbest lives, who killed Bergen, suddenly stopped broadcasting the Bergen movie today! The riot police came to the premiere of the movie in Istanbul. Producers who receive death threats live with bodyguards (see Figure. 10.)” 180 of these comments are criticism of the applied censorship, 6 of them are supportive of the applied censorship, 9 of them are neutral, 14 of them are not related to the topic, and the rest are comments on other user’s comments. The tweet received 56,043 likes, 719 quoted tweets, and 7,044 retweets. Candaş Tolga Işık, who has fewer followers than the other Twitter accounts examined, has more interaction coming to his tweet than the others. Considering the comments on Işık’s tweet, such blocking of a movie in the place specified as the murderer’s hometown has been associated with the murderer’s former mafia relations. Criticism of the situation is made clear with the language preferred by the user, the exclamation mark used, and the blaming phrases in the sentences used. Candaş Tolga Işık continues his thoughts by commenting again under this tweet. The user expressed the following statement this time: “I just called Kozan Mayor Kazım Özgan and said, ‘Why was the movie that was booked 1 month ago suddenly removed from the vision the day it was released?’ I asked. ‘It was deemed appropriate,’ he said. Mr. President did not give any other answer despite all my insistence. (see Figure 11).”

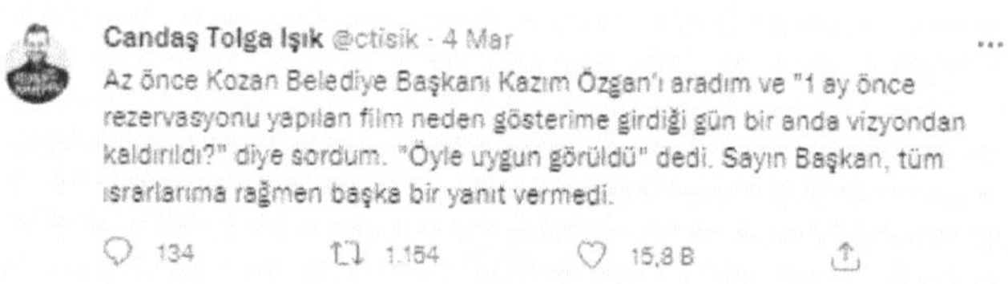

Figure 11. Screenshot showing Candaş Tolga Işık’s other comment from his account under the username @cisik on March 4, 2022.

This tweet, which he wrote in response to his previous tweet, received half the attention of the former tweet. The vast majority of followers indicate their thoughts on the subject by liking both of the tweets. The second biggest group show their support to the person by quoting the tweet. The interaction option of the tweet that has the least amount of interaction in both of Işık’s tweets is the comment option. In the comment section, users especially focus on certain topics such as censorship, femicide, mafia, and murder.

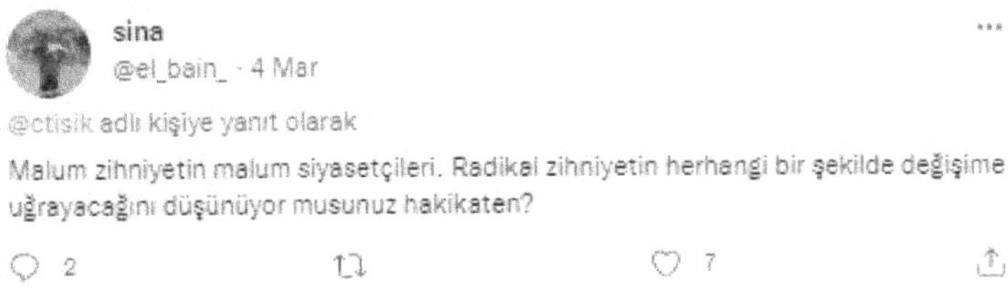

Figure 12. Screenshot showing the response of user @el_bain_ to the comment made by Candaş Tolga Işık from his account under the username @cisik on March 4, 2022.

In addition, unlike other Twitter accounts discussed earlier, the ruling political party was intensely criticized in the comments made under Candaş Tolga Işık's Bergen tweet, as shown in Figure 12. The user with the username @el_bain_ has commented on Işık's tweet as follows: "Expected politicians of the known mentality. Do you really think there will be any change in the radical mentality?" Femicide and censorship are associated with the ruling party in Figure 12.

In his second tweet, Candaş Tolga Işık states that he has communicated with the Mayor of Kozan and adds the answers of the mayor. In that tweet, unlike his first tweet, Işık doesn't make a personal comment on the topic. Işık, who took a biased stance by referring to International Women's Day with the words March 8 at the beginning of his first tweet, preferred to use language that is far from personal comments while using his journalist identity to prove the accuracy of the news in his second tweet.

When the tweets about the banning of the Bergen movie which was made by 5 accounts, 3 corporate and 2 individual, and the comments under it are examined, these tweets can be associated with the Fourth Wave feminist movement's utilization of social media to criticize the patriarchal system and to make women's problems visible. The user @CNN_YMN has used the following statement, similar to Figure 13: "There is no need to make big sentences about women's rights. Even this event is enough to show the hypocrisy of the dominant masculine mentality in the country, and even increases." Many tweets similar to this example have been shared to criticize the bans on the Bergen film and its connection with the patriarchal system.

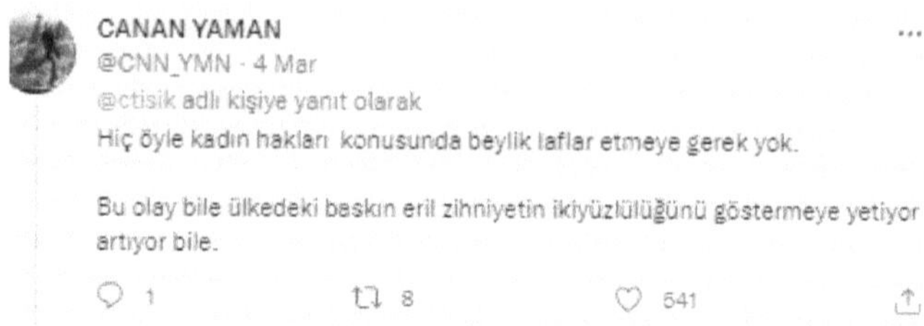

Figure 13. Screenshot of @CNN_YMN's comment.

In particular, Bergen's murder and the subsequent ban of the movie in the murderer's hometown was heavily criticized. When the responses of different Twitter users to these tweets from the 5 Twitter accounts mentioned earlier were analyzed, the mass response to the ban can be considered as a digital activist movement. Most of the users criticize the cancellation of the screening of the film and state that this cancellation is a kind of censorship. In addition, it was heavily criticized that violence against women was repeated with this censorship practice. When we look at the comments under the tweets, there are certain changes in the comments and criticisms according to the ideological perspectives of the 5 accounts that tweeted about the ban. Under the tweet of the official account of the newspaper Sözcü, which opposes the ruling party of the period, it can be seen that users heavily associate the femicide and censorship with the ruling party. Increasing femicide, the repeal of the Istanbul Convention, and the fact that this movie which is about femicide was not screened in the hometown of the murderer are associated with the ruling party. The majority of the comments under the tweet posted by journalist Candaş Tolga Işık, who is known for his oppositional attitudes, are about criticism of the ruling party. It is emphasized that the censorship applied to the film stems from the ruling government and that violence against women increased during this government's ruling period. It is seen that the comments on violence against women and femicides are predominant in the tweets of NTV Culture and Arts and BBC News Turkey accounts.

The tweets that are supportive of the ban are very few compared to the tweets that criticize the censorship. The majority of the support tweets are sent under the tweet of Kozan Mayor, where the screening of the film was banned. Excluding the support or anti-censorship tweets, it is stated in some of the tweets that this news of banning are related to the promotional campaign of the movie. Twitter users who make such comments are more than those who tweet in support of censorship.

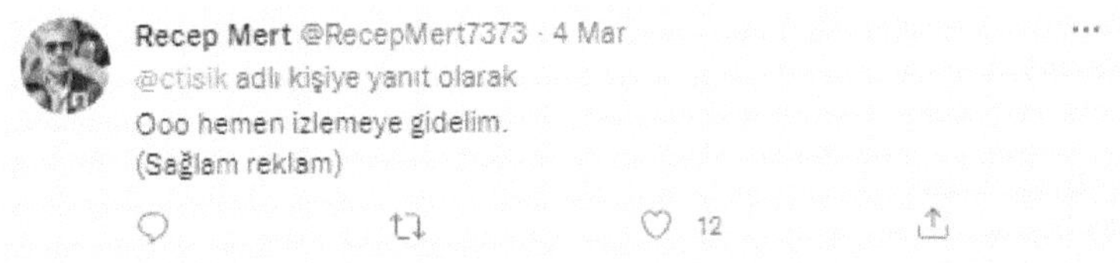

Figure 14. Screenshot of @RecepMert7373's comment.

In the comments section of the 5 Twitter accounts examined in this study, tweets under Candaş Tolga Işık's tweet, which perceive the ban as a marketing strategy, can be observed, as shown in Figure 14. This figure like, A user named @ RecepMert7373 commented, "Let's go watch now. (nice name)". The high number of likes on such tweets show that this idea is accepted by certain audiences. Comments agreeing with this idea that it is a marketing trick used to attract the audience to the film were evaluated under the title of irrelevant because they did not have any positive or negative implications for the censorship applied.

Table 2. Tabular form of data

Categories	Number	Frequency (%)
Support for Censorship	16	2,65
Criticism of Censorship	540	89,70
Unbiased	17	2,82
Irrelevant	29	4,81
TOTAL	602	

In the comments section of the 5 Twitter accounts examined in this study, tweets under Candaş Tolga Işık's tweet, which perceive the ban as a marketing strategy, can be observed, as shown in Figure 14. This figure like, A user named @RecepMert7373 commented, "Let's go watch now. (nice name)". and only 16 supported censorship. In addition, there were 17 unbiased and 29 irrelevant tweets in the comments. The intense reaction for the *Bergen* movie on the digital platform and the criticism of many particular Twitter users shows that this reaction is a digital activist movement. A large audience criticized the censorship applied to the film via digital media. As a result of these criticisms and digital activist movement, the Mayor had to make a public statement. In addition, the fact that majority of the comments coming under the 5 Twitter accounts' tweets are about femicide and the woman's voice being turned down can be interpreted as that this reaction is a digital activist movement of Fourth wave feminist movement.

4. Conclusion

Turkish cinema has been exposed to certain forms of censorship in the past. Sometimes more strictly sometimes more relaxed. In this study, 5 different tweet accounts' tweets and the comments below them which were posted on the Twitter platform in Turkey after the Bergen movie was banned from the screening in the Kozan district by the decision of the Mayor of Kozan, were examined. First of all, the number of tweets that support and oppose the censorship were determined. When the tweets on the banning of the *Bergen* movie which were posted from 3 corporate and 2 personal Twitter accounts were analyzed different data were obtained. According to this examination; the form of discourse changes depending on whether the accounts that send the relevant tweets are corporate or individual accounts and their ideological stances. In addition, the comment tweets that come under these tweets vary according to the ideological views of the account.

In this study, tweets sent between 04.03.2022 and 14.03.2022 regarding the banning of the Bergen movie were analyzed using van Djik's discourse analysis method in the context of the digital activist movement. The comments under the analyzed tweets were categorized as support for censorship, criticism for censorship, undecided and irrelevant. 602 comments that are made under 5 tweets were examined and placed in one of these categories. The tweets of 3 corporate accounts are in the form of a news title that introduces the incident and direct the followers to the news page. Tweets from 2 personal accounts are formed in a language that is more open to interpretation.

Looking at the comments below the 5 tweets posted, the number of tweets criticizing the censorship of the *Bergen* movie is by far the highest with 89.70 %. While making this criticism, it is emphasized that this practice is a kind of censorship. Almost all tweets criticizing censorship talk about femicide and violence against women. In addition, the criticism tweets mainly emphasize that this practice took place in Kozan because Kozan is the hometown of Halis Serbest, who murderer Bergen. Criticism of the censorship is heavily concentrated under the tweets that was sent by Twitter accounts which stand in opposition to the current ruling government. In these comments, it is stated that femicides are in line with the policies carried out by the current government and that the murderer is protected with the censorship applied.

Only 2.65 % of the comments made to the 5 tweets justify and side with the censorship. They defend this justification in line with the statement made by the Mayor of Kozan. Censorship is supported by comments that the film contains violence and that it will negatively affect society. 10 of the 16 censorship supporting comments came to the tweet posted by the Kozan Mayor. When the accounts were examined, it was determined that individuals who were ideologically close to the Mayor and followed him tweeted in support of censorship.

While 2.82 % of the comments under 5 tweets are neutral, 4.61 % are irrelevant. The vast majority of unbiased tweets are that this news is an advertising campaign. Although the mayor of the aforementioned district has confirmed the authenticity of the information mentioned and has stated his reason, it is insisted by the neutral section that this news are aimed at increasing the audience of the movie. 29 comment tweets under the 5 main tweets have nothing to do with the topic and users tweet to increase their own followers.

Against the censorship applied by Kozan Municipality for the *Bergen* movie, individuals criticized the situation on Twitter. It is seen, based on the likes and comments coming to the tweets about the banning of the *Bergen* movie from the 5 Twitter account with high number of followers, majority of the users criticize the censorship. Individual user accounts have brought criticism, that is, a digital activist attitude, to the situation through the accounts they have created on the Twitter platform to display an attitude against the current situation.

Fourth Feminist Wave, that is, Digital Feminism, aims to make women's struggles more visible through digital platforms and social networks and aims to legitimize the presence of women in the public sphere. As Sandoval stated, through the hashtags used on Twitter, women are provided with the opportunity to raise their voices by distinguishing themselves from class and social differences. The reaction to the 5 Twitter accounts' tweets about the banning of the *Bergen* movie in Bergen's murderer's hometown shows us that this online reaction is a digital feminist movement. Digital feminism walks on the same path as digital activism and they feed from each other. For this reason, the tweets posted over the banning of the *Bergen* movie are an example of digital activism as well as an example of Digital Feminism.

References

Altun, A., Gencel Bek, M., & Altun, E. (2007). Aile İçi Şiddet Haberlerinin Üretim Süreci ve Medya Profesyonelleri. *İletişim Araştırmaları Dergisi*, 5(2), 9–61.

Bergen. (2022, 29 June). Box Office: https://boxofficeturkiye.com/film/bergen--2015133.

Bergen kimdir? Acıların Kadını Bergen'in trajik hayat hikayesi. (2022, 29 June). Hürriyet: https://www.hurriyet.com.tr/galeri-bergen-kimdir-acilarin-kadini-bergenin-trajik-hayat-hikayesi-40801357/23.

Budgeon, S. (2011). *Third-Wave Feminism and the Politics of Gender in Late Modernity*. Houndmills: Palgrave Macmillan.

Bülbül, R. (2001). *Haberin Anatomisi ve Temel Yaklaşımlar*. İstanbul: Atlas Press.

Donovan, J. (2001). *Feminist Teori*. İstanbul: İletişim Yayınevi.

Dursun, Ç. (2010). Kadına Yönelik Şiddet Karşısında Haber Etiği. *Fe Dergi*, 2(1), 9–32.

Elkin, F. (1962). Censorship and Pressure Groups. *Phylon*, 21(1), 71–80.

Hook, B. (2000). *Feminism Is for Everybody Passionate Politics*. Cambridge: South End Press.

Hooks, B. (1981). *Ain't I a Woman: Black Women, and Feminism*. Boston: South End Press.

İnuğur, N. (2002). *Basın ve Yayın Tatihi*. İstanbul: Der Press.

Kadın Cinayetlerini Durduracağız Platformu 2021 Yıllık Veri Raporu. (2022, 29 July). Kadın Cinayetlerini Durduracağız Platformu: https://kadincinayetlerinidurduracagiz.net/veriler/3003/kadin-cinayetlerini-durduracagiz-platformu-2021-yillik-veri-raporu.

Kaiser, S. B. (2012). *Fashion and Cultural Studies*. London.: Berg Publishers.

Kaya, Ş. (2018). Kadın ve Sosyal Medya. *Gaziantep University Journal of Social Sciencess*, 17(2), 563–576.

Knappe, H., & Lang, S. (2014). Between Whisper and Voice: Online Women's Movement Outreach in the UK and Germany. *European Journal of Women's Studies*, 21(4), 361–381.

Mitchel, J. (1985). *Kadınlık Durumu* (Çev. G. İnal) İstanbul: Kadın Çevresi Yayınları.

Mitchel, J., & Oakley, A. (1998). *Kadın ve Eşitlik* (Trans. F. Berkta,) İstanbul: Pencere Yayınları.

Onaran, A. Ş. (1968). *Sinematografik Hürriyet*. Ankara: Gürsoy Basımevi.

Öngören, M. T. (1979). Türk Sinemasının Sorunları. *Kurgu Anadolu Üniversitesi İletişim Bilimleri Fakültesi Uluslar arası Hakemli İletişim Dergisi*, 1(1), 23–79.

Özgüç, A. (1976). *Türk Sineması Sansür Dosyası*. İstanbul: Koza Press.

Özön, N. (1970). *İlk Türk Sinemacu Fuat Uzkınay*. İstanbul: Türk Sinematek Derdeği Press.

Özuyar, A. (2004). *Babıali'de Sinema*. İstanbul: İzdüşüm Press.

Person, R. E., & Simpson, P. (2001). *Critical Dictionary of Film and Television Theory*. London: Routledge.

Sandoval, C. (2000). *Methodology of the Oppressed*. Minneapolis: University of Minnesota Press.

Sevim, A. (2005). *Feminizm*. İstanbul: İnsan Press.

Taş, G. (2016). Feminizm Üzerine Genel Bir Değerlendirme: Kavramsal Analizi, Tarihsel Süreçleri ve Dönüşümleri. *The Academic Elegance*, 3(5), 163–1753.

Tatar, M. (1979). *Türkiye'de Film ve Film Senaryoları Sansürü*. Ankara: Türkiye ve Ortadoğu Amme İdaresi Enstitüsü Kamu Yönetimi Lisans Üstü Uzmanlık Programı Tezi.

Tekvar, S. O. (2017). Türkiye'de Feminist Alternatif Medyanın İşlevselliği: Bir Alternatif Medya Örneği "Kadınların Postası" "Projesininİncelenmesi". *İnsan ve Toplum Bilimleri Araştırmaları Dergisi*, 6(1), 426–436.

Tişvek, Ö. (1968). *Mukayeseli Hukukta ve Türk Hukukunda Sinema Filmlerinin Sansürü*. İstanbul: İstanbul University Press.

Wollstonecraft, M. (2012). *Kadın Haklarının Gerçekleştirilmesi* (Trans. D. Hakyemez) İstanbul: Türkiye İş Bankası Kültür Press.

Asst. Prof. Orhan Faik[1]

Nomophobia triggered by digital activism and its place in academic studies

Abstract: In communication where technology plays a central role, new forms such as social platforms, e-mail and sites have emerged. Although technology offers some advantages to forms of communication, it has also given rise to the certain disadvantages. Nomophobia can be given as an example to this. This concept expresses the fear of being disconnected from communication provided by mobile phone. In this context, the research will encompass current situation of nomophobia as well as incorporating relevant studies on the subject. We will also examine results of internet and media use, which are thought to be used beyond their intended purpose in recent years, as well as the addiction of individuals who spend time on social media. Besides we will present information about today of digitalization and digital activism. Later we will examine and explain in detail how digital activism, which triggers nomophobia as a type of digital addiction, is produced through phones.

In the introduction of the study will incorporate a literature review on the concept of nomophobia. In addition, we will carry out a research on 78 theses on Nomophobia published in "YÖK Thesis" (Council of Higher Education Thesis Center). We will compile the number and percentage of theses published in 19 fields in the YÖK Thesis related to the concept. Additionally we will uncover the number and content of master's, doctoral and medical specialty studies. Moreover we will provide, the annual sharing indicator of research conducted in 19 areas related to nomophobia. In this context.

Keywords: Addiction, digital activism, nomophobia, activism, digital addict.

1. Introductıon

Individuals are becoming a part of digital activism by taking advantage of the opportunities provided by technology in our developing world. The internet, which was used passively at first, later has begun to be used actively by individuals. Thus, different types of content have emerged. Today, the increased speed of individuals in communicating has caused the interaction to be carried out and organized more quickly. The Internet and, accordingly, new media and technologies emerge as a new concept in the lives of individuals. However, they

1 Istanbul Arel University, Faculty of communication, New Media and Communication Department, orhanfaik@arel.edu.tr, ORCID: 0000-0003-4560-9007.

cause a number of changes, and increases individuals' addiction instincts. This type of addiction, which acts as a digital drug, acts with individuals throughout their lives and affects their lifestyle. Individualds now easilly get bored in an environment without digital technologies. Even if someone does not have it, they can travel close or long distances by relying on the technology that their close friends have with them. Otherwise, they may think that they will face with emptiness and fear of danger, and this fear seriously affects individuals during the entire time they are away from technology. The fear of staying away from technology and the feeling of not feeling well without technology suggest that the individual may be Nomophobic. It is possible to reveal whether an individual suffers from nomophobia or not by testing a series of experimental questions and physical movements.

The issue of digital addiction attracts the attention of researchers every day, and studies are carried out on where this addiction has evolved. The aim of our study is to interpret the emergence of the concept of Nomophobia, which emerged as a result of technology addiction in Turkey, what causes Nomophobia, which is the type of addiction brought by digitalization, and its dimensions by examining them in the context of interaction theory. Also, the aim of the study is to uncover the emotions of the individual as a part of society with the emergence of digitalization and to uncover whether individuals are affected by other individuals by revealing awareness. Digitalization highlights the relationships between the internet and the individual, revealing the connection between concepts that have turned into diseases.

In the study, we present information to the readers about the consequences of internet and media use, which are thought to be used beyond their intended purpose in recent years, as well as the addictions of individuals who spend time on social media. The aim of the study is to review the time that internet users unknowingly miss while online and to try to convey what needs to be done in the fight against nomophobia in the context of communication. In the research, we conducted a literature review on the concept of nomophobia, and examined the studies on nomophobia through theses published in 'YÖK Thesis'. In this context, we presented the ideas about the future of technology addiction and combating digital addiction. Research has been conducted on this day of digitalization, and a detailed analysis has been carried out on the current place and definition of digital activism.

1.2. Today of the digitalization and digital activism

It is seen that rapid breakthroughs have emerged in many areas with the development of digitalization. Communication and education are at the forefront of these developments. With the development of education, communication technologies are increasing day by day. Digitalization not only makes communication easier in every field, but also adds many innovations to the living standards of individuals. We can undoubtedly point to digitalization in communication as one of the revolutions of our digital age (Parlak, 2017: 1741). Although there is no clear idea about the future of digitalization of communication, there is no doubt that we will see more of the difference we see today when we compare the communication habits of twenty years ago with today's communication habits in the near future, in a few years.

Technology causes individual and social change. Change also causes the transformation of some old movements into new social movements. The reason for the change of old social movements, that is, the basis of their transformation into digital activism, is technology. Since digital activism has emerged as a new concept, a clear consensus has not been reached regarding its level of effectiveness, and there is no clear framework for its definition. In short, we can define digital activism as the use of digital technologies to cause social and political change. We can also define digital activism as using digital media to organize public campaigns by triggering social, political and economic change (Zinderen, 2021: 13–14).

Digital activism mobilizes the individual to participate in events, but this can also lead to addiction. For this reason, digital addiction as a type of addiction was further investigated and information on the subject was explained in the paragraph below.

1.3. Digital addiction as a type of addiction

Addiction can occur for many reasons. Although substance addiction is one of the most talked about and researched topics in the literature, technology addiction, internet addiction, in short, digital addiction are also among today's addiction issues. Against the feeling of boredom and loneliness caused by the daily routine, experts warn individuals to engage in hobbies suitable for them, such as theater and sports (Kılıç, 2016: 59). Researchers' support in the fight of society members against digital addiction can make the work even easier. As stated before, technological developments attract people of all ages to screens in our digitalizing world. When we say screen, the idea of only a television screen has disappeared. Phones and computers have started to take more place in memories. Content producers, who see that the number of people focusing on screens is increasing and try to turn this into an advantage, produce for individuals of all ages. It is seen that the competition is increasing day by day in order to attract more viewers to the screen and to direct the attention of a limited number of viewers to their own content. But there are two parties caught up in this competition. The first side is the producer side, and the second side is the consumer (Ertemel & Aydın, 2018: 666). Without realizing it, both parties fall into a digitally dependent situation. For this reason, one of the current issues of recent times is how this addiction should be reduced and how to get rid of the damages that addiction may cause more cheaply.

There are now new addictions in our lives, and they begin to take their place more deeply over time. As a result of technological developments, the factors that we think make our daily lives easier are now a part of our lives. Technologies and digital content production channels have progressed so much towards becoming a part of people that it seems that they have reached a level where people even accept their existence. We have started to feel incomplete without a computer, tablet, phone or TV screen on long journeys. Even when we do not have these digital technologies with us anymore, we display resentful attitudes towards the people around us and become unable to maintain communication physically. A study titled "The difference between gender in terms of nomophobia in Turkey: a meta-analysis" in 2022 revealed that women are more nomophobic than men, but it was stated in the study that applying nomophobia studies to different sample groups is important in determining the difference between genders. Digital equipment that triggers increasing technology addiction varies according to gender and the structure of society, as stated in the paragraphs above. Detailed research was conducted in the paragraph below on how smartphones and digital technologies trigger nomophobia and how this addiction could be combated.

1.4. Nomophobia triggered by smartphones and digital technologies

Smartphones, which were born with the addition of computer features to mobile phones, are also spreading rapidly around the world and today there are 6.92 billion smart mobile phones in the world compared to 7.33 billion mobile phones. This reveals that 86.11 % of the world owns smartphones, and it has been observed that there has been an increase of 36–37 % in smartphones in 7 years since 2016. According to the "Smartphone users 2022 by countries around the world" data published on Statista.com; While the country with the most smartphones in the world is China (more than 974 million), the top 5 after China are India (659 million), the United States (more than 276 million), Indonesia (more than 187 million), Brazil (more than 143 million) and Russia (more than 106 million). Turkey ranks 15th after Vietnam with 64 million smartphone users. In African countries with large populations, such as Egypt, Kenya, Ethiopia, Congo, Tanzania and Nigeria, smartphone usage is still far behind these figures. However, today the difference between mobile phone owners and smartphone owners has decreased to 5 %, indicating that almost everyone will have a smartphone in a few years.

The fact that smartphones can do many things that computers can do directs people to use smartphones more than computers. In addition to the fact that old mobile phones only allow making calls and messaging, smart phones can be connected to the internet, provide news from the world 24/7, allow receiving and sharing information, play games online or through applications, take photos and videos, send e-mails, etc. In addition to the convenience they provide in daily tasks such as being able to use office programs, smartphones can cause psychological harm to individuals at a level that can lead to phobia.

The concept of nomophobia, which we can briefly describe as the phobia of being deprived of smartphones, first emerged in 2008 with a survey conducted by the United Kingdom Post Office with 2100 mobile users. As a result of this study, which is also important as it is the first research on mobile phone addiction, it was revealed that approximately 53 % of people in the United Kingdom experience a constant and irrational fear of being disconnected from their mobile devices. More than half of the people who participated in the research stated that they could never turn off their phones for this reason, and one in ten people stated that having their phones turned off caused them anxiety because they felt the need to be constantly reachable. Experts also revealed that 48 % of women and 58 % of men among the participants in the research experienced this feeling of anxiety, and the situations that gave the participants a feeling of anxiety were; They found that this happens when they run out of charge or credit, lose their phone, or are out of network coverage. Later, another study conducted by the British mobile phone company SecurEnvoy in 2012 revealed that 66 % of the population suffers from nomophobia and that people experiencing nomophobia experience stress similar to the level of stress experienced when going to the dentist.

People with nomophobia may also feel restless and anxious when their phones are not with them or when their batteries are about to run out. Apart from these symptoms, some symptoms are commonly observed in people suffering from nomophobia.

These are:

- Anxiety (anxiety disorder)
- Respiratory changes such as shortness of breath
- Tachycardia (increased heart rate)

- Sweating
- Agitation
- Tremors
- Disorientation.

Apart from these common symptoms, people;

- Nausea
- Dizziness
- Feeling of discomfort
- Panic and fear
- Symptoms.

Additionally, individuals who experience excessive stress, low self-confidence, poor social relationships, spend an extensive amount of time online, suffer from anxiety (particularly social anxiety disorder), struggle to maintain social connections, have a traumatic experience of being without a mobile phone, or have family members who suffer from nomophobia are more likely to develop nomophobia.

2. Findings of the research

In the research, we examined 78 theses published in YÖK National Thesis Center. These theses were catogrized into 19 fields. The fields are as follows:

- Expertise in Medicine,
- Physiotherapy and Rehabilitation,
- Health Management,
- Sports,
- Psychology,
- Science and Technology,
- Education and Training,
- Journalism,
- Public Relations,
- Public Health,
- Business,
- Nursing,
- Tourism,
- Family Medicine,
- Psychiatry,
- Sociology,

- Religion,
- Labor and Industrial Relations,
- Communication Sciences.

When we examined the distribution of theses written within the framework of these fields by year, we encountered the following Table 1:

Table 1. Number and Percentage of Studies Conducted on the Subject of Nomophobia in the National Thesis Center.

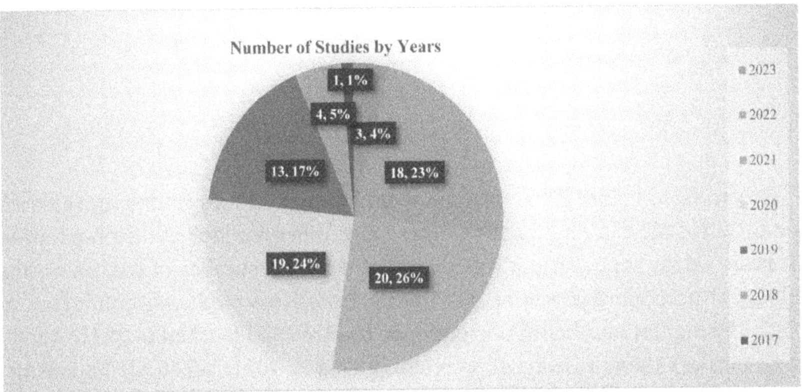

As seen in Figure 1, thesis studies on nomophobia started in 2017. However, only 1 study was conducted in 2017. If we give information about the content of the study, the research was a master's degree research in the field of Science and Technology. The most studies on the subject were found in 2021. On this date, 20 theses were written in Turkey, 16 of which were master's degrees, 2 were doctoral studies, and 2 were medical specialization studies. The research conducted in 2017 constitutes 1 % of the overall thesis studies, and a total of 20 studies conducted in 2021 constitute 26 %.

When we look at the place of graduate studies among general research on the subject of nomophobia, we encountered he following Table 2:

Table 2. Number and Percentage of Master's Theses on the Subject of Nomophobia

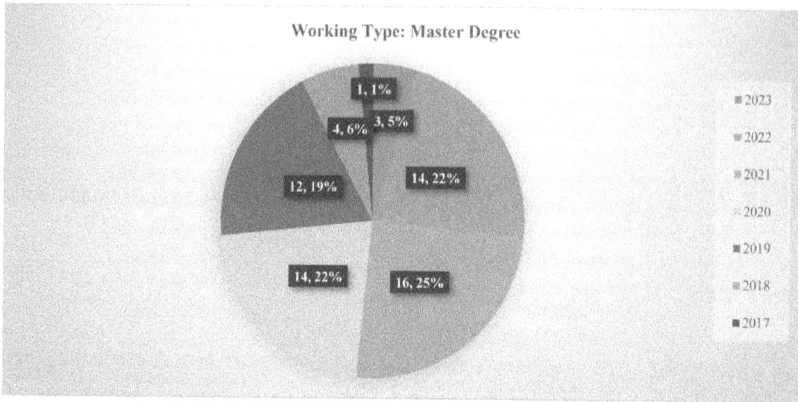

According to Figure 2, the total number of master's theses among the research conducted at the National Thesis Center is 78. When we look at the preparation of theses on an annual basis, it is seen that the least number of studies on the subject of nomophobia was in 2017. Only 1 thesis research was conducted in 2017. The highest number of postgraduate research was reached in 2021. A total of 16 master's thesis researches were conducted in 2021. When we look at the percentage, we see that the rate is 1 % with at least 1 number and 25 % with a maximum of 16 numbers.

When we reviewed the doctoral theses made at the National Thesis Center, we encountered the following Table 3:

Table 3. Doctoral Theses Made at the National Thesis Center on Nomophobia

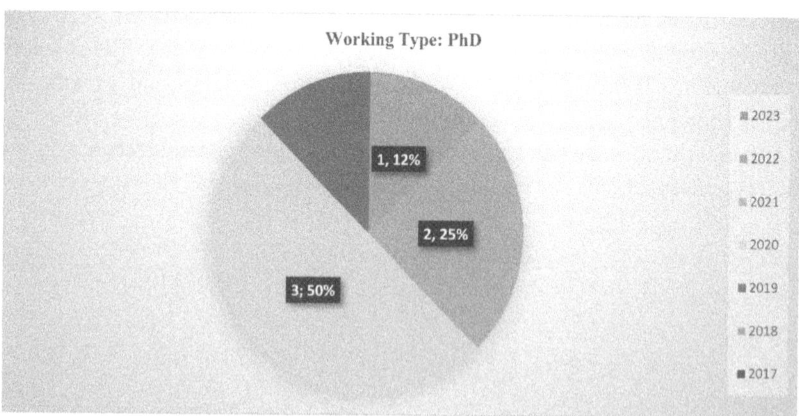

According to the research conducted at the National Thesis Center on the subject, a total of 6 studies were conducted on the subject of nomophobia. Among these studies, 3 studies conducted in 2022 constitute 50 % of the general doctoral theses. In 2021, 2 doctoral studies were carried out and this number constitutes 33 % of the total doctoral studies. When we examine the doctoral thesis studies conducted in 2020, we see that only 1 research was conducted. This constitutes 17 % of overall doctoral thesis studies. It has been that the subject of nomophobia, which has been included in thesis research as literature in Turkey since 2017, has been studied 6 times in total in the last 7 years. Notably the subject of nomophobia was absent from doctoral theses in 2023, 2019, 2018 and 2017.

When we examined the Medical Specialization studies at the National Thesis Center on the subject, we encountered the data in the Table 4 below:

Table 4. Number and Percentage of Studies Conducted in the National Thesis Center in the Field of Medical Specialization on the Subject of Nomophobia

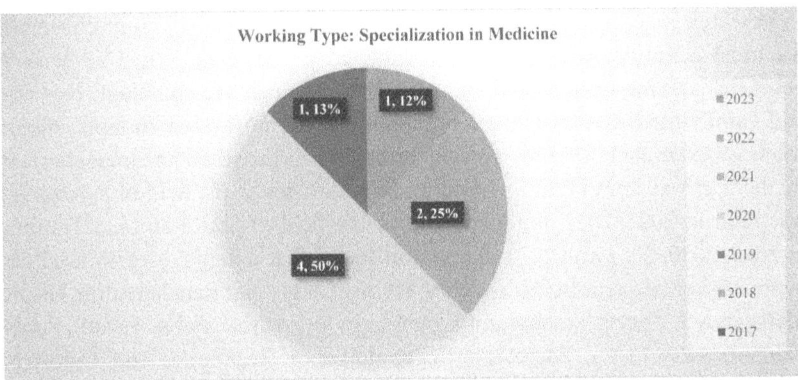

In the research conducted in the field of Medical Specialization on Nomophobia at the National Thesis Center, we saw that a total of 8 studies were conducted. It was found that 50 % of the studies were carried out in 2020. On this date, 4 studies were conducted in the field of medical specialization. Among the general studies on the field, 2 studies were conducted in 2021, 1 in 2022, and 1 in 2019.

When we look at the distribution of the studies conducted at the National Thesis Center on the subject of nomophobia by years, we can see the following graph:

Table 5. Annual Sharing Indicator of Studies Conducted at the National Thesis Center on the Subject of Nomophobia within 19 Fields

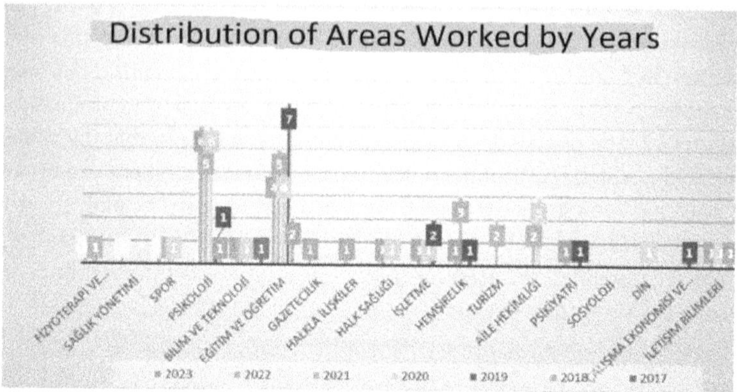

Research reveals that in 2022, the field of Education and Training received the most attention, with 7 studies conducted in this area. When we look at other fields, it has been seen that studies in fields such as Psychology, Nursing, and Family Medicine have made nomophobia the most research topic. Again, when we examined the content of the research conducted on an annual basis in the field, it was found that the number of researches in the field of Psychology was high in 2022, 2021 and 2020, and in the field of Education and Training in 2019, 2020, 2021 and 2022. It was also found that a thesis research has been conducted once a year in fields such as Physiotherapy and Rehabilitation, Health Management, Sports, Science and Technology, Journalism, Public Health, Public Relations, Psychiatry, Sociology, Religion, Labor Economics and Industrial Relations, and Communication Sciences.

3. Conclusion

As a result of the literature review conducted specifically focusing on the theses stored in the YÖK National Thesis Center on nomophobia, it was found that the subject is relatively new and has been included in the thesis contents of universities as of 2017. It was found that the subejct has been studied in both master's and doctoral theses, and is also the subject of Medical Specialization research in the field of health. At the same time, when examining academic articles addressing nomophobia, it is evident that the studies are mostly conducted on students and young people.

Nomophobia is among the new research studies conducted in Turkey and is also among the issues that will be examined for the future. According to the data obtained, the subject has been studied 78 times as thesis research in Turkey. These studies include Medical Specialization, Physiotherapy and Rehabilitation, Health Management, Sports, Psychology, Science and Technology, Education and Training, Journalism, Public Relations, Public Health, Business, Nursing, Tourism, Family Medicine, Psychiatry, Sociology, Religion, Labor and Industry. It was observed that research has been conducted in 19 fields, including Relationships and Communication Sciences. 20 of the total 78 theses were conducted in 2021 and were recorded as the highest number in the distribution of research on this subject by year. 16 of the 20 theses made in 2021 are master's theses. The total number of master's theses on nomophobia is 64. While only one study was conducted on the subject in 2017, it appears that the most studies were conducted in 2021. In 2021, there were a total of 16 master's theses on the subject.

In the research conducted on the subject, we see that the number of doctorates in the YÖK National Thesis Center is 6. The date when nomophobia was most researched as a doctoral thesis is 2022 and the number is 3. It was found that no research on the subject was conducted in doctoral theses in 2023, 2019, 2018 and 2017. A total of 8 studies were conducted in the field of Medical Specialization. When we look at the results of the research conducted on the fields, it was revealed that a total of 19 studies were conducted on Education and Training. It was also observed that studies in fields such as Psychology, Nursing, and Family Medicine have made nomophobia the subject of most research. It was found that the number of researches in the field of Psychology is high in 2022, 2021 and 2020, and in the field of Education and Training in 2019, 2020, 2021 and 2022.

Finally, it is possible to see that the issue of nomophobia has recently begun to be researched frequently as a type of addiction in Turkey. It is examined further as a master's thesis. It should be noted that there are researches in the form of medical specialization and doctoral thesis. Examining the subject in other academic studies may add value to the field. It would be beneficial to examine nomophobia as a type of addiction in more detail in the field of communication.

References

Avcı, E. (2022). The Difference between Gender in Terms of Nomophobia in Turkey: A Meta-analysis. *The European Research Journal*, 74–83.

Avicenna. (2020, Eylül 17). Nomofobi: Nedir, Belirtileri ve Tedavisi. Avicenna: https://avicennaint.com/nomofobi/.

Bahl, R. R., & DeIuliis, D. (2019, Ocak 4). Substance Abuse and Addiction: Breakthroughs in Research and Practice. *Nomophobia* (I. R. Association, Dü.). https://doi.org/10.4018/978-1-5225-7666-2.ch015.

Bankmycell. (2023, Temmuz 15). How Many Smartphones Are in the World? Bankmycell: https://www.bankmycell.com/blog/how-many-phones-are-in-the-world adresinden alındı.

Bhattacharya, S., Bashar, M. A., Srivastava, A., & Singh, A. (2019). Nomophobia: No Mobile Phone Phobia. *Journal of Family Medicine and Primary Care*, 1297–1300.

Ertemel, A. V., & Aydın. G. (2018). Dijital Ekonomide Teknoloji Bağımlılığı ve Çözüm Önerileri. *Addıcta: The Turkısh Journal On Addıctıons*, 5(4), 666–667.

Mailonline. (2008). Nomophobia İs the Fear of Being Out of Mobile Phone Contact – And İt's the Plague of Our 24/7 Age. Mailonline: Retrieved from. https://www.dailymail.co.uk/news/article-550610/Nomophobia-fear-mobile-phone-contact--plague-24-7-age.html

Murphy, N. (2023, Mayıs 4). What Is Nomophobia? CPD Online College: Retrieved from. https://cpdonline.co.uk/knowledge-base/care/what-is-nomophobia/

Parlak, B. (2017). Dijital Çağda Eğitim: Olanaklar Ve Uygulamalar Üzerine Bir Analiz. *Süleyman Demirel, Üniversitesi İktisadi ve İdari Bilimler Fakültesi Dergisi*, 22(15), 1741.

Statista. (2023, Temmuz 15). Number of Smartphone Users by Leading Countries in 2022. Statista: Retrieved from. https://www.statista.com/statistics/748053/worldwide-top-countries-smartphone-users/

Statista. (2023, Temmuz 25). Statista Technology & Telecommunications. Statista: Retrieved from. https://www.statista.com/statistics/218984/number-of-global-mobile-users-since-2010/#:~:text=In%202021%2C%20the%20number%20of,projected%20to%20reach%207.49%20billion

Zinderen, A. (2021). *Dijital Sosyoloji Çalışmaları* (s.13–14). Ankara: Nobel Akademik Yayıncılık

Kılıç, F. S. (2016). Bağımlılık ve Uyarıcı Maddeler. *Osmangazi Tıp Dergisi*, 38(1), 59.

Annex-1: The theses used in the research are as in the appendix

Theses:
Adıgüzel, A. (2018). Üniversite öğrencilerinde gündemi kaçırma korkusu, problemli akıllı telefon kullanımı, problemli internet kullanımı ve yaşantısal kaçınmanın cep telefonu bağlantısını kaybetme korkusuna yönelik modelin sınanması Muğla ili örneği. *Yüksek Lisans Tezi*, 121. Muğla Sıtkı Koçman Üniversitesi Eğitim Bilimleri Enstitüsü.
Ağduk, S. (2021). Nomofobinin OKÜ İİBF öğrencilerinin demografik özellikleri ve akademik başarıları ile olan ilişkisinin incelenmesi. *Yüksek Lisans Tezi*, 177. Osmaniye Korkut Ata Üniversitesi Sosyal Bilimler Enstitüsü.
Akhoroz, M. (2019). Examining the relationship between personality traits and nomophobia among preservice teachers. *Yüksek Lisans Tezi*, 71. Orta Doğu Teknik Üniversitesi Fen Bilimleri Enstitüsü.
Akın, H. M. (2021). İntörn hemşirelik öğrencilerinde nomofobi ve aleksitimi ilişkisinin değerlendirilmesi. *Yüksek Lisans Tezi*, 95. Atatürk Üniversitesi Sağlık Bilimleri Enstitüsü.
Aktaş, Y. (2019). Nomofobi düzeylerinin yaşam doyumu ve iş performansı üzerindeki etkisi: Kütahya kent merkezinde bir uygulama. *Yüksek Lisans Tezi*, 144. Kütahya Dumlupınar Üniversitesi Sosyal Bilimler Inst..
Al, A. F. (2021). Sağlık çalışanlarında iş tatmin düzeyi ile nomofobi ve sosyal medya bağımlılığı ilişkisinin değerlendirilmesi. *Tıpta Uzmanlık*, 70. Sağlık Bilimleri Üniversitesi Gaziosmanpaşa Taksim Eğitim ve Araştırma Hastanesi.
Altan, B. (2019). Nomofobi ile aleksitimi arasındaki ilişkide bilinçli farkındalık ve üst bilişin aracı rolünün incelenmesi. *Yüksek Lisans Tezi*, 91. İstanbul Aydın Üniversitesi Sosyal Bilimler Inst..
Arslan, B. (2023). Belediye ofis çalışanlarının nomofobi düzeylerinin, üst ekstremite fiziksel performansı, sosyal kaygı ve iş performansına olan etkisinin incelenmesi. *Yayınlanmamış Yüksek Lisans Tezi*, 88. Muğla Sıtkı Koçman Üniversitesi Sağlık Bilimleri Inst..
Atan, İ. B. (2020). Telefondan uzak kalma korkusunun (Nomofobi) hayat memnuniyeti ve dini yönelim ile ilişkisine dair bir araştırma. *Yüksek Lisans Tezi*, 114. Marmara Üniversitesi Sosyal Bilimler Enstitüsü.

Theses:
Ataş, M. (2021). Ergenlerin mobil telefonsuz kalma korkusu (nomofobi), stresle başa çıkabilme ve algılanan sosyal destek düzeyleri arasındaki ilişkinin incelenmesi. *Yüksek Lisans Tezi*, 145. Necmettin Erbakan Üniversitesi Eğitim Bilimleri Enstitüsü.
Avcı, S. (2020). Öğretmenlerin nomofobi düzeylerinin sosyodemografik değişkenler açısından incelenmesi. *Yüksek Lisans Tezi*, 82. Çağ Üniversitesi Sosyal Bilimler Enstitüsü.
Ay, J. (2021). Üniversite öğrencilerinde nomofobi, dijital oyun bağımlılığı ve internet bağımlılığı arasındaki ilişkinin incelenmesi. *Yüksek Lisans Tezi*, 73. Üsküdar Üniversitesi Sağlık Bilimleri Enstitüsü.
Aydın, K. (2022). Üniversite öğrencilerinin nomofobi ve netlessfobi düzeylerinin ilşkisel desen ile incelenmesi. *Doktora Tezi*, 272. Atatürk Üniversitesi Sosyal Bilimler Enstitüsü.
Bal, S. (2023). Sporun nomofobi, netlessfobi, internet bağımlılığı ve gelişmeleri kaçırma korkusu üzerine etkisi. *Yüksek Lisans Tezi*, 100. Yozgat Bozok Üniversitesi Lisansüstü Eğitim Enstitüsü.
Bayrak, B. (2017). İstanbul'da bir grup ergen üzerinde cep telefonundan ayrı kalma korkusu (Nomofobi), bağlanma özellikleri, ruhsal ve davranışsal sorunlar arasındaki ilişkinin incelenmesi. *Yüksek Lisans Tezi*, 79. İstanbul Aydın Üniversitesi Sosyal Bilimler Enstitüsü.
Bilkay, S. (2020). Pozitif psikolojik sermayenin çalışanların ilişki ağı kurma yeteneği üzerindeki etkisinde nomofobinin düzenleyici rolü: Havacılık sektöründe bir araştırma. *Doktora Tezi*, 217. İstanbul Arel Üniversitesi Sosyal Bilimler Enstitüsü.
Büyükalim, M. (2020). Üniversite öğrencilerinde genel aidiyet, nomofobi ve yaşam doyumu arasındaki yordayıcı ilişkiler. *Yüksek Lisans Tezi*, 106. Necmettin Erbakan Üniversitesi Eğitim Bilimleri Enstitüsü.
Büyükçolpan, H. (2019). Üniversite öğrencilerinde nomofobi, bağlanma biçimleri, depresyon ve algılanan sosyal destek. *Yüksek Lisans Tezi*, 119. Hacettepe Üniversitesi Eğitim Bilimleri Enstitüsü.
Can, D. (2022). Mobil telefon yoksunluğu korkusu (nomofobi) öncülleri üzerine bir araştırma. *Yüksek Lisans Tezi*, 96. Atatürk Üniversitesi Sosyal Bilimler Enstitüsü.

Theses:
Can, E. (2019). Nomofobi ile online satın alma davranışı ilişkisinde mobil ticaret kullanımının rolü. *Yüksek Lisans Tezi*, 123. Eskişehir Osmangazi Üniversitesi Sosyal Bilimler Enstitüsü.
Canatar, F. (2020). Nomofobi ve akıllı telefon bağımlılığının bağlanma stilleri, kimlik duygusu ve kişiler arası problemler açısından incelenmesi. *Yüksek Lisans Tezi*, 163. İstanbul Sabahattin Zaim Üniversitesi Lisansüstü Eğitim Enstitüsü.
Çakmakçı, B. (2022). Hemşirelik fakültesi öğrencilerinde nomofobi, depresyon ve psikolojik iyi oluş düzeyleri arasındaki ilişkinin incelenmesi. *Yüksek Lisans Tezi*, 73. Aydın Adnan Menderes Üniversitesi Sağlık Bilimleri Enstitüsü.
Çelik, A. G. (2022). Üniversite öğrencilerinde sosyal medya kullanımının ve nomofobinin beden imajı ve benlik saygısı ile ilişkisi. *Yüksek Lisans Tezi*, 110. İstanbul Gelişim Üniversitesi Lisansüstü Eğitim Enstitüsü.
Çelik, Y. S. (2022). Ergenlerde riskli akıllı telefon kullanımı ve ilişkili etkenler. *Tıpta Uzmanlık*, 144. Hacettepe Üniversitesi Tıp Fakültesi.
Çırak, M. (2021). Üniversite öğrencilerinde nomofobi: Dijital bağımlılık, sosyal bağlılık ve yaşam doyumunun rolü. *Yüksek Lisans Tezi*, 120. Hacettepe Üniversitesi Eğitim Bilimleri Enstitüsü.
Çolak, M. (2019). Ortaokul öğrencilerinin nomofobi düzeylerinin bazı değişkenler açısından incelenmesi. *Yüksek Lisans Tezi*, 67. Çanakkale Onsekiz Mart Üniversitesi Eğitim Bilimleri Enstitüsü.
Demirel, B. R. (2021). Hemşirelerde nomofobi ile sosyal iyilik hali arasındaki ilişki. *Yüksek Lisans Tezi*, 90. Sağlık Bilimleri Üniversitesi Gülhane Sağlık Bilimleri Enstitüsü.
Derinyar, T. (2022). Nomofobi, sosyal bağlılık ve yaşam doyumu ilişkisi: Beden eğitimi öğretmen adayları örneği. *Yüksek Lisans Tezi*, 78. Trabzon Üniversitesi Lisansüstü Eğitim Enstitüsü.
Doğrusoy, S. (2021). Online uygulanan çözüm odaklı kısa süreli psikolojik danışma programının nomofobi ile aleksitimi üzerine etkisinin incelenmesi. *Yüksek Lisans Tezi*, 72. Ufuk Üniversitesi Sağlık Bilimleri Enstitüsü.
Düner, Z. (2022). Üniversite öğrencilerinde aile aidiyeti ile nomofobi arasındaki ilişki: Fırat ve Medipol Üniversiteleri örneği. *Yüksek Lisans Tezi*, 71. Fırat Üniversitesi Sosyal Bilimler Enstitüsü.

Theses:
Ekşi, N. N. (2020). Öğretmenlerin nomofobi ve örgütsel hafıza düzeyleri arasındaki ilişki. *Yüksek Lisans Tezi*, 132. İstanbul Sabahattin Zaim Üniversitesi Sosyal Bilimler Enstitüsü.
Eldemir, S. (2021). Psikolojik ihtiyaçlar, bilinçli farkındalık ve nomofobi arasındaki ilişkinin incelenmesi. *Yüksek Lisans Tezi*, 70. Tokat Gaziosmanpaşa Üniversitesi Eğitim Bilimleri Enstitüsü.
Enez, Ö. (2021). Investigation of nomophobia and related psychological variables with cross-sectional and experience sampling methods: the effect of emotion dysregulation, affect, boredom, psychopathology, and social context. *Doktora Tezi*, 267. Ankara Yıldırım Beyazıt Üniversitesi Sosyal Bilimler Enstitüsü.
Er, S. (2021). Boyun ağrılı bireylerde ağrı şiddeti, özürlülük, postür, uyku kalitesi ve nomofobi arasındaki ilişki . *Yüksek Lisans Tezi*, 69. Bahçeşehir Üniversitesi Lisansüstü Eğitim Inst..
Erdoğan, Ş. N. (2021). Nomofobi ile dikkat eksikliği hiperaktivite bozukluğu belirtilerinin ilişkisi. *Tıpta Uzmanlık*, 83. Sağlık Bilimleri Üniversitesi Ankara Dışkapı Yıldırım Beyazıt Eğitim Ve Araştırma Hastanesi.
Ergin, Z. Ö. (2020). Lise öğrencilerinin nomofobi düzeylerini etkileyen faktörler. *Yüksek Lisans Tezi*, 127. Hacettepe Üniversitesi Eğitim Bilimleri Ins.
Ertan, G. (2019). Mobil telefonsuz kalma korkusunun (nomofobi) iş tatmini, işe bağlılık ve sosyal izolasyon üzerine etkisi. *Yüksek Lisans Tezi*, 144. Marmara Üniversitesi Sosyal Bilimler Enstitüsü.
Fırıncı, B. (2020). Akıllı telefon kullanımı ve nomofobinin uyku kalitesi ve gündüz uykululuk durumuna etkisinin incelenmesi: İnönü Üniversitesi örneği. *Tıpta Uzmanlık*, 126. İnönü Üniversitesi Tıp Fakültesi.
Göçü, Y. E. (2022). Ergenlerde nomofobi durumunun dikkat eksikliği ve hiperaktivite ile ilişkisi. *Yüksek Lisans Tezi*, 67. İstanbul Gelişim Üniversitesi Lisansüstü Eğitim Enstitüsü.
Göktaş, H. (2019). Lise öğrencilerinin akıllı telefon bağımlılığı, mobil telefon yoksunluğu korkusu (Nomofobi) ve akademik başarıları arasındaki ilişki. *Yüksek Lisans Tezi*, 110. Süleyman Demirel Üniversitesi Eğitim Bilimleri Enstitüsü.

Theses:
Gördağ, Ö. E. (2020). Trakya Üniversitesi araştırma görevlilerinde nomofobi ve nomofobiyi etkileyen faktörlerin araştırılması. *Tıpta Uzmanlık*, 141. Trakya Üniversitesi Tıp Fakültesi.
Gül, M. (2020). Akıllı telefondan uzak kalma korkusu (nomofobi) nun uyku ve yaşam kalitesi üzerine etkisinin değerlendirilmesi. *Tıpta Uzmanlık*, 87. Sağlık Bilimleri Üniversitesi İstanbul Haydarpaşa Numune Eğt. ve Arş. Hastanesi.
Günlü, A. (2021). Üniversite öğrencilerinde nomofobinin temel psikolojik ihtiyaçlar doyumu, öz kontrol ve duygu düzenleme değişkenleriyle modellenmesi. *Doktora Tezi*, 189. Dokuz Eylül Üniversitesi Eğitim Bilimleri Enstitüsü.
Güveli, R. (2022). Niğde ili çiftlik ilçesi'ndeki yetişkinlerin nomofobi, yalnızlık ve depresif belirti düzeyleri. *Doktora Tezi*, 116. Erciyes Üniversitesi Sağlık Bilimleri Enstitüsü.
Helvacıoğlu, H. N. (2022). Nomofobi, sosyal medya bağımlılığı ve psikolojik iyi oluş arasındaki ilişkinin incelenmesi: Z kuşağı üzerine bir araştırma. *Yüksek Lisans Tezi*, 134. Selçuk Üniversitesi Eğitim Bilimleri Enstitüsü.
İlik, F. Z. (2021). Konaklama işletmeleri çalışanlarının nomofobi düzeylerinin işe bağlılıklarına etkisinin belirlenmesi: Eskişehir örneği. *Yüksek Lisans Tezi*, 107. Anadolu Üniversitesi Sosyal Bilimler Enstitüsü.
Kabakcı, M. (2022). Üniversite öğrencilerinde akıllı telefondan yoksun kalma korkusu. *Yüksek Lisans Tezi*, 103. İstanbul Gelişim Üniversitesi Lisansüstü Eğitim Enstitüsü.
Kadıoğlu, G. (2022). Üniversite öğrencilerinde akıllı telefondan yoksun kalma korkusu (Nomofobi) ile sosyal bağlılık, sosyal onay ihtiyacı ve kişilerarası ilişki tarzları arasındaki ilişkinin incelenmesi. *Yüksek Lisans Tezi*, 120. Üsküdar Üniversitesi Sosyal Bilimler Enstitüsü.
Karadaş, T. (2020). Kredi ve Yurtlar Kurumunda kalan kız öğrencilerin dijital temas alışkanlıklarının incelenmesi. *Yüksek Lisans Tezi*, 100. Sivas Cumhuriyet Üniversitesi Eğitim Bilimleri Enstitüsü.
Karatay, S. (2018). Hyperconnectivity Kavramı Bağlamında Mobil Sosyal Medya Uygulamaları: Nomofobi ve Fomo Rahatsızlıklarına Yönelik Bir Araştırma. *Yüksek Lisans Tezi*, 127. İstanbul Üniversitesi Sosyal Bilimler Inst..

Theses:
Kars, A. (2020). Akıllı telefon bağımlılığı'nın (nomofobi) kişilerarası ilişkiler üzerindeki etkisinin incelenmesi: Atatürk Üniversitesi öğrencileri üzerinde bir araştırma. *Yüksek Lisans Tezi*, 134. Atatürk Üniversitesi Sosyal Bilimler Enstitüsü.
Koç, E. (2021). Yetişkinlerde ayrılma anksiyetesi ve nomofobi arasındaki ilişkinin incelenmesi. *Yüksek Lisans Tezi*, 91. İstanbul Gelişim Üniversitesi Lisansüstü Eğitim Enstitüsü.
Kuzu, M. (2020). Üniversite öğrencilerinin nomofobik profilleri ile rekreatif etkinliklere katılım düzeyinin farklı değişkenlerle karşılaştırılarak aralarındaki ilişkinin incelenmesi. *Yüksek Lisans Tezi*, 59. Çanakkale Onsekiz Mart Üniversitesi Sağlık Bilimleri Inst..
Meral, D. (2022). Ergenlerde nomofobinin yordanmasında gelişmeleri kaçırma korkusu, sosyal medya bağımlılığı ve aleksitiminin rolü. *Yüksek Lisans Tezi*, 169. Gazi Üniversitesi Eğitim Bilimleri Enstitüsü.
Orucoğlu, O. (2020). Üniversite öğrencilerinde akıllı telefon bağımlılığı, nomofobi ve yaşam doyumu arasındaki ilişkinin incelenmesi. *Yüksek Lisans Tezi*, 84. Üsküdar Üniversitesi Sosyal Bilimler Enstitüsü.
Öz, H. (2018). Üniversite okuyan genç yetişkinlerin mobil telefon yoksunluğu korkusu (nomofobi) ile kişilik tipleri arasındaki ilişkinin incelenmesi. *Yüksek Lisans Tezi*, 75. İstanbul Aydın Üniversitesi Sosyal Bilimler Enstitüsü.
Özbek, V. (2022). Lise öğrencilerinde farklı bağlanma stilleri ve yetiştirilme tutumlarının nomofobi düzeyleri ile ilişkileri ve duygu düzenleme becerilerinin bu değişkenler arasındaki biçimlendirici rolü. *Yüksek Lisans Tezi*, 110. İSTANBUL AYVANSARAY ÜNİVERSİTESİ Lisansüstü Eğitim Inst..
Özden, Ö. (2019). Üniversite öğrencilerinin nomofobi düzeyi ile psikolojik ihtiyaçların doyumu ve kişilik özellikleri arasındaki ilişkinin incelenmesi. *Yüksek Lisans Tezi*, 96. Atatürk Üniversitesi Eğitim Bilimleri Enstitüsü.
Özgöz, F. Z. (2020). Ondokuz Mayıs Üniversitesi Tıp fakültesi öğrencilerinde nomofobinin ayrılma anksiyetesi ve dürtüsellik ile ilişkisi. *Tıpta Uzmanlık*, 89. Ondokuz Mayıs Üniversitesi Tıp Fakültesi.
Özlü, B. N. (2020). Üniversite öğrencilerinde nomofobi ile sosyal anksiyete ve iletişim becerileri arasındaki ilişkinin incelenmesi. *Yüksek Lisans Tezi*, 86. Üsküdar Üniversitesi Sosyal Bilimler Enstitüsü.

Theses:
Öztürk, M. A. (2023). Sağlık çalışanlarında nomofobinin sanal kaytarma üzerindeki etkisi. *Yüksek Lisans Tezi*, 115. Atılım Üniversitesi Sosyal Bilimler Enstitüsü.
Saatçı, F. (2021). Üniversite öğrencilerinin nevrotik eğilimleriyle sosyotelizm düzeyleri arasındaki ilişkide gelişmeleri kaçırma korkusunun ve nomofobinin aracılık rolü. *Yüksek Lisans Tezi*, 110. Trabzon Üniversitesi Lisansüstü Eğitim Enstitüsü.
Sadan, Ş. (2022). Ortaöğretim öğrencilerinin psikolojik belirtilere göre nomofobi düzeylerinin yordanması. *Yüksek Lisans Tezi*, 92. Sakarya Üniversitesi Eğitim Bilimleri Enstitüsü.
Sülüngür, M. A. (2020). Üniversite öğrencilerinin nomofobi düzeylerinin, korku düzeyleri ve obsesif kompulsif yakınmalarının türü ve şiddeti arasındaki ilişkinin incelenmesi üzerine karşılaştırmalı bir araştırma . *Yüksek Lisans Tezi*, 117. Üsküdar Üniversitesi Sosyal Bilimler Enstitüsü.
Şeker, Ö. (2022). Examination of the relationship between high school students' strategies to cope with cyberbullying and the levels of nomophobia. *Yüksek Lisans Tezi*, 138. Yeditepe Üniversitesi Eğitim Bilimleri Enstitüsü.
Şengör, Y. (2020). İyi oluşun yordayıcıları olarak yalnızlık ve nomofobi. *Yüksek Lisans Tezi*, 113. Tokat Gaziosmanpaşa Üniversitesi Eğitim Bilimleri Enstitüsü.
Şimşek, K. (2019). Türkiye'de ortaöğretim öğrencilerinin akıllı telefon bağımlılık düzeyleri ve kullanım alışkanlıkları: Kahramanmaraş örneği. *Yüksel Lisans Tezi*, 150. Gazi Üniversitesi Eğitim Bilimleri Enstitüsü.
Tanır, G. (2021). Fiziksel aktivitenin teknoloji çağı hastalıkları netlessfobi ve nomofobi ile ilişkisi. *Yüksek Lisans Tezi*, 59. Aydın Adnan Menderes Üniversitesi Sağlık Bilimleri Enstitüsü.
Tanrıverdi, S. (2022). Tüketim olarak nomofobi: Sinemada medya bağlımlılığının ele alınışı. *Yüksek Lisans Tezi*, 180. Ankara Hacı Bayram Veli Üniversitesi Lisansüstü Eğitim Enstitüsü.
Tarakcı, H. D. (2022). Yaratıcı düşünme becerisinde akış deneyimi ve nomofobinin etkisi. *Doktora Tezi*, 151. Kırıkkale Üniversitesi Sosyal Bilimler Enstitüsü.

Theses:
Taştan, S. (2020). Spor yapan ve yapmayan üniversite öğrencilerinde internet bağımlılığı ve nomofobi düzeylerinin incelenmesi. *Yüksek Lisans Tezi*, 95. Süleyman Demirel Üniversitesi Sağlık Bilimleri Enstitüsü.
Turgut, M. (2021). Öğretmenlerin eğitim teknolojileri kullanım düzeyleri ile mobil telefon yoksunluğu korkusu arasındaki ilişkinin incelenmesi. *Yüksek Lisans Tezi*, 98. Zonguldak Bülent Ecevit Üniversitesi Sosyal Bilimler Enstitüsü.
Uğuz, G. (2019). Kişilik özellikleri ve nomofobi ilişkisi: Kamu hastanelerinde çalışan hemşireler ile bir araştırma. *Yüksek Lisans Tezi*, 103. İstanbul Üniversitesi-Cerrahpaşa Lisansüstü Eğitim Enstitüsü.
Uza, C. D. (2019). Üniversite öğrencilerinde akıllı telefon bağımlılığı ve nomofobi ile mizaç karakter arasındaki ilişkinin incelenmesi. *Tıpta Uzmanlık*, 124. Hatay Mustafa Kemal Üniversitesi Tıp Fakültesi Ruh Sağlığı ve Hastalıkları Ana Bilim Dalı.
Yıldırım, O. (2019). Ergenlerde akıllı telefondan yoksun kalma korkusu (Nomofobi) ile sosyodemografik değişkenler, temel psikolojik ihtiyaçlar, sürekli kaygı ve mutluluk arasındaki ilişkinin incelenmesi. *Yüksek Lisans Tezi*, 132. İnönü Üniversitesi Eğitim Bilimleri Enstitüsü.
Yıldız, E. (2021). Ortaokul 8.sınıf öğrencilerinin nomofobi düzeyleri ile liseyegeçiş sınavı (LGS) puanları arasındaki ilişkinin sosyo-demografik değişkenler açısından incelenmesi. *Yüksek Lisans Tezi*, 139. Bursa Uludağ Üniversitesi Eğitim Bilimleri Enstitüsü.
Yıldız, R. (2021). Nomofobinin sanal kaytarma üzerindeki etkisi: Antalya Belek örneği. *Yüksek Lisans Tezi*, 91. Akdeniz Üniversitesi Sosyal Bilimler Enstitüsü.
Yoğurtçu, D. D. (2018). The relationship between five factor personality traits and nomophobia levels among university students. *Yüksek Lisans Tezi*, 120. Yeditepe Üniversitesi Eğitim Bilimleri Enstitüsü.

Assoc. Prof. Nur Emine Koç[1], Assoc. Prof. Ayşegül Akaydın Aydın[2], Asst. Prof. Sema Bulat Demir[3], Res. Asst. Elif İnceismail[4], Res. Asst. Meltem Başaran[5]

Virtual Reality and Digital Gaming Experiences in Turkey

Abstract: Digital and virtual reality game market has been growing day by day both in the world and in Turkey. Youngesters prefer games rather than television programmes. By presenting a simulation of different emotions about real life with the various games it contains, game world affects lifestyles, preferences and emotional states of the users. Digital and virtual reality games also make a difference in the severity of their emotional states with the different experience opportunities they offer to their users. There are limited number of studies in the field that focus on the mood differences between virtual reality games and digital games. Therefore, within the scope of the research, it was aimed to measure EEG performance metrics for virtual and digital gaming experiences in Turkey, conduct comparative analysis, and deepen the findings with interview data. During the research, university students were played two different games in virtual and digital environment by using the Emotiv EPOC X device. Thus, it is aimed to determine mood changes by analyzing the EEG performance metrics of the players in the digital and virtual reality environments. As a result of the research, it is found that the excitement, interest, relaxation, and stress values of the participants playing virtual reality games are significantly higher than those of the participants playing digital games. There is no significant difference between gaming experiences depending on gender. The participants find virtual reality game more exciting and realistic than console game. They are more affected by violent elements than the elements in console game. Digital games have become an important form of entertainment and interaction that has gained popularity with the rapidly developing technology in recent years. However, it is seen that digital games are not only used for

1 Istanbul Aydın University, Faculty of Communication, New Media and Communication Department, nurkoc@aydin.edu.tr, Orcid ID: 0000- 0002- 3477- 8019.

2 Istanbul Aydın University, Faculty of Communication, Journalism Department, aakaydinaydin@aydin.edu.tr, Orcid ID: 0000-0001-5772-4008.

3 Istanbul Aydın University, Faculty of Communication, TV News and Broadcasting Department, semabulat@aydin.edu.tr, Orcid ID: 0000-0002-5473-3424.

4 Istanbul Aydın University, Faculty of Communication, Advertising Department, elifinceismail@aydin.edu.tr, Orcid ID: 0000-0002-3424-8034.

5 Istanbul Aydın University, Faculty of Communication, TV News and Broadcasting Department, meltembasaran1@aydin.edu.tr, Orcid ID: 0000-0002-1912-4703.

entertainment but also as a social, cultural and political tool. At this point, it is important to understand how digital games have potential for digital activism. This article will also examine the role of digital games in digital activism and make suggestions on how it has created and will create a change in this field.

Keywords: Virtual reality games, digital games, epoc^x, participant experiences, digital activism.

1. Introduction

Game is entertainment that usually has certain rules, allowing people to spend their time pleasantly; moreover, it can be defined as every kind of competition improving both mental and physical abilities (Harris, 2001: 7). It is a cultural phenomenon that dates back to ancient times and is common in every society. Playing allows people to interact with each other cognitively, physically, emotionally and socially from an early age. It is also at the center of human development. In the process from the past to the present, game emerges as an entertainment tool that is played in many different ways and for different purposes for all ages of individuals. According to Osborne, within the main principles of game theory, games are interlinked with real life not only economically, but also socially (2004: 10). With its different styles and purposes, the act of playing games is an integral part of people's lives.

With the rapid development of technology, games have begun to be transferred to digital space by adapting from their traditional forms, like every structure that changes; further more, gaming habits have evolved from traditional to digital. Gaming experiences, which are fun free time activities, have become more preferred due to the easy accessibility of Internet and digital gaming tools, and their exemption from time and space, yet they become more preferable these days with their high level presentation of reality by their graphics, stories, characters. Digital games refer to games that can be played with the gaming tools without computers, consoles, tablets, mobile phones or Internet connection to play computer-based games. One of the most important reason why digital games are so popular is their being interactive and allowing players to role-playing. These games can be played by a single player or multiplayer online so that digi-social activities and cultural interactions of digital world can be tranferred easily. Virtual reality games are taken as games which are much closer to reality than all the other digital games and promise the players to get lost in the game and stay in the reality of virtual technology. By the virtual environment; sensory feedback, interaction, mental and physical immersion can be experienced much more than any other digital games (Sherman & Craig, 2002: 6).

Digital games also offer experiences that take place in an interactive environment, allowing players to step into different worlds and be a part of fictional stories. This experience encourages players to empathize, understand different perspectives, and become sensitive to social issues. With these features, digital games become a powerful platform to convey an activist message.

For example, a game called "Papers, Please" encourages players to play as an immigration officer and shows the impact borders and bureaucracy have on people's lives. This game allows players to reflect by experiencing the hardships of asylum seekers and facing ethical challenges.

> As in the rest of the world, the digital game sector in Turkey has shown great development. According to the reports examined, it is stated that the sales of digital games will reach 93% by the end of 2023. According to "We are social 2022" report, 91.5% of games are played on mobile platforms in Turkey (We are The Social Global Digital, 2022).

When the studies conducted in the field of virtual reality and games in the digital game sector are examined, it can be stated that the research applied in the article titled "Are the Effects of Unreal Violent Video Games Pronounced When Playing With a Virtual Reality System?" coincides with this study. In this research, the short-term effects of violent games played with and without Virtual Reality (VR) glasses on provoking aggressive behavior are analyzed. An indirect relationship has been found between physiological arousal (heart rate, HR), preparation of aggressive thoughts, and hostility to the situation, violent gaming, (VG), and aggression (Arriga et al., 2008). With another study, "Video Games and Aggressive Thoughts, Feelings, and Behavior in the Laboratory and in Life", it is found that having been exposured to violent video games increases aggressive thoughts and behaviors. However, it has been reported that men trigger aggressive behavior at a higher rate than women. Exposuring to violent video games leads to increased aggressive behavior in both the short term and the long term (Anderson & Dill, 2000). In the research titled "Comparative Evaluation of the EEG Performance Metrics and Player Ratings on the Virtual Reality Games", three Virtual Reality games were played by 14 participants using EEG device. In the brain maps drawn at the end of the research, it is found that the players have different emotional reactions while playing the Virtual Reality game. Of these, the sense of violence has come to the fore (Paranthaman et al., 2021).

By this study, console and VR game experiences of participants are going to be identified due to their emotional changes by using EEG device EPOC X as for revealing the differences of them and for the gaming sector to understand the needs of the users more effectively.

1.1. Literature review

Computer games started to cover a big place in people's lives early in 1900s. The first known computer game called OXO was created in 1952 and after ARPA project in 1958, W.A. Higinbotham created a tennis game for his workers in his laboratory and that game is taken as the first computer game in history called Odyssey. In 1961, Steve Russell, Martin Graetz and Wayne Wiitanen designed a spaceship game and named it as Spacewar which can be played by two players. Steve Jobs and Steve Wozniak started to work for Atari firm of which Nolan Bushnell is the founder. They created a game called Breakout before Jobs left Atari firm to found Apple (Gentile, 2006: 1306).

In the beginning, almost all the game scenarios are simple, for fun and violent, but the more technology has grown, the more complicated the scenarios became. After Nintendo games gained popularity in 1981 by its graphics and scenario, computer games has its place as an entertainment tool accepted by the whole world and open a huge market for consumers.

When the format of digital games are analyzed, it is seen that many games take their infrastructure from movies, and many movies take their infrastructure from games (Özsoy & Turan, 2021: 637). This cycle, which directs popular culture in mutual interaction, has brought many important movies and digital games to the audience and users. Story telling has also changed into digital one and feeds both cinema and game sector (Miller, 2004: 14). For instance, "Episode IV: A New Hope", the first of the Star Wars movie series, a science fiction legend, was released in 1977. In 2019, last serial film of 12 films is released. Having high fanbase and millions of followers increasing each day, it has become a much more popular cultural item than its films. From cartoons to souvenirs, many Star Wars products have attracted attention of people and have taken their place among quality games in the digital game market with the advancement of technology. Following the computer revolution of the 1980s, video games found themselves in the spotlight of mass media. Yet, it wasn't until the widespread adoption of the internet from 1995 onwards that they truly cemented their place as an indispensable commodity for users. With the increasing importance of the stories as well as the contents of the games, popular virtual heroes, sections from movies and real lives have brought the reality fictions of the games to the fore. Star Wars: Shadow of Empire was fictionalized as a sub-story in the Star Wars universe during and after the release of Star Wars: Episode V: The Emperor in 1997, and then in 2004 Star Wars: Battlefront, Lego Star Wars, Lego Star Wars II: The Released with the debuts of 10 popular game movie franchises, such as the Original Triology. Spider Man, Alien: Isolation, Golden Eye, Mad Max,

Friday the 13th, Jurassic World Evolution, Middle- Earth: Shadow of Mordor, King Kong, X-Men-Origins: Wolverine are some notable examples of games adaptations from movies.

Looking at the movies adapted from games to movies, it is seen that Resident Evil is one of the most popular movies. It has been chosen as the research of our study because of its popularity. First released by Capcom in 1996 for Playstation, Sega Saturn and PC, there are 26 games in the Resident Evil series. The first Resident Evil movie was released as a sci-fi thriller in 2002 in accordance with the game's format. The 6th and last movie of the series, Resident Evil: Last Chapter, was released in 2016 and earned a total of 136 million dollars at the box office in 18 days. With the Resident Evil movie series, which broke the record with over 1 billion dollars worldwide, the game elements were successfully transferred to the cinema by targeting the existing customer base of the game world (Digitalspy, 2022). Examples such as Mortal Kombat, Street Fighter, Tomb Raider, Doom, Need for Speed, Pokemon, Final Destiny, Hitman, Rampage, Max Payne and Warcraft: The Beginning are among the most important movie adaptations from games. Digital games, which offer the maximum level of reality to their users by combining the stories with the right fictions, the formats that taste like the movie scenario, and the superior graphics, broke new ground in the game industry with the introduction of virtual reality applications into our lives.

However digital games become very attractive to especially youngsters, at first Virtual Reality games were not preferred due to the high costs, limited activities while playing, lots of cables and a headset need. By presenting its users a highly interactive experience, VR games immerse users' senses in an artificial virtual environment which creates a new reality and a new presence feeling (Burdea, 2003: 3). Therefore with the increase in the usage experience of VR technologies, VR games are made more convenient to use. With the use of devices such as HTCVive, Samsung VR, Oculus Rift in popular games, VR games have become one of the important parts of digital gaming culture. When the motivations for VR games are examined in the researches, the reasons for choosing VR games are listed as excitement, entertainment, escape, relaxation, making friends and becoming a habit (Huang, 2010: 1172). Among the most important features of Virtual Reality games are immersion, imagination and interactivity. Immersion means by VR technology, changing all the natural sense into digital ones. VR simulates the environment and the user closes his/her perception to the real world (Bowman, 2007: 37). According to Slater, there are three stages of immersion: engagement, engrossment and total immersion. Engagement is the first level of immersion and up to the users' attention and effort (2009: 3550). The more empathy have the users, the more committed they are. According to Sherman and Craig, immersion is used in two ways: mental and physical immersion. Mental immersion is the state of preoccupation and physical immersion is the synthetic stimulation of the body senses within the help of technology (Sherman & Craig, 2002: 10). Imagination is up to the users' performance while solving a problem (Gallace, 2012: 5). Interactivity is a kind of bridge between the users and the objects so as to use them within the simulated world by giving presence feeling to the users (Fuchs, 2011: 6).

It has been seen fewer health problems in VR games than in other games, as they provide digital mobility, mutual communication and perception of reality at the maximum level. On the other hand, since it gives the feeling of presence directly in the game, it can also trigger situations such as dizziness, nausea and stress (Steinicke, 2016: 16). For this reason, users may not spend time in VR games for a long time; however, studies on reducing these negative effects are still on progress. The exercise and healing power of virtual environments is a therapeutic feature, especially in the development of physical skills and overcoming fears. It also has the features of reducing and treating anxiety by warning by going over the fear of flying or acrophobia (Zyda, 2005: 26).

First VR games is Space Harrier 3D Sega using VR-Powered Shades, developed in 1988. It is a fast-paced three- dimensional action game. The characters use weapons and different kind of guns to beat rivals. Second one is created by Nintendo in 1995 called Virtual Boy. It is played with video game console having stereoscopic 3D graphics. Then in 1990s, Red Alert, Teleroboxer and Mario's Tennis are released (Digitalspy,2022). Nowadays, the most popular VR Game examples are, Half Life: ALYX (released in 2020) which is a VR version of Half-Life series. Its plot is about a war against an alien race (Steam, https://store.steampowered.com/app/546560/HalfLife_Alyx/). It is a singleplayer game. Another example is Batman: Arkham VR is also a singleplayer game, released in 2017 by Warner Bros. Interactive Entertainment. It is again a fight game experiencing Dark Knight's Universe (Steam, https://store.steampowered.com/app/502820/Batman_Arkham_VR/). One more example is No Man's Sky, an online multiplayer, offline one player VR game, released in 2016. Its topic is about exploration and survival in different galaxies (Steam, https://store.steam powered.com/app/275850/No_Mans_Sky/).

Until Dawn: Rush of Blood, one of the VR games, was used in our research. Rush of Blood, a PlayStation game developed by Supermassive Games. It was released by Sony Interactive Entertainment for PlayStation 4's VR headset on 13th, October, 2016. It is a shooting-focused rail shooter with an increasing dose of fear and tension in a horror-themed amusement park. With its fiction, story, music and realism, it puts users at the center of the game. 7 Various weapons are used in the game, which has different roller coasters. As a single player game, Rush of Blood is the sequel to Until Dawn, which was released in October 2015 (PlayStation, n.d.).

1.2. Digital game industry in Turkey

There are a lot of controversies about the terminology of digital games. Games are referred to as video games, computer games, electronic games, handheld games, mobile games, and digital games (Wolf, 2012: 15–16). Various researchers have preferred and used one of these terms in their studies. As an example, Mark Wolf preferred the term "video game" and stated that the use of this term in "games" and its use in "video technology" should be addressed (2008). From the 1980s to the present, these games have generally been defined as computer games, video games, or electronic games. In Turkey, the term "computer game" is mostly used, but with the 2000s, the expression "digital game" has become an accepted concept to include all genres of arcade games, PC (personal computer games), console games, and mobile games (Binark & Bayraktutan Sütcü, 2008: 42–43).

The first known digital game examples in Turkey are: The pioneering works of a game developer named Mevlüt Dinç in 1985, Keloğlan released in 1986, Dagger released in 1992; further more, Legends of Istanbul: Tulip Warriors released in 1994. After 2000, it is possible to talk about the world of digital games and video games at a definite level that dates back to the present day with games such as Corridor, Ambush, Sovereign Symphony, Nightmare 22, Chief Admiral Barbaros Hayrettin Pasha, Istanbul Doomsday Time, Mount and Blade, Umaykut and Uruz: The Return of Man. (Sarpkaya, 2020: 192–196).

The digital game sector, which has become one of the most important industries in the world, has started to make a serious contribution to the Turkish economy. As awareness of its economic potential increases, governments continue to ramp up their support and incentives for this sector. In Turkey, support and incentives provided to the gaming industry have contributed to its rapid development and growth in recent years. The efforts undertaken by Turkey in the gaming sector contribute positively to the country's economic development and employment. Significant developments were also experienced in the game sector in Turkey in 2020. The pandemic period has played a major role in the development of this sector. During this period, it was announced that Turkish games received twice as much attention compared to the world average, with an average of 759,470 downloads. Additionally, the number of game development companies in Turkey increased to 239 (BTK 2O2O Dijital Oyunlar Raporu, 2020). Morever, as Turkey's gaming ecosystem gained prominence on the world stage with its achievements since 2018, the number of active game studios in Turkey reached 522, with 331 in Istanbul and 108 in Ankara (Anadolu Ajansı, 2023).

2. Methods

Within the scope of the research, it was decided to use the mixed method as a research method in order to ensure data diversity and to interpret quantitative research results more fiducial inference. The common aim of this study is to support the data to be obtained by brain waves with the qualitative data to be obtained in the interview. The pattern of the study among the mixed methods was determined as an explanatory sequential mixed design. The purpose of this design is to use qualitative data to explain quantitative findings in more detail (Creswell, 2017: 224). In accordance with the design, it was decided to use the method of measuring brain waves, which is often used in neuroscientific research, and is a quantitative method, and the semi-structured interview method, which is one of the qualitative research methods, in a mixed way.

The sample of the study was determined by the proportional stratified random sampling method. According to the research, this feature was determined to be for Istanbul Aydın University Faculty of Communication students who have digital game playing experience and have experienced playing any "Resident Evil" game before. The sample is divided into two layers. One layer consists entirely of male participants, and the other layer consists entirely of female participants. Then it was planned to select a sample from each layer without selection. The reason university students are chosen as researchers is that both console games and Virtual Reality games are frequently played by the 18–24 age group. A digitally prepared participation form was sent to the participants to investigate the game experience. 125 students filled the participation form. 58.1 % (72 people) of the participants stated that they regularly play digital games. Of these participants, 33 stated that they had played "Resident Evil" before. However, only 10 of the 33 participants were women. In order to receive an equal number of participants from the strata, all female participants were included in the study, and 10 students were taken from male participants, and the number of sample participants was limited to 20 people.

In the first stage of the study, the brain activity of the participants was measured with the Emotiv EPOCX device during the gaming experience. Each participant, who was fitted with an EPOCX device, played a digital game followed by a Virtual Reality game. For each game, the contestants had a four-minute playing time allotment. The main reason of the time restriction is the health risks that Virtual Reality glasses carry. In the second and qualitative part of the research, semi-structured interview questions were asked to the participants and the users about their gaming experiences, duration, wishes, and the violent elements they encountered in the games.

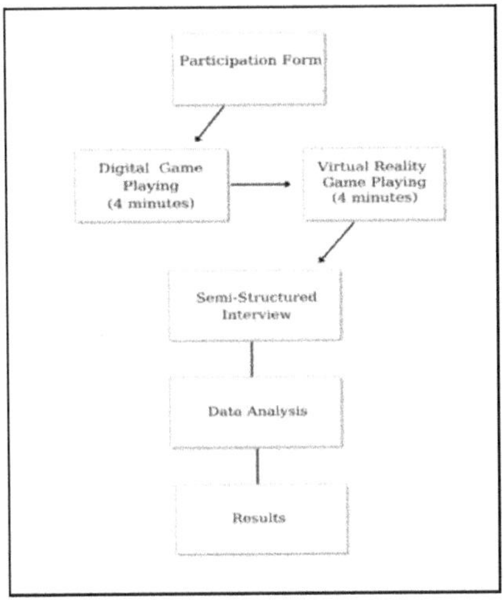

Figure 1. Research model.

The three problem sentences from the research are as follows:

H1: *"Is there a difference in users' cognitive activities (engagement, excitement, interest, focus, relaxation, stress) between the digital gaming experience and the virtual reality gaming experience?"*

H2: *"Are there any differences in gender-related cognitive activities (engagement, excitement, interest, focus, relaxation, stress) during the gaming experience?"*

H3: *"What are the differences between virtual and digital gaming experiences between participants' tastes for gaming, violent elements in games, and willingness to continue playing?"*

2.1. Analysis of data and findings

The analysis of the research data were performed using the SPSS 25.0 program. The average, standard deviation, lowest (minimum), and highest (maximum) scores related to the measurement results were evaluated as descriptive statistics. As a result of the Shapiro-Wilk normality test applied to the measurement results, it was determined that the engagement and interest data were suitable for the normal distribution, while the excitement, focus, relaxation, and stress data were not suitable for the normal distribution. For comparisons according to game type and gender, the Independent Samples T test was used in data suitable for normal distribution, while the Mann-Whitney U test was used in data that were not suitable for normal distribution.

Table 1. Descriptive statistics on participants' engagement, excitement, focus, ınterest, relaxation, stress levels

Measurement	N	Lowest	Highest	X	SS	Shapiro-Wilk	
						The Test Value	p
Engagement	40	47	95	71,08	9,79	,959	,158
Excitement	40	13	88	35,48	16,77	,903	,002
Focus	40	32	84	44,28	10,35	,860	,000
Interest	40	47	81	59,26	7,01	,946	,055
Relaxation	40	15	62	31,95	10,68	,925	,011
Stress	40	30	75	42,95	10,48	,820	,000

When the table is examined, it is seen that the average engagement score (X=71.08) and the average interest score (X=59.26) of the participants were above the medium level, the average excitement score (X=35.48), the average focus score (X=44.28), the average stress score (X=42.95) was medium level; and the average relaxation score (X=31.95) was low.

Table 2. Comparison of measurement results by game type and gender

Measurement	**Game type**	**Female**	**Male**	**Total**	**Significance**		
					Game type	**Gender (digital game)**	**Gender (virtual game)**
Engagement	Digital	69,24±6,00	75,83±10,07	72,54±8,75	T=0,944	T=1,777	T=0,526
	Virtual	68,32±7,85	70,90±13,37	69,61±10,75	p=0,351	P=0,092	P=0,605
Excitement	Digital	28,99±13,75	30,64±11,58	29,82±12,40	U=121,0	U=43,0	U=27,0
	Virtual	35,74±19,65	46,56±17,34	41,15±18,87	P=0,033	P=0,597	P=0,082
Focus	Digital	42,81±8,91	41,88±6,24	42,34±7,51	U=164,0	U=50,0	U=32,0
	Virtual	43,00±11,47	49,44±13,18	46,22±12,47	P=0,330	P=0,999	P=0,173
Interest	Digital	56,48±4,64	56,66±6,38	56,57±5,43	T= -3,738	T=0,072	T=0,036
	Virtual	61,90±8,45	62,03±6,83	61,96±7,48	P=0,001	P=0,943	P=0,972
Relaxation	Digital	26,46±6,71	26,51±6,27	26,49±6,32	U=81,0	U=48,0	U=48,0
	Virtual	36,09±9,80	38,74±13,30	37,42±11,45	P=0,001	P=0,880	P=0,880
Stress	Dijital	40,13±6,57	37,30±4,90	38,71±5,83	U=104,0	U=35,5	U=46,0
	Sanal	45,45±10,90	48,91±14,12	47,18±12,41	P=0,009	P=0,307	P=0,762

**p<0,01

When the table is examined, it is seen that there is no significant difference between the genders in engagement, excitement, focus, interest, relaxation, and stress measurements in both the digital game group and the virtual game group (p >0.05). When the differences according to game types are examined, there is no significant difference between the engagement and focus levels of digital game and virtual game players (p>0.05), however, it is seen that the excitement level of virtual game players (X=41.15) is higher than the excitement level of digital game players (X=29.82), the interest level of virtual game players (X= 61.96) is higher than the interest level of digital game players (X=56.57), the relaxation level of virtual game players (X=37.42) is higher than the relaxation level of digital game players (X=26,49), and the stress level of those who play virtual games (X=47.18) is significantly higher than the stress level of digital game players (X=38.71).

According to the findings of the semi-structured interview, the majority of the participants were affected by the violent elements in the virtual game and listed these elements as pigs, blood scenes, creepy sounds, and a dark environment. In this context, it was concluded that the violent elements in the virtual game affected the participants more. The majority of the participants stated that they did not have difficulty when playing digital games, but they had more difficulty with virtual games. In this direction, it is possible to say that the participants have more difficulty in the virtual game than in the digital game. Another findings obtained within the scope of the study is related to the desire and duration of continuing the digital and virtual game. The majority of participants stated that they wanted to continue the virtual game. This shows that the majority of participants want to continue the virtual game for a longer period of time.

2.2. Discussion and suggestion

In the study, it was determined that there was no significant difference in terms of the gender variable among the participants who played console games and Virtual Reality games. This situation shows that this may be due to the limited number of participants in the research. In future studies, when the sample of the research is expanded, hypotheses can be re-evaluated in terms of the gender variable.

However, it can be thought that games on different themes preferred within the scope of the research may affect stress and relaxation values in different ways. Therefore, in terms of developing the research, the experiment model can be repeated with different types of games on different themes.

On the other hand, the research can also be repeated with console game and Virtual Reality game versions of a single game. Thus, the differences between games that affect the results of the research (e.g., the elements of the story line) can be minimized.

In addition, the participants'wearing of virtual reality glasses and EEG device is one of the more challenging aspects of the research. For this reason, the development of a new virtual reality glasses design that can be designed for virtual reality and EEG- themed studies is also among the suggestions.

3. Conclusion

In the study, engagement, excitement, focus, interest, relaxation, and stress values between the virtual reality game experience and the console game playing experiences of the participants were examined. As a result of the research, the excitement, interest, relaxation, and stress values of the participants who played virtual reality games were significantly higher than those of the participants who played digital games. This is reconciled with the fact that virtual reality games offer a virtual environment experience that is immersive and similar to reality.

The virtual environment allows the person to adapt to the game and get away from the physical environment in which they are located. Thus, the participant reacts to the horror and suspense elements offered by the game at a higher level than console games. In contrast, the focus and engagement values are related to the story of the game. The fact that the console game played has a more complex story arc and contains mystery and puzzles has increased the participants' focus and engagement value. Thus, there was no significant difference between the focus and engagement value of the participant playing the virtual reality game, which has a simpler story arc. In other words, while the virtual reality game takes its power in focus and engagement values from illusion, the console game has shown that it takes it from the story arc. In addition, another research result there is no significant difference in the partcipants' experiences of the playing games depending on gender, in the research.

In addition to all this, participants found the virtual reality game more exciting and realistic than the console game. It was stated that the participants were affected by the pig, blood scenes, creepy sounds, dark environment, violence, and horror elements in the virtual reality game. It was found that participants were more affected by the violence and horror elements in the virtual reality game compared to the elements in the console game. The virtual reality game was described as more realistic and impressive by the participants, while the console game was evaluated as simple and artificial. It is stated that the participants want to play the virtual reality game for a longer time, which makes the game more impressive because it increases the feeling of being in the game with the glasses used in the virtual reality game.

Game designs used in research can be applied in activist movements. By this way, individuals who share the same thought and view can come together to form virtual communities and engage in social movements . As for the game design, when "Blood Rush" and "Resident Evil" are taken into consideration, it can be said that the realistic images in the game, the graphics used, the resolution of the game, the cinematic effects and the light used in the space have an effect on the users. For this reason, it is thought that the image quality and design of the games also allow the user to be involved in the game.

Digital games have become platforms that encourage active participation of players and unleash their creativity. Games give players a sense of control and freedom, allowing them to customize the experience and take initiative. Players make decisions, create stories and interact with other players in the game world. Gaming communities encourage sharing and communication, enabling the flow of knowledge and inspiration among players. In the future, it is expected that digital games will further strengthen participation and further reveal the creative potential of the players.

Beyond their recreational use, digital games reveal a new facet of digital activism. Games become a powerful tool for social change, encouraging players to raise awareness, empathize and engage in collective action through interactive experiences. The role of digital games in activism provides new and innovative ways to address and transform societal issues. Therefore, the relationship between digital games and digital activism should be further explored and supported.

References

Anderson, C. A., & Dill, K. E. (2000). Video Games and Aggressive thoughts, Feelings, and Behavior in the Laboratory and in Life. *Journal of Personality and Social Psychology*, 78(4), 772–790.

Anadolu Ajansı, 2023. Türk Oyun Sektörü Yatırımda Avrupa'nın Zirvesinde. Retrieved from [11.03.2023], from https://www.aa.com.tr/tr/bilim-teknoloji/turk-oyun-sektoru-yatirimda-avrupanin-zirvesinde/2921042

Arriaga, P., Esteves, F., Carneiro, P., & Monteiro, M. B. (2008). Are the Effects of Unreal Violent Video Games Pronounced When Playing with a Virtual Reality System? *Aggressive Behavior: Official Journal of the International Society for Research on Aggression*, 34(5), 521–538.

Binark, M., & Bayraktutan-Sütcü G. (2008). *Digital Play as a Product of the Culture Industry*. Istanbul: Kalkedon Publishing.

Bowman, D. A., & McMahan, R. P. (2007). Virtual Reality: How Much Immersion is Enough?. *Computer*, 40(7), 36–43.

Burdea, G. C., & Coiffet, P. (2003). *Virtual Reality Technology* (p. 3). John Wiley & Sons.

BTK 2O2O Dijital Oyunlar Raporu, 2020. BTK 2020 Dijital Oyunlar Raporunu Yayınladı. Retrieved from [01.02.2022], from https://www.btk.gov.tr/haberler/btk-2o2o-dijital-oyunlar-raporunu-yayinladi

Creswell, J. W. (2017). *Research Pattern: Qualitative, Quantitative and Mixed Method Approaches* (3. Printing b.). (Trans. S. B. Demir). Ankara: The Book that Educates.

Digital Spy. (2022). Resident Evil Timeline: The chronological order explained. Retrieved on: [1 March 2023]. https://www.digitalspy.com/tv/ustv/a40622563/resident-evil-timeline-chronological-order/

Fuchs, P., Moreau, G., & Guitton, P. (2011). *Virtual Reality: Concepts and Technologies* (p. 6). London: CRC Press.

Gallace, A., Ngo, M. K., Sulaitis, J., & Spence, C. (2012). Multisensory Presence in Virtual Reality: Possibilities & Limitations. In *Multiple Sensorial Media Advances and Applications: New Developments in MulSeMedia* (pp. 1–38).

Gentile, D. A., & Anderson, C. A. (2006). Video Games. In N. J. Salkind (Ed.), *Encyclopedia of Human Development* (Vol. 3, pp. 1303–1307). Thousand Oaks, CA: Sage Publications.

Huang, H. M., Rauch, U., & Liaw, S. S. (2010). Investigating Learners' Attitudes toward Virtual Reality Learning Environments: Based on a Constructivist Approach. *Computers & Education*, 55(3), 1171–1182.

Miller, C. H. (2004). *Digital Storytelling: A Creator's Guide to Interactive Entertainment.* USA: Focal Press, Elsevier.

Osbourne, M. J. (2004). *An Introduction to Game Theory.* Oxford: Oxford University Press.

Özsoy, Ö., & Turan, B. T. (2021). Video Oyunlarından Uyarlanan Filmlerin Başarı ve Başarısızlık Analizi. *The Turkish Online Journal of Design Art and Communication*, 11(2), 635–658.

Paranthaman, P. K., Bajaj, N., Solovey, N., & Jennings, D. (2021, August). Comparative Evaluation of the EEG Performance Metrics and Player Ratings on the Virtual Reality Games. *In 2021 IEEE Conference on Games (CoG)* (pp. 1–8). IEEE.

PlayStation. (n.d.). Until Dawn: Rush of Blood. Retrieved from [01.02.2022], from https://store.playstation.com/tr-tr/product/EP9000-CUSA02350_00-RUSHOFBLOOD00001/

Sarpkaya, S. (2020). *Digital Game and Mythology: A Content Analysis on the Elements of Turkish Mythology in Digital Games*, Mythology Research II. (Ed. İbrahim Gümüş, pp. 185–201). Çanakkale: Paradigm Academy.

Sherman, W. R., & Craig, A. B. (2002). *Understanding Virtual Reality: Interface, Application, and Design* (pp. 1–17). U.S.A: Morgan Kaufmann Publishers.

Slater, M. (2009). Place Illusion and Plausibility Can Lead to Realistic Behaviour in Immersive Virtual Environments. *Philosophical Transactions of the Royal Society B: Biological Sciences*, 364(1535), 3549–3557.

Steam, (n.d.). Batman™: Arkham VR. Retrieved from [01.02.2022], from https://store.steampowered.com/app/502820/Batman_Arkham_VR/

Steam, (n.d). Half-Life: Alyx. Retrieved from: [01.02.2022], from https://store.steampowered.com/app/546560/HalfLife_Alyx/

Steam. (n.d.). No Man's Sky. Retrieved from [01.02.2022], from https://store.steampowered.com/app/275850/No_Mans_Sky/

Steinicke, F. (2016). *Being Really Virtual* (p. 16). Switzerland. Springer.

We Are The Social Global Digital 2022 Report. (2022). 10 May 2022. https://periscope.com.tr/we-are-social-global-dijital-2022-raporu/. Accessed Date: 12 November 2022.

Wolf, Mark J. P. (2012). Building Imaginary Worlds: The Theory and History of Subcreation. New York and London: Routledge.

Zyda, M. (2005). From Visual Simulation to Virtual Reality to Games. *Computer*, 38(9), 25–32.

Notes on Contributors

Asst. Prof. Buket Akdemir Dilek born in 1992 in Izmir, Buket AKDEMİR DİLEK graduated from Marmara University, Faculty of Communication, Department of Radio, Television and Cinema. She completed her master's degree in Marmara University, Institute of Social Sciences, Department of Radio Television Cinema, Cinema Program. She completed her doctorate in the same program. She works at Hasan Kalyoncu University, Faculty of Communication, Department of Radio, Television and Cinema as assistant professor. She works on subjects such as Women's Studies, Turkish Cinema, Cinema and Ideology, Accented Cinema, World Cinema and Cinema Readings.

Assoc. Prof. Ayşegül Akaydın Aydın studied Television Journalism (B.A) in İstanbul Bilgi University and Media Management (M.A.) in Marmara University. She got her PhD degree from Radio-TV Cinema department in Istanbul University. She worked as research assistant in İstanbul Bilgi University between 2009–2017. She has been working as associated professor at Istanbul Aydın University, Journalism Department, Faculty of Communication. Her interests include communication theories, new television technologies, television culture.

Res. Asst. Meltem Başaran is a Research Assistant in Department of TV News and Broadcasting at Istanbul Aydın University and Assistant Editor of the Journal of Communication Studies. She is also a PhD student in Radio, Television and Cinema from Kocaeli University. She is an Assistant Prof in Department of TV News and Broadcasting at Istanbul Aydin University.

Res. Asst. Bilgesu Biber is currently working as a research assistant at Istanbul Arel University, Faculty of Fine Arts, Department of Cartoon and Animation. She completed her graduate education at Anadolu University, Faculty of Communication Sciences, Department of Journalism. She did her master's degree at Ankara University, Department of Journalism. Her master's thesis title is Reflections of conservatism on art journals in Turkey: The case of New Arts Journal. She is currently studying for my PhD at Başkent University, Department of Radio, Television and Cinema. Her research interests include communication, communication theories and cinema.

Asst. Prof. Sema Bulat Demir has finished Bachelor degree in Ege University Radio and Television Department in 2016. She has completed master degree in Ege University Radio and Television Department in 2019. She has studied "an intertextual analysis of Shakespeare's plays in the narrative structures of animation films" as her Master degree thesis. She got her PhD degree from Istanbul University, Department of Journalism. She is an Assistant Prof in Department of TV News and Broadcasting at Istanbul Aydın University since May, 2023.

Asst. Prof. Muhammet Dilek born in 1990 in Antalya. Muhammet Dilek graduated from Ege University, Department of Radio Television and Cinema in 2013. In 2015 he started working as research assistant at Marmara University, Institute of Social Sciences. He completed his master's degree in 2018 at Marmara University, Institute of Social Sciences, Department of Radio Television and Cinema, Cinema Program and since 2018 he completed on his doctorate in the same department. He mainly works on Hollywood Cinema.

Assoc. Prof. Kenan Duman was born in 1981, in Sakarya, Turkey. He completed his higher education at Istanbul University, Faculty of Communication Department of Journalism. He also earned his master's and doctoral degrees at Istanbul University, Institute of Social Sciences between 2004–2013. He discussed the subject of "The Minority Press and Its Problems in Turkey" for his thesis. In the 2007–2008 academic year, he was in Italy at the Suor Orsola Benincasa University of Naples as a doctoral student and studied Sephardi Jews and their life style. He still continues his academic studies as a faculty member at Istanbul Arel University, Faculty of Communication. His studies focus on digial culture, minorities and media culture.

Asst. Prof. Büşra T. Durmuş was born in 1979. She started her undergraduate studies at Istanbul University Sociology Department in 1996 and completed them in 2013. She completed her master's degree at Istanbul University Journalism Department in 2016 with a thesis titled "The Idea of Decentralisation in Terakki Journal (1906–1907)". She received her PhD degree from the same department in 2020 by presenting a thesis titled "Reconstruction of Women Identity by Positivist and Materialist Ottoman Intellectuals Through Press Activities (1908–1912)". She served as a founding member of GLOBERA (Global Educational Research Association) between 2018 and 2020. She currently works as a doctoral faculty member in the Department of Journalism at Marmara University. Her main research areas are the representation of women in the media, gender and media, press history, and new media studies.

Asst. Prof. Orhan Faik was born in 1988 in Saatli district of the Republic of Azerbaijan. After graduating from school, he started his undergraduate education in Baku at Khazar University, Institute of Social Sciences, Department of Journalism. He attended the "Tarzan Media Training" training seminar in the Netherlands and gained knowledge about the field. After completing his undergraduate education, he started his master's degree at Atatürk University, Institute of Social Sciences, Department of Radio, Television and Cinema. After the completion of his education, he returned to Azerbaijan and worked in Ses TV and News Agency for a short time. In 2020, he completed his doctorate education at Kocaeli University Institute of Social Sciences, Department of Communication Sciences. Faik, who worked as a scholarship holder in Tübitak Sobag 1001 Project during his education, has papers on identity, old age, and psychology of exile. In addition to Turkish, he speaks Azerbaijani, Russian and English. Since 2021, he has been working as a faculty member at Istanbul Arel University Faculty of Communication, Department of New Media and Communication.

Res. Asst. Elif İnceismail is a Research Assistant in Department of Advertising at Istanbul Aydın University. She is also a PhD student at Ege University, Department of Advertising. She is an Assistant Prof in Department of Advertising at Istanbul Aydin University in Turkey.

Assoc. Prof. Nur Emine Koç born in 1980, in Istanbul, has her BA and MA degree in English Language and Literature Department. She got her Phd degree on Communication Studies, Maltepe University in 2016 with the thesis of "An Example of Reality Shows on TV within the Context of Consumption Culture: Evim Şahane Program". She got her Assoc. Prof degree in April, 2023. Between 2002–2009, she worked as an English teacher at colleges and in 2010, she continued her career as a lecturer in Istanbul Aydın University and after getting her degree as an Assistant Prof Doctor in 2016, not only has she given different kind of courses to vocational school, BA, MA and PhD students, but also she has many administrative duties such as Vice Manager at Foreign Languages Vocational School, Head of Foreign Languages and Cultures Department, Head of Applied English and Translation, Head of English Translation Department, Vice Manager at New Media and Application and Research Center. Having a lot of studies on New Media field, especially on digital exhaustion and digital culture, Koç has been the Head of New Media and Communication Department both for BA and MA degree students in Communication Faculty of Istanbul

Aydın University since 2020. She also volunteers as the Film and TV Series Analysis Supervisor of "Let's End Violence Together" Platform.

PhD. Erdem Koç was born in 1977, in Istanbul. He had BA and MA degrees on English Language and Literature. After completing his MA degree, he started studying at communication department and he had PhD degree on Communication Studies in 2016. He is interested in Media Literacy. Since 2000, he has been working at Ministery of Education as an English teacher. Throughout his career, he taught English from primary to high school levels besides he worked as a part time instructor at English Translation Studies department at Istanbul Aydın University. He had 5 years of school manager assisstant and 5 years of school manager experinces. He is still continuing his studies on communication sciences.

Res. Asst. Hatice Öksüz holds a BA in Erciyes University, Faculty of Communication, Radio Television and Cinema Department (2014) and achieved an MA in Marmara University, Radio Television (2019) and currently a PhD Candidate in Istanbul University, Radio Television Cinema (2020). She served as a research assistant at Istanbul Aydın University, Faculty of Communication, Visual Communication Design Department since 2020.

Assoc. Prof. Begüm Aylin Önder completed her undergraduate education at Beykent University in 2008. In the same year, she worked as a graphic designer at Ciner Yayın Holding within Habertürk. She obtained her master's degree in 2012 from Istanbul Kültür University, Social Sciences Institute, Department of Communication Design. Since 2015, she has been working as a visual designer at Aljazeera Türk Network. In 2020, she received her Proficiency in Art from Istanbul Arel University, Institute of Social Sciences. Until 2021, she served as a full-time faculty member at Istanbul Bilgi University, Graphic Design Department. From 2020 to 2022, she worked as an Assistant Professor and Head of Visual Communication Design Department at Istanbul Aydın University, Faculty of Communication. Since 2022, she has been serving as an associate professor and head of the Visual Communication Design Department at Istanbul Arel University, Faculty of Communication. Since April 2024, she has been serving as the vice dean of the relevant faculty. Additionally, she teaches practical and theoretical courses at Marmara University, Faculty of Education, and Yalova University, Art and Design Department. Önder, who also teaches at the graduate, doctoral, and proficiency levels, has participated in numerous exhibitions and served as a jury member in many national and international competitions. Her interests include artificial intelligence, computer graphics, digital art, visual culture, new media, and Generation Z.

Dr. Yakup Toktay holds a bachelor's degree from Atatürk University, Faculty of Communication, Department of Radio Television and Cinema (2016), a master's degree from Marmara University, Department of Radio Television (2019) and a PhD from Istanbul University, Department of Radio Television and Cinema (2023). He is currently working as a lecturer in the Department of Media and Communication at Bandırma Onyedi Eylül University.

www.ingramcontent.com/pod-product-compliance
Ingram Content Group UK Ltd.
Pitfield, Milton Keynes, MK11 3LW, UK
UKHW021848100926
8556IPUK00020B/1124

9 783631 880944